The Incredulous Reader

ALSO BY CLAYTON KOELB

Thomas Mann's "Goethe and Tolstoy": Notes and Sources

The Incredulous Reader

LITERATURE AND

THE FUNCTION OF DISBELIEF

CLAYTON KOELB

Cornell University Press

ITHACA AND LONDON

First published 1984 by Cornell University Press.
Published in the United Kingdom by Cornell University Press, Ltd., London.

International Standard Book Number 0–8014–1645–0
Library of Congress Catalog Card Number 83–18840
Printed in the United States of America
Librarians: Library of Congress cataloging information
appears on the last page of the book.

The paper in this book is acid-free and meets the guidelines
for permanence and durability of the Committee on Production
Guidelines for Book Longevity of the Council on Library Resources.

To Susan

"... il libro, e chi lo scrisse."

Contents

CONTENTS

/ 8

Preface

THIS BOOK BEGAN with a question that I considered simple, not to say naive: What happens when we read things that we do not and perhaps could not believe? I was not very much concerned with the relatively well-plowed field of allegorical fantasy, that is, with hermeneutic strategies for discovering what might be "true" about these tall tales. The problem seemed to me that, after all our best allegorical efforts were tried, there remained a body of works that presented an incredible surface and stubbornly resisted all attempts to make them believable. Works such as Aristophanes' *Birds,* Poe's tales of terror, and the nonsense verses of Carroll and Morgenstern, along with a great deal of more contemporary "fantasy and science fiction," still seem incredible no matter how criticism tries to interpret them. But if they do so, if there are such absolutely unbelievable fictions, how and why do we read them? How does our disbelief affect the reading process?

This issue, which I at first regarded as simple, proves to be very difficult, complicated by its intimate connection with many problems of literary theory and the philosophy of language. It is all the more difficult because our tradition has made special efforts to eliminate the problem by converting disbelief in the surface of texts to belief in their inner truth. Another complication is that the question of disbelief appears to be at once very old-fashioned and aggressively modern. Phrases such as "how does the drama move if it is not credited?" and "the willing suspension of disbelief" belong to the bedrock of our critical tradition. Their very familiarity might lead some of us to think that the problem had been solved long since. At the same time, the question has a number of implications that are closely tied to issues of critical theory associated with structuralist and post-structuralist thought, with the work of Barthes and Derrida. The danger on this side is that some readers may suspect that the problem is merely an artifact of a special theoretical ortho-doxy, that indeed it would disappear if the deconstructionists (or whoever) stopped grinding their double axes. One of my chief efforts has been to convince the reader that neither of these assumptions is warranted.

The book's subject, then, is a particular problem of reading. It will quickly become evident that reading, too, is in the main its method. My text proceeds, for the most part, by examining other texts that reveal something about the problem of disbelief. My criteria for selecting the texts I read were, first, that they contribute to the understanding of this problem and, a distant second, that I be able to read them in the languages in which they had been written. The texts I have chosen thus come from widely separated places and times and from authors of differing renown. Some readers may find it puzzling that I take Robert Nye as "seriously" as Aristophanes, that I read David Gerrold as carefully as Thomas Mann. I can only reply that I have done so not to promote authors I happen to like, but to satisfy the de-mands imposed by the topic.

In order to spare the reader some of the discomforts of deal-ing with texts in many languages, I have provided translations of all material quoted from foreign language sources. In almost all cases the original is given, in whole or in part, either in the notes or in the text beside the translation; a few quotations appear in English only, on the assumption that the reader is unlikely to want to consult the originals when they are not central to the argument. I try to use standard translations when available, but often, for various reasons, I have felt the need to provide my own. Translations other than mine are always acknowledged in the notes. In the case of materials in ancient Greek, I have given originals in transliteration (not phonemic transcription), and have made no attempt to represent quantity.

My book has its distant origins in the 1950s, when I started reading the works of Robert Heinlein and developed what became a lifelong fascination with science fiction and fantasy. More immediately, the impulse to write this volume and not another came from the encouragement and support of Susan Noakes, whose combination of theoretical sophistication and insight into my deepest critical concerns made her advice always compelling. Anne Burnett, Sun Hee Kim Gertz, Samuel Jaffe, James Redfield, Monica Setterwall, George Walsh, and Anthony Yu read parts of the manuscript as it progressed and gave me the benefit of their learning and experience. I have not taken as full advantage of their advice as I should have, I am sure. Eli Rosenow will recognize elements in this book as products of conversations long past, as will Betsy Dawson and Richard Weisberg.

I also acknowledge the valuable assistance I received from Linda Brodkey and Donald G. Marshall. Both read the manuscript with great care and sympathy, and both offered suggestions for revisions that resulted in major improvements in the book's final form. The intention buried in earlier versions would never have been realized without their insight and encouragement.

CLAYTON KOELB

Chicago, Illinois

Part One /

DISBELIEF AND UNTRUTH

CHAPTER 1 /

Literature and Incredulity

SINCE PRACTICALLY the moment of its composition, "The Rime of the Ancient Mariner" has been the center of critical debate about the relation of disbelief to literature. To be more accurate, Coleridge's own theorizing about his poem has received the critical attention, particularly the famous passage in the fourteenth chapter of the *Biographia Literaria* in which he proposed the "suspension of disbelief" as the definition of "poetic faith." This formulation has become such an integral part of our critical culture that it is now virtually impossible to mention the issue of literary disbelief without being told that, of course, it is what we suspend.

Coleridge evidently supposed that the possibility of his reader's disbelief in the "shadows of imagination" in his poem presented a problem. He offers a solution in the form of a theory of "dramatic truth," arguing that even if the objects of imitation are supernatural "shadows of imagination," there is a need for poetic faith. That faith arises from our *inward nature*, whence the unreal objects take on human interest and a semblance of truth. Coleridge does claim truth for the "Ancient Mariner," but he calls it "dramatic truth," in which the Aristotelian demand for probability is satisfied. The emotions described and engendered by the poem are "such emotions as would naturally accompany such situations, supposing them real. And real in *this* sense they have been to every human being who, from whatever source of delusion, has at any time believed himself under supernatural agency."[1] The suspension of disbelief is necessary only for the shadows of imagination, the supernatural things themselves, and it is requested in the service of a poetic faith that is justified by the truth of the poem to inward nature.

Coleridge thus proposes the suspension of disbelief as a kind of bridge to take us from one secure shore of faith to another. Our belief in the poem does not require our belief in the supernatural events it describes, since those supernatural events are not—according to Coleridge the theorist—the poem's real subject. I will argue below that Coleridge's poetic practice can be understood in another way, according to a theory other than Coleridge's, which reasserts the central importance of the supernatural events and the disbelief they engender. In this context, however, it is enough for us to note Coleridge's claim that it was not those situations themselves but rather the "emotions as would naturally accompany such situations" that were the poem's central concern and that in effect those emotions depicted by the poem are indeed a just picture of a real original, that real original being our inward nature.

A different approach might be to suppose that the reader's disbelief, far from being a problem, far from needing to be suspended, is actually something without which the poem would fail to work. And we can be certain that there has been at least one reader of the "Ancient Mariner" whose disbelief remained intact: the self-reader, the poet himself. We can see this in the passage quoted above, in which he talks about the person who has believed himself under supernatural agency "from whatever source of delusion." Two points of view emerge here: the one belongs to the person suffering from the delusion, the one who "believes"; the other apparently belongs to the writer, who recognizes that this belief has its source in *delusion*. The word "delusion" derives from a Latin expression meaning "playing [someone] false" whose root is *ludus*, "game." Coleridge's formulation proposes that such a game is present in his story, a false reality that creates a boundary around itself, an inside and an outside. On the inside there is belief, which is generated out of the game

---

[1]*Biographia Literaria*, chap. 14. Quoted here from I. A. Richards, ed., *The Portable Coleridge* (New York: Viking, 1950), 512.

itself, whereas on the outside there is only the recognition that this game is a falsehood. The boundary is marked by the change from belief to disbelief, from thinking that the game is in fact not a game but the real world, to recognizing that such thinking can exist only because the game fences off the real world. Inside that boundary, one may suppose the existence and indeed supreme power of "supernatural agency." Outside it, one recognizes such agency as part of the game, as result of the delusion, or perhaps even that which itself constitutes the delusion.

The Wedding Guest is one of the clearest examples of literature of a character who is the audience of an incredible story, and what happens to him seems to me an excellent poetic illustration of the effects of such an incredible text on a reader who is brought from disbelief to belief in that text's word. The process begins, not with a willing suspension of disbelief in the story, but with the *un*willing suspension of belief in the world. The Guest is at first unwilling even to listen to the mariner. It is only the power of the story, the hypnotic power that glitters in the old man's eye, that compels his reluctant assent. "He cannot choose but hear" (l. 18). It forces him to pay attention to the long narrative rather than to the wedding celebration, to advert to the word in preference to the world, to suspend his belief in that world and to transfer it finally to the word. Much effort has been expended by critics in attempts to find connections between the matter of the mariner's tale and the safe, happy, convivial world of the wedding feast. But the point is surely that they are not connected, that in spite of the enormous attraction of this wedding world, and in spite of its *reality*, the narration simply wipes it from the consciousness of the Wedding Guest. He becomes possessed and under compulsion, and he is thereby transformed from simply a reader of the tale into a character in it.

This possession suffered by the Guest exactly parallels the experience of the mariner himself. We learn toward the poem's end, as a kind of reply to the Hermit's question ("What manner of man art thou?" [l. 577]), that the mariner, too, is under compulsion. The "strange power of speech" that compels the attention of the Guest also drives the mariner to tell his tale. The poem makes quite explicit the fact that the mariner is possessed by the need to tell his story:

Forthwith this frame of mine was wrenched
With a woful agony,
Which forced me to begin my tale;
And then it left me free.

Since then, at an uncertain hour,
That agony returns:
And till my ghastly tale is told,
This heart within me burns.

I pass, like night, from land to land;
I have strange power of speech;
The moment that his face I see,
I know the man that must hear me:
To him my tale I teach.

[Ll. 578–90]

It turns out, then, that it is not the mariner who is victorious ("hath his will") in his encounter with the Guest but rather that "strange power of speech." The Guest "cannot choose but hear"—that is, he is forced by the power that glitters in the mariner's eye to be nothing but an audience, to turn his attention away from the world that calls him and to the word:

"The Bridgegroom's doors are open wide,
And I am next of kin;
The guests are met, the feast is set:
May'st hear the merry din."

[Ll. 5–8]

But the mariner himself cannot choose but speak; he is the medium through which the supernatural agency of the power of speech does its work. When he uses his eye to immobilize the Guest, he is really using the power derived from his possession by language.

The mariner is indeed, as Wordsworth suggested, passive; he "does not act, but is continually acted upon." But this observation, though it is absolutely accurate, is not the criticism it was meant to be, since this passivity before the word is exactly what the poem sets out to depict. The "Rime" elaborates its own phrase, "he cannot choose but hear." It takes this locution in deadly earnest, so that an initially metaphorical "compulsion" is transformed into a physical one: both the dead crew and the living mariner are physically "possessed" by speech. The frame story shows that one of the features of this particular compulsion is that it is transferable. The mariner is able to "have his will" over the Wedding Guest, to compel him to be a listener to his word, precisely because the mariner has no will apart from the volition of the power that possesses him. The Guest, too, is made into a believing reader, as he is wrenched completely free of his own context of wedding and fellowship, music and feasting, just as the mariner himself is driven by main force out of the normal world and into the word.

But we, the readers who recognize all that happens as a "delusion," remain outside the game and indeed want to remain there. We need the protection of our disbelief to keep from becoming, like the Wedding Guest, "stunned" and "of sense forlorn." If we were to do as the mariner does, understand the power that overwhelms him as a *real* power, we would then have to see the mariner's tale as the Guest does, as a terrifying force that eclipses the ordinary world of daily experience and leaves us in a condition deprived ("forlorn") of sense.

The "Ancient Mariner" vividly demonstrates that the "willing suspension of disbelief" is the last thing a writer of supernatural tales should want in his readers. Coleridge himself never participated in the "delusion" that overcomes his characters, and neither should we. Of course this statement does not mean that the reader should rise up and condemn the untruth he recognizes, as some readers occasionally have done. But to yield our incredulity altogether would be no better. We must preserve, not suspend, our disbelief if we are to avoid the distressing fate of that paradigm of the naive reader, the Wedding Guest.

Still, one frequently hears arguments that disbelief is irrelevant to the reading of literature. We find such an argument in the doctrine that poetic statements are not really statements at all; that, in short, the poet "nothing affirmeth, and therefore never lieth," to use Sidney's glistening and authoritative phrase.[2]

[2]*Defense of Poesy.*

According to the sophisticated elaboration of this sentiment, poetic utterances are a special class of utterance, to be labeled "pseudostatements" or "quasi-judgments" or the like and not to be believed or disbelieved. J. L. Austin may be quoted as an advocate of such a view:

> Many utterances which have been taken to be statements . . . are not in fact descriptive, nor susceptible of being true or false. When is a statement not a statement? When it is a formula in a calculus: when it is a performatory utterance: . . . when it is part of a work of fiction. . . . It is simply not the business of such utterances to "correspond to the facts" (and even genuine statements have other businesses besides that of so corresponding).[3]

Austin's remarks seem to hold good for most of the assertions of novels and stories, since many of them are in any case not obviously either true or false. When Thomas Mann tells us that "Director Weinschenk's afternoon visits repeated themselves in quick succession," we accept the information as part of the story and pass no further judgment on it. But when Mann goes on to say that Weinschenk "gave utterance to the opinion that *Romeo and Juliet* was a play by Schiller," it is essential to the effectiveness of the fiction that we take exception to Weinschenk's opinion.[4] A reader who was unable to detect the falsity of Weinschenk's attribution of authorship would be incapable of understanding the text.

It is easy to see, then, that *all* statements that are parts of a fiction cannot be immune from criteria of truth or falsity. Numerous true and false statements—statements that indeed are only effective in the fiction if they are believed to be true or false—can be embedded in a matrix of fictional statements not subject to such criteria. It is extremely important to regard carefully the distinction between criteria of truth and criteria of fictionality. Suppose I were to state with conviction the following: "Julius Caesar frequently remarked that Tokyo is the

---

[3] *Philosophical Papers*, 2d ed. (New York: Oxford University Press, 1970), 131.
[4] *Buddenbrooks* (Frankfurt: Fischer, 1960), 300. "Die Nachmittagsbesuche Direktor Weinschenks wiederholten sich in rascher Folge. . . ." ". . . der Meinung Ausdruck gab, 'Romeo und Julia' sei ein Stück von Schiller."

largest city in Japan." Such a statement would obviously be false, though in such a circumstance it would not be fictional. The statement attributed to Caesar and embedded in my utterance is perfectly true (Tokyo is indeed the largest city in Japan) even though Caesar's remark is also fictional (Caesar obviously never said any such thing). Readers ordinarily take such things in their stride, easily recognizing fictional true statements, fictional false statements, and so forth. Certain rhetorical effects depend on the reader's ability to make such distinctions.

Criteria of truth and falsity (and thus also of belief) are applicable as well to statements not so much embedded in the fiction as constitutive of the fiction itself. Statements like "Weinschenk gave utterance to the opinion that" are ordinarily neutral with regard to such criteria, but they need not be. Suppose Mann had written, "The Buddenbrooks' dog frequently embarrassed the family by giving utterance to the opinion that *Romeo and Juliet* was a play by Schiller." Such a fiction, based on an incredible premise, uses the evident untruth of its constitutive statements to entertain the reader. We *accept* such statements as necessary to the telling of the story, but our acceptance does not entail belief or prevent disbelief or require disbelief's "suspension." The case of the Buddenbrooks' dog is an imaginary one, but Thomas Mann did occasionally employ incredible elements in his fictions. The following example illustrates how Mann presupposes our disbelief and uses it for literary effect. Schridaman, one of the principal characters in *The Transposed Heads*, overcome with depression, takes up a sword and severs his own head from his body.

> Such a thing is quickly said, and it was not otherwise than quickly done. And yet the narrator has here only one wish: that the listener not accept with indifference and thoughtlessness this statement as something ordinary and natural, simply because it is so often reported and appears in the records as ordinary, that people go around cutting off their own heads. The individual case is never ordinary. . . . Self-beheading, no matter how often reported, is a practically undo-able deed, for the performance of which is needed a monstrous determination and a terrible combination of all the vital and volitional powers; and that Schridaman with the soft spiritual eyes and the not particularly strong

brahmanly merchant's arms managed to bring it off should not be accepted as something ordinary but should rather be taken with almost incredulous amazement."[5]

Mann's ironic game depends upon his expectation that the reader will find his narration incredible, will not in fact believe it. The pose of the earnest narrator, trying hard to convince a credulous audience that self-beheading is really quite unusual, is entertaining precisely because the audience is actually more inclined to disbelief than is the narrator himself. The narrator's sophistication is unmasked as relative naivete, since to believe such outrageous nonsense at all, lengthy protestations notwithstanding, shows the narrator to be more credulous than the reader. Thomas Mann therefore not only expects and tolerates his readers' disbelief in this constitutive statement; he contrives the narration in such a way as to make this disbelief an essential element in the tale's ironic rhetoric.

Neither Mann nor his reader has "suppressed" or "suspended" disbelief with regard to the marvelous elements in *The Transposed Heads*. But neither his nor our disbelief prevents our taking the story seriously or keeps us from being "good readers" in the New Critical sense. As a result we are led to an apparent contradiction, since we would probably all agree that—to take a classic example—importing disbelief in Christianity into a reading of *Paradise Lost* would indeed keep a person from being a "good reader." The events of the Christian salvation history are constitutive elements in Milton's poem, just as self-beheading and magical healing are constitutive elements of Mann's story.

---

[5]*Sämtliche Erzählungen* (Frankfurt: Fischer, 1971), 594–95. "Das ist schnell gesagt, und auch nicht anders als schnell zu tun. Und doch hat hier der Überliefernde nur einen Wunsch: es möchte nämlich der Lauscher die Aussage nicht gleichmütig-gedankenlos hinnehmen als etwas Gewohntes und Natürliches, nur weil es so oft überliefert ist und in den Berichten als etwas Gewöhnliches vorkommt, dass Leute sich selber den Kopf abschnitten. Der Einzelfall ist nie gewöhnlich. . . . Die Selbstenthauptung, so oft sie berichtet sein mag, ist eine fast untunliche Tat, zu deren gründlicher Ausführung eine ungeheure Begeisterung und eine furchtbare Versammlung aller Lebens- und Willenskräfte auf den Punkt der Vollbringung gehört; und dass Schridaman mit den gedankensanften Augen und den wenig wackeren brahmanischen Kaufmannsarmen, sie hier vollendete, sollte nicht wie etwas Gewohntes, sondern mit fast ungläubigem Staunen hingenommen werden."

How is it that we can (indeed must) bring our disbelief to bear on the latter but cannot (indeed must not) on the former?

The answer must be that Mann and his story invite and expect a disbelieving audience, while Milton and his poem invite and expect a believing one. Mann's narrator, like the reporter of Lucian's *True History*, is one who "solicits the reader's incredulity."[6] It is of course rare to find a text whose writer explicitly proclaims, as Lucian does, that he is a liar. The reader's disbelief is usually solicited in some other, less direct fashion, as it is in *The Transposed Heads*. Whatever their method, however, a large class of fictions does solicit incredulity by speaking untruth.

My interest in this investigation is principally in such fictions and in the function of disbelief in our reading of them. I do not mean to imply by this restriction that disbelief cannot have a useful function in the reading of texts that do not invite it. I shall try to show below that Italo Calvino pursues just such a policy in reading scientific texts. Moreover, deconstructionist criticism might be seen as the productive application, to texts that present a surface calling for belief, of an uninvited (and perhaps unwelcome) skepticism about the possibilities of language. As Geoffrey Hartman describes it, deconstruction is a refusal to believe that "the 'presence of the word' is equivalent to the presence of meaning. [It urges instead the opposite,] that the word carries with it a certain absence or indeterminacy of meaning." Indeed, one form of deconstructionist commentary shows that literature "subverts all possible meanings by its 'irony'—a rhetorical or structural limit that prevents the dissolution of art into positive and exploitative truth."[7] Deconstruction, thus understood, is a kind of exploration of the relationship between poetry and untruth. It is a valid and entirely justifiable use of disbelief, one that bears some interesting relationships to the process I seek to describe. But it remains something different. Deconstruction derives from a conception of language's protean nature: just as we think we have caught hold of it, it turns into

[6]*True History (Alethes historia)*, A 4. Lucian's story will be discussed in detail in Chapter 7.
[7]Harold Bloom et al., *Deconstruction and Criticism* (New York: Seabury Press, 1979), viii.

something else. The fictions in which I am interested display a kind of faith in language to pin down the nonexistent, to make something out of nothing, to manipulate the void. The difference between "the untruth of poetry" that deconstruction discloses and "the poetry of untruth" that I am about to describe may seem a small one. But it is, for the moment, decisive.

Another critical concern lying close to this inquiry, and yet crucially different, is the definition of the genre of "the fantastic." Such a definition has already been provided by Tzvetan Todorov in his well-known book on the subject. An examination of Todorov's explanation of the fantastic will show clearly how different is the object of my interest:

> The fantastic requires the fulfillment of three conditions. First, the text must oblige the reader to consider the world of the characters as a world of living persons and to hesitate between a natural and a supernatural explanation of the events described. Second, this hesitation may also be experienced by a character; thus the reader's role is so to speak entrusted to a character, and at the same time the hesitation is represented, it becomes one of the themes of the work—in the case of naive reading, the actual reader identifies himself with the character. Third, the reader must adopt a certain attitude with regard to the text: he will reject allegorical as well as "poetic" interpretations. These three requirements do not have equal value. The first and third constitute the genre; the second may not be fulfilled.[8]

An ideal example of "the fantastic" thus defined (though it is once again my example and not Todorov's) is Thomas Mann's early short story "The Wardrobe" (*Der Kleiderschrank*). Mann describes a certain Albrecht van der Qualen who, while riding the Berlin-Rome express and feeling somewhat sick and sleepy, decides to interrupt his journey at a particular little town at which the train happens to stop. He finds the place attractive somehow and decides to rent a room from a woman who reminds him of a "character out of E. T. A. Hoffmann."[9] In this room is a perfectly ordinary wardrobe, but as van der Qualen is

[8]*The Fantastic: A Structural Approach to a Literary Genre*, trans. Richard Howard (Ithaca: Cornell University Press, 1975), 33.
[9]*Sämtliche Erzählungen*, 122.

preparing for bed he notices that it is not empty. "Someone was standing inside, a shape, a being, so pure that Albrecht van der Qualen's heart stood still a moment. . . . She was perfectly naked and held one of her thin, tender arms upright and grasped with her index finger one of the hooks on the wardrobe's ceiling."[10] She emerges from the wardrobe, that night and who knows how many nights afterward, to tell Albrecht stories, "sad stories offering no consolation." The tale ends with the narrator's asking,

> How long did it last? Who knows? Who knows indeed if Albrecht van der Qualen actually awoke that afternoon and stopped over in that unknown town; if he did not rather remain sleeping in his first class carriage to be borne with incredible speed by the Berlin-Rome express over all the mountains? Who among us would undertake to provide with certainty and acting on his own authority an answer to this question? The whole thing is uncertain. "Everything must be up in the air."[11]

The narrator himself emphasizes the ambiguity of the presentation. Either there really was a naked girl living in the wardrobe, or there was not. If there was not, perhaps van der Qualen had a vision. Perhaps the whole stopover in the town was a dream dreamed in the train. This hesitation between an understanding of the events of the story as marvelous or as natural (as the dream or hallucination of a sick man) is the essence of Todorov's notion of the fantastic. The reader cannot know with certainty how to "explain" the events of the fiction.

One need only compare "The Wardrobe" to *The Transposed Heads* to see the difference between Todorov's subject and mine. There is nothing ambiguous about the self-beheadings or the

[10]Ibid., 124–25. "Jemand stand darin, eine Gestalt, ein Wesen, so hold, dass Albrecht van der Qualens Herz einen Augenblick stillstand. . . . Sie war ganz nackt und hielt einen ihrer schmalen, zarten Armen empor, indem sie mit dem Zeigefinger einen Haken an der Decke des Schrankes umfasste."
[11]Ibid., 126. "Wie lange dauerte das . . . , wer weiss es? Wer weiss auch nur, ob überhaupt Albrecht van der Qualen an jenem Nachmittage wirklich erwachte und sich in die unbekannte Stadt begab; ob er nicht vielmehr in seinem Coupe erster Klasse verblieb und von dem Schnellzuge Berlin-Rom mit ungeheurer Geschwindigkeit über alle Berge getragen ward? Wer unter uns möchte sich unterfangen, eine Antwort auf diese Frage mit Bestimmtheit und auf seine Verantwortung hin zu vertreten? Das ist ganz ungewiss. 'Alles muss in der Luft stehen.'"

healing that follows in the latter tale. They are the central events of the fiction, and they are plainly and clearly incredible. The narrative allows the reader no possibility for a "natural" explanation of what happens to Schridaman and his friends. If the self-beheading is a delusion, it at any rate encompasses the entire universe of the novella. The naked girl in the wardrobe, on the other hand, is readily understood as a dream vision, given the hero's abnormal state of mind at the time he sees her. In *The Transposed Heads,* nothing "is up in the air"; in "The Wardrobe," everything is.

The unambiguous quality of the incredible elements in *The Transposed Heads* is a characteristic of another genre examined, though less centrally, by Todorov. This is the so-called marvelous. The realm of the marvelous is characterized by the presence of "supernatural" elements that remain unexplained (as for example the miraculous healing of the severed heads), though in various subgenres "the supernatural is somewhat justified." Thus the "hyperbolic marvelous" simply exaggerates (serpents that could swallow elephants and so forth) but "does not do excessive violence to reason." Other subgenres present other reasons to prevent the reader's outright incredulity. Only in the pure state of the marvelous is the reader given no explanation, justification, or excuse for the supernatural events described.[12]

This "pure marvelous" comes very close to coinciding with my subject. It does not quite do so, for this reason: Todorov focuses on the "supernatural" quality of events narrated to characterize his genre. I am interested instead in that which is incredible, whether supernatural or not. What are we to make of the "divine," or "Christian," marvelous, in which some narrated events are clearly supernatural but are nevertheless intended to be (and by a sympathetic reader in fact are) believed? With God all things are possible. Todorov would probably call this another "imperfect" subgenre, but my point is still the same. I wish to focus attention more on the matter of disbelief, the reader's and also the writer's, and less on the character of the events that for whatever reason, are disbelieved. To cut off one's own head may

[12]Todorov, *Fantastic,* 54–57.

or may not be "supernatural," depending on how we understand that term, but it is certainly incredible. That *Romeo and Juliet* is a play by Schiller is something we do not believe, but the notion does not partake of the supernatural. Still, the literature of the marvelous will figure prominently in this study, since the incredible and the marvelous form very similar, though not identical, classes.

CHAPTER 2 /

A Taxonomy of Untruth

MY SUBJECT, then, is the function of disbelief as an integral part of the process of reading literature. It is evident, however, that we do not always apply disbelief to all literary texts, nor, when we do, do we apply it always in the same way. We have reasons for not believing texts, and the usual reason we would give, surely, is that these texts are untrue. Since the relationship between disbelief and untruth is not necessarily self-evident, it is appropriate now to explain why I see the two as indissolubly connected and to indicate what I understand that connection to be.

First of all, we should note that believing (and thus also disbelieving) a statement or collection of statements is not quite the same thing as believing, or believing "in," other things. Belief in statements always means an acceptance of those statements as true, while believing other things may not carry such an implication. A good illustration of the distinction, and of its difficulties, is provided by the case of the man who claimed that, while he *knew* that the earth turned on its axis, he did not believe it; he believed, he said, that the sun rose in the east and went down in the west. His difficulty might suggest that belief and truth are separable and that one can believe something that one knows to be untrue. Such a notion of belief would stress a kind of intuitive grasp of a state of affairs, a correspondence between our perceptions and actuality, between phenomenon and noumenon. It would suggest that belief comes from the powerful (though deceptive) evidence of the senses, while knowledge of the truth has a distant source removed by many steps of reasoning from the evidence of the senses. Belief would be immediate, while truth would be mediated by processes of reasoning. Actually, though we can understand and can even accept such distinctions, we must recognize that, far from implying the incompatibility of truth and belief, the man's confession implies only the distinction between believing statements and believing states of affairs. If asked "Do you believe the statement that the earth rotates on its axis?" the man would have had to reply in the affirmative: he would have had to believe because that is all he could mean by saying that he "knew" that the earth did so. What he "knew" was the truth of the statement. That he did not believe the fact did not mean that he did not believe the statement of the fact. Believing a statement entails accepting it as true.

For the purposes of this investigation, it is appropriate to understand "untruth" as the product of disbelief applied to statements. To say that a *text* is untrue is to say that someone does not believe it. Statements are true if and only if someone believes them. I realize that such a definition of untruth ignores certain difficulties of interest to philosophers, but the simplification involved is a necessary and proper one. It is possible, of course, to posit such interesting complications as the case of "accidental" or unintentional truth, that is, when someone suggests something neither he nor his auditors believe but that turns out to be true. Are not such statements actually "true" even though no one believes them at the time they are uttered? If Aristophanes, for example, were to have said that the "fixed stars" were hurtling through space at very high speeds, his statement would not have been believed even by himself. We know, however, that such a statement is true, and since we believe it, we readily suppose that our belief in some sense transcends time.

Since our interest here is language and specifically literary language, it follows that we are concerned with the relation not simply between states of affairs in the world and statements about them but rather between speakers/writers, listeners/readers, utterances/texts, and states of affairs in the world. It is not appropriate for us to investigate the correspondences or lack of them between the world and the word—that is the province of philosophy and science. We must be concerned rather with what those who speak and apprehend words suppose about the relation between language and reality. The scientist may, perhaps even must, disregard the attitude of the writer and the reader in assessing the truth of statements, but literary theorists must place those attitudes at the center of their attention. They must do so because their aim is, after all, knowledge not about the "actual" relationship between statements and reality, but rather about the way in which literary language functions in its human context of authors and readers.

Considered in such a context, "untruth" can only come into being when a text is disbelieved either by its author or by one of its readers. A simple taxonomy of untruth might be made, one would suppose, by arranging the various combinations of believing and disbelieving authors/speakers with believing and disbelieving readers/listeners. Such a taxonomy would be simple, but it would also be relatively useless. When we say something we do not believe or disbelieve something said to us, we invariably make certain assumptions about the attitude of the other party, speaker or listener, involved in the speech act. When, for instance, we disbelieve a statement made to us, we do so in the specific context of an attitude toward the speaker whose utterance we do not believe. In the first place, we try to decide whether the speaker believed the statement he or she made. If we suppose that the speaker did believe what we do not, we are likely to suppose that the statement was an error, while if we suppose that the speaker did not believe it, we will probably suspect that he or she was trying, unsuccessfully, to deceive us. Any taxonomy of untruth must take into account this kind of assumption.

There is a further complication. Because we make assumptions not only about the other party's attitude toward the statement but also about that party's expectations about our attitude, the disbelieving listener will not only try to guess whether or not the speaker believed the statement uttered but will also attempt to decide whether or not the speaker expected our belief. A disbelieving listener who posits a disbelieving speaker may, as I said, suppose that the speaker was lying but will do so only if it is also posited that the speaker expected and wanted the listener's belief. If, on the other hand, the disbelieving listener posits a disbeliving speaker who in fact expects the listener's disbelief, the situation is quite different, and something other than lying is involved. Boccaccio's argument in *The Genealogy of the Pagan Gods* that poets are not liars can be restated in terms of precisely this distinction, which we see made explicit in Sidney's defense of poetry: poets are not liars because they do not expect their readers' belief, even though they do in fact say things they know to be untrue. We may not call a speaker/author a liar unless we have reason to suppose both conditions: first, that he or she did not believe the statement, and second, that he or she expected and solicited the audience's belief. These belong to the "felicity conditions" for the illocutionary act of lying.

A similar set of distinctions must be made when we regard "untruth" from the point of view of the disbelieving speaker. If he or she expects a believing listener who will in turn posit the speaker's belief, the goal in speaking will be lying as we normally understand it. If, on the other hand, that same disbelieving speaker expects a believing listener who will suppose that the speaker disbelieves, we have a different form of deception that we might call "Iagoism." When Othello asks Iago, "Was not that Cassio parted from my wife?" and Iago replies, "Cassio, my lord! No, sure, I cannot think it, / That he would sneak away so guilty-like, / Seeing your coming," Iago explicitly disbelieves his statement about "sneaking away" (he *knows* Cassio has no reason to sneak, having arranged the whole business), he wants Othello to suppose that he disbelieves it (since he wishes Othello to think Iago is Cassio's defender and friend), and he confidently expects Othello to believe it (as Othello indeed does). This convoluted deception follows directly on the heels of another in a slightly different form. When Iago denies that it was Cassio, he disbelieves his statement, expects Othello to disbelieve it, but intends Othello to think that Iago *does* (erroneously) believe it. This "intentional error" differs from both ordinary lying and Iagoism because of the different assumptions and intentions of the speaker in making a statement which he (or she) does not believe.[1]

[1]We can make a table showing the various possibilities derived from this scheme of three differentiae:

My interest lies in texts that solicit the reader's disbelief, that is, in literary situations in which the reader supposes that the author neither believed the text nor expected the audience to believe it. Such texts form a particular illocutionary mode, a special way of doing something in the act of speaking/writing. We do not have a common name for utterances in this illocutionary mode, as we do for "lies," but the absence of such a name shows only that insufficient attention has been paid to this class of speech acts, not that it does not exist. I will call utterances in this mode "apistic fictions" ("apistic" from the Greek *apistos,* "incredible") and will limit my study to that form of untruth. An incredible fiction is one we disbelieve; an apistic fiction is one we disbelieve because our disbelief is somehow solicited. I will leave to other theorists the examination of the other modes (lying, Iagosim, and so forth) indicated by the taxonomy.[2]

But even the limitation of the apistic mode does not sufficiently define the kind of text I wish to examine. We will have to add one more criterion to complete this taxonomy of untruth, and that criterion will have to separate the genuinely "untrue" fictions from the others. The criterion I propose is the presence or absence of an intention to communicate the truth.

As everyone knows who has ever spoken ironically, it is possi-

---

I. The speaker/author disbelieves his own utterance and
    A. expects a believing listener/reader who
        1. posits the speaker's belief [successful lying]
        2. posits the speaker's disbelief [Iagoism]
    B. expects a disbelieving listener/reader who
        1. posits the speaker's belief [intentional error]
        2. posits the speaker's disbelief [apistic fiction]
II. The listener/reader disbelieves what is said to him and
    A. posits a believing speaker/author who
        1. expects the listener's belief [simple error]
        2. expects the listener's disbelief [dogged assertion]
    B. posits a disbelieving speaker/author who
        1. expects the listener's belief [unsuccessful lying]
        2. expects the listener's disbelief [apistic fiction]

Cases IB2 and IIB2 are explained below. IIA2 has not been discussed, but it is not centrally relevant to this inquiry.

[2]On the various mendacious modes, the best introduction is Sissela Bok, *Lying: Moral Choice in Public and Private Life* (New York: Random House, 1978). She includes a useful appendix of excerpts from various philosophers and theologians on the subject of lying.

ble to make an incredible statement and at the same time to intend that statement to convey true information. The name commonly given to this manner of speaking is allegory, though Boccaccio used *fabula* to designate its use in poetry. "In the simplest terms," says Angus Fletcher, "allegory says one thing and means another."[3] Such an intentional breakdown in the relation between signifier and signified makes allegory one of the most interesting and at the same time most dangerous modes of expression. But the term "allegory" and the concept to which it refers are in reality far broader than the apistic mode I wish to discuss. Although the "hidden" meaning of an allegory is often intended to be some form of truth, it need not be so. One can imagine allegories in which the deeper sense would be non-sense (though it is hard to think of examples). Furthermore, the superficial level of an allegory need not be, and often is not, incredible. An allegory need not solicit our disbelief to be an allegory. For these reasons, I propose that a more accurate name for the submode of apistic fictions that intend to communicate the truth would be "aletheic" (which I intend here to mean "truthful though incredible") fictions. Many, though not all, al-legories are aletheic fictions, though *all* aletheic fictions may be called allegories. One common form of the aletheic apistic mode (and thus also of "allegory") is irony. We are all familiar with this form of utterance in which what is said is intended to be disbelieved but in the service of some other (often opposite) truth: I return home from the snowy, traffic-choked streets say-ing, "Lovely weather we're having!"

Although I will have to pay some attention here to the alethe-tic mode, and particularly to its important literary forms, alle-gory and irony, my concern is really with the *other* sort of apistic fiction, the kind that does not seek to convey any truth at all. This is untruth in its purest form, the opposite of "truthful" or aletheic fiction, the *lethetic* mode. This is the manner of speak-ing in which neither the speaker nor the listener believes what is said, neither posits belief on the part of the other, and neither supposes that the untruth spoken is merely a surface behind

---

[3]*Allegory: The Theory of a Symbolic Mode* (Ithaca: Cornell University Press, 1964), 2.

which some sort of truth is hidden. It is not duplicitous, for it is neither mendacious nor "allegorical." It speaks, and it intends nothing more than what it says, thought what it says may be very complex and though what it says is credited by no one.

Since I have coined the terms "alethetic" and "lethetic," I should tell the reader precisely what I intend and do not intend by them. I have derived my designations from the Greek *aletheia* ("truth") rather than from the more familiar Latin *verus* for a number of reasons. First and foremost, I want to distinguish clearly between the notions developed here and the more common conceptions of literary truth derived from mimetic theories of poetry. From the Latin we have "verisimilar" and "verisimilitude," familiar ways of naming the quality of being "true to life." These ideas of poetic truth obviously depend upon a concept of "likeness," and that concept is far removed from the fictional mode I have called alethetic. Verisimilar literature strives to be "like" the world, so like it in fact that we are brought as far as to believe it. Aristotle's theory of poetry, even including his theory of the marvelous, supposes that the "incredible" (*apithanos*) is the thing most studiously to be avoided if a poem is to be successful. Alethetic fictions, on the other hand, like Boccaccio's *fabulae*, are deliberately incredible; they use the reader's disbelief to force the reader to look for the hidden kernel of truth promised by tradition. Alethetic fictions are truthful, in their fashion, but they are never verisimilar.

Another, though far less important, reason for my choice of the term "alethetic" is that is possesses no extraneous and confusing meanings derived from other contexts. I advance this claim in spite of the fact that the notion of aletheia has been treated at length and in detail by Martin Heidegger in various writings, including particularly the essay "The Origin of the Work of Art."[4] Only readers with some acquaintance with Heidegger's writings could make a connection between his thoughts on art and aletheia and mine on alethetic fictions. But such readers, familiar as they would be with Heidegger's philosophy, would recognize instantly that I have in mind nothing as

---

[4]Quotations from this essay are from the translation by Albert Hofstadter in the anthology of Heidegger's essays *Poetry, Language, Thought* (New York: Harper & Row, 1971).

complex and suggestive as his concept of the "unconcealed" and
its central role in the poetic process. Heidegger understands the
Greek notion of truth (aletheia) to be a coming out of concealment, a dis-covery, and on this basis he argues for a view of art as
essentially truthful in its capacity to discover (that is, to bring out
of hiding) beings. The artist through his art *"brings forth* present
beings as such beings *out of* concealedness and specifically *into*
the unconcealedness of their appearance" (p. 59). Since that
unconcealedness is aletheia, truth, art becomes by Heidegger's
definition the discoverer of truth.

My notion of untruth rests on the simple assumption that
when we do not believe that the words of a statement or text
correspond with the world, then that statement or text is, for us,
untrue. Heidegger, though he would surely accept that it is possible for language to be "untrue" in this sense, evidently does not
see this feature of language as central or salient, especially in
poetic language. The language of poetry, which Heidegger con-
siders to be the best example of "authentic" language, does not
concern itself with making representations that are to be compared with "real" states of affairs. Of course it is possible for
language to do so, but Heidegger perceives the "truth" of *authentic* language to be more fundamentally and more important-
ly the truth of aletheia, the bringing forth into unconcealment.
Language speaks: that is the central proposition upon which
Heidegger builds his theory of language,[5] meaning among
other things that authentic, poetic language performs real actions in the world of beings. It does not simply make representations. Considered from this perspective, the proposal of a study
of literature and untruth is not merely trivial or even immensely
profound; it is impossible, a contradiction in terms. Literature
(as "authentic" language) is always truth (as aletheia).

The concept of an alethetic apistic mode as defined here had
best, then, not be linked to a Heideggerian aletheia, since my use
of the term "alethetic" and his use of *aletheia* have very little in
common. In one sense it could even be said that they are opposed, for Heidegger's aletheia brings out of concealment, while
the most prominent feature of alethetic fictions is that they

[5]In the essay "Language" from the same anthology.

"hide" the truth they *mean* behind the untruth they *speak.* Heidegger sees the intermixture of truth and untruth as part of the fundamental structure of truth itself, whereas I (who deliberately equate truth with belief) find this intermixture only in certain modes of utterance.

Heidegger's concept of truth as "unconcealedness" is of course based on an etymological understanding of *aletheia,* a noun formed from the adjective *alethes.* It is an interesting accident of the Greek language that this common word meaning "true" is a negative formed by the addition of the alpha privatum to a root that can mean "to escape notice, to be unknown, unseen, unnoticed" but also "to let something escape notice, to forget."[6] This latter sense of the root is represented by the noun *lethe,* "forgetfulness, oblivion." The noun *aletheia,* then, can mean "that which is not hidden, that which has not escaped notice," as Heidegger's interpretation stresses, or it can be understood as "that which is not forgotten, that which has not been allowed to escape one, that which is remembered." Because of the way the Greek word is formed, it can have no negative—it is a negative already. There can be nothing in Greek analogous to the English "untruth." In terms of the structure of the Greek language, the opposite of *aletheia* (in the "root sense" of the word) is *lethe:* untruth is "forgetfulness."

My term "alethetic" should be understood to refer to what is "not forgotten" rather than to what is "unconcealed." The alethetic apistic mode brings forth texts that are incredible but that do not forget the "real" world. It uses the readers' disbelief to make them remember what they do believe or would believe and to find that believable thing "under the surface" of the fiction. It appears to break apart the relation between the word and the world, but by remembering the world it urges the reader to reestablish that relation by reinterpreting the word in such a way as to make it correspond to the world.

Lethetic fictions, on the other hand, present words that are oblivious of the world of things (not, as we will see, of the world of language). The reader does not believe them, and knows they

[6]Liddell and Scott, *An Intermediate Greek-English Lexicon,* (7th ed. Oxford: Oxford University Press, 1964).

do not correspond to the world, but solves the problem created by that disbelief by letting the words go their own way independently. I do not mean that such a reader sees the words as forming a new or other world worthy of belief. He or she does not simply transfer allegiance from the "real" world to an imaginary one, because disbelief continues to function. Rather, readers allow the world for a time to escape them—or themselves to escape the world—by attending to a sovereign form of language.

Because the lethetic fiction lets the world slip away, it has nothing but the word to sustain it, and it becomes radically language centered (a "logocentrism" that is the exact opposite of the logocentrism Derrida finds in the orthodox Western tradition), spinning its marvels from the commonplaces of everyday speech. By taking language seriously—and it has nothing else to take seriously—a lethetic fiction turns that language into a fantasy world such as that which we find in the genres of science fiction and "the marvelous." The term "lethetic," however, may refer not only to a genre but also to a *mode*, not only to a kind of literature but also to a way in which literature may be written or read. We are at liberty to disbelieve anything we hear or read, and it follows that we can read any genre of literature in the apistic mode. We are also at liberty to remember the world or to forget it, so that anything we disbelieve may be interpreted either lethetically or alethetically. In practice, of course, the choice we make will depend to a great degree on what the text encourages us to do, so that we may speak of a "lethetic text" as well as of a "lethetic reading" of a text. While the lethetic mode of reading may be applied to any text, only a relatively small number of works solicit such reading and may be properly assigned to the lethetic genre.

It will be important to keep in mind this distinction between the lethetic genre and the lethetic mode in the following discussion. The center of my interest is the genre, with texts that provide in various ways clues that they do not want our belief. We cannot ignore the fact, however, that the application of lethetic reading to texts that seek to be believed is an option that always remains open. That the option is there, however, does not mean that it must always be exercised. If it were appropriate or necessary to read all fiction lethetically, there would in fact be no need for the set of distinctions for which I argue here.

Still, a small group of writers are concerned, both theoretically and practically, with the results of reading lethetically texts that quite obviously do not invite lethetic reading. Although the lethetic genre is my main interest, then, completeness requires that I pay some attention (in Part 3) to at least a few representatives of those authors who make regular use of the lethetic mode.

On the other side, there are readers who will not wish to read lethetically, no matter what encouragement they are given to do so. Angus Fletcher notes that "all literature, as Northrop Frye has observed, is from the point of view of commentary more or less allegorical,"[7] and Boccaccio suggested centuries earlier that every conceivable text, even the fireside tales of a "maundering old woman," can be understood as a *cortex* beneath which some *intentio* is hidden.[8] Indeed, a strong tradition, which Boccaccio helped establish, informs the training of most sophisticated readers and urges that all reading of incredible texts be alethetic reading. In part, I hope to show how we might learn to resist this urge to alethetic reading and why and in what circumstances we would want to resist it.

This contrast between lethetic and alethetic reading is essential to the theoretical foundation of my inquiry, but it is not upon the distinction itself that my ultimate interest centers. The core of my concern is specifically the lethetic mode. The alethetic mode, particularly its ironic and allegorical versions, has already received extensive theoretical attention from scores of subtle minds. Though the element of disbelief essential to it has not been, from my point of view, sufficiently stressed, on the whole our critical tradition has provided us with a substantial framework for discussing alethetic reading. Lethetic reading, on the other hand, has been misunderstood and neglected to such a degree that its very existence is likely to be a matter of controversy.

Because it renounces any claim to discover the "true" refer-

---

[7] *Allegory*, 8.
[8] Vincenzo Romano, ed., *Genealogie deorum gentilium libri* (Bari: Laterza & Figli, 1951), 2:705 ff.

ence of the text it disbelieves, lethetic reading runs counter to the most powerful tendencies of philosophical and critical orthodoxy. The alethetic reader swims with the current. Though he or she may disbelieve the letter of the text being read, this reader seeks and indeed finds an "interior," some semantic structure related to the text by analogy or another definable relationship, and thus finds "truth." This process is predicated on deeply held assumptions, including the trust in language that urges the belief that *all* texts, no matter how incredible they may seem, convey valuable information about the world. The world about which true information is conveyed may prove to be very small: in the case of psychoanalytic hermeneutics, for example, the "world" about which truth is assumed to be told is the microcosm of the speaker's psyche. Nevertheless, given that restriction, *every* text produced by a single mind is assumed by psychoanalysis to be a storehouse of true information about that mind, no matter how incredible or absurd the text may look. Indeed, the mechanisms of the mind, as Freud describes them, are such that the more absurd a text looks, the more important is likely to be the information that it covers up and distorts. Psychoanalysis goes even further than the biblical hermeneutics Boccaccio wanted to apply to secular poetry, for it combines the most radical skepticism about the surface of its texts (readers of the Bible were on the whole committed to the value of the literal level) with the sincerest faith in the capability of language to embody the truth. This is as true of Lacan's practice as of Freud's.

Lethetic readers neither believe the text nor "believe in" the power of language to represent the world. I do not say that they have less reverence for language than alethetic readers—as we will see, just the opposite is true—but that they are not interested in language as an instrument to describe or discover reality. They may suppose it possible for texts to convey information about the world, but as readers such a possibility has no reality and thus no meaning for them. Lethetic readers do not find hidden truths, but neither do they seek to demonstrate the difficulty or impossibility of conveying truth through language. They may want to deconstruct a text in an explicatory fashion, as a way of seeing how the language of a text works, but they would not do so as a way of demonstrating the inadequacies of language (or of that text) as an epistemological tool, because it does not matter to them whether language may be so used or not. Such questions, important though they certainly are in their own terms, are of no importance to the reader of lethetic fictions. Indeed, it is very possible that one becomes a lethetic reader in order to "escape" just such questions.

An escape of this sort is a matter not of deception or of pretending that the questions do not exist but of "forgetting" them in the sense of focusing attention elsewhere, of simply adverting to something else. The person who writes a lethetic fiction is not deceptive in drawing our attention away from the world to which his text does not correspond. Since by definition such a lethetic text is one the reader does not believe, there can be no deception. Readers, having determined that the text before them does not correspond to reality, may then ignore reality without being deceived and without deceiving themselves.

The "forgetting" that takes place in reading lethetic fictions is of a particular sort. The lethetic reader in the act of reading forgets not that the world exists—he or she could not then exercise disbelief—but rather that the world is powerful, far more important under normal circumstances than peculiar objects, such as lethetic fictions, that ignore it. But even this much forgetfulness is a great deal when we consider its object. The text must offer much in return to justify finding it more powerful and more valuable than the world of things, events, values, and feelings usually called "reality." The crucial point at issue in the chapters that follow, then, will be precisely this: What prompts a reader to prize, for the moment of reading at least, a fiction he does not believe more highly than the world he knows and inhabits?

CHAPTER 3 /

The Imitation of Language:
Logomimesis in David Gerrold
and Thomas Mann

A TEXT THAT solicits our disbelief severs its language from the world and requires us either to reject it out of
hand (and thus cease reading) or to acknowledge the power of
language, of that text's language, as superior to any other
power. If its power is superior to that of the world in general, it
is certainly superior to our own personal power. Forgetting the
world and forgetting ourselves thus amount to the same thing
insofar as both sorts of oblivion result from submission to the
sovereignty of the word. We submit willingly not only because
the text seems benevolent in its obvious disinclination to deceive;
not only because submitting is itself enjoyable; but also because
submission to the authority of the word-as-signifier (rather than
the word-as-trace of some aspect of the world) liberates us from
another, potentially oppressive authority.

Acknowledgment of the sovereign power of language is an
essential feature of lethetic fictions: the definition of the mode
entails it. There is nothing to be obtained from a text wherein
the word does not correspond to the world except the word
itself. And there is no "action" for the lethetic fiction to imitate
except such "actions" as language itself provides. Lethetic narratives are thus often *logomimetic* in that they reproduce or elaborate structures found not in the nonlinguistic world but in the
resources of language itself. I have coined the term "log-

omimesis" on the model of Gérard Genette's *mimologiques* but of course with the opposite signification.[1] Genette is interested in what he calls "Cratylism," the *"myth* of a *motivation* of the linguistic sign . . . , the idea of a motivation by *analogy*—a relation of resemblance, a mimetic relation—between 'the word' and 'the thing.'"[2] I see in lethetic literature an actual motivation of "myths," that is, of fictional texts as narratives, by analogy with the microstructures of ordinary speech. Figurative language in particular provides, as we will see, a rich storehouse upon which the writer of lethetic fictions can draw. Of course, any fiction, lethetic or not, can make use of logomimesis in various parts of its structure, but the lethetic fiction tends to make the reproduction and elaboration of linguistic structures the fundamental impulse or "moment" of its coming into being. The transformation of a trope into a narrative moment is thus one of the most characteristic strategies of lethetic literature.

A good illustration of this process is provided by David Gerrold's short story "With a Finger in My I."[3] Like many works in the field of fantasy and science fiction, this story pursues the implications of a linguistic structure, usually some common expression from ordinary language, when that structure is assumed to govern the structure of the fictional world. In this story, the commonplace of language that interests Gerrold is the one that says "the world is going to pieces—falling apart at the seams" (p. 410). The action of the story concerns the reactions of a man to his discovery that the world is, quite literally, coming apart.

Disintegration begins in a small way with an echo of Gogol's "Nose":[4] the hero discovers that a part of his body is mysteriously missing, in this case not his nose but the pupil of his left eye. This finding would distress most of us, but the narrator protests that the really disturbing thing is that he can still see out of that left eye: "If I hadn't been able to see out of it, I wouldn't

---

[1]See *Mimologiques* (Paris: Seuil, 1976).

[2]"Valéry and the Poetics of Language," in Josué V. Harari, ed., *Textual Strategies* (Ithaca: Cornell University Press, 1979), 359.

[3]Anthologized in Harlan Ellison, ed., *Again Dangerous Visions I* (New York: Signet, 1972), 402–11. Citations below in the text refer to this edition.

[4]See Chapter 6 for a discussion of "The Nose" as a logomimesis.

have worried. It would have meant only that during the night I had gone blind in that eye. But for the pupil of the eye to just fade away without affecting my sight at all—well, it worried me. It could be a symptom of something serious" (p. 402). Taking the larger view, which the narrator does most unselfishly here, these sentiments are quite correct. For an individual's body to start coming apart is, after all, not so very unusual. True, people do not often "lose" a pupil overnight, but they do from time to time lose their sight. What does not ordinarily happen, and what could cause some genuine philosophical anxiety, is for the ability to see to "come apart" from the organ of sight. This event is evidence that the world, not just the narrator, is indeed beginning to come apart.

The problem is serious enough to prompt the narrator to consult a physician. After numerous difficulties, he finally arranges a visit to a doctor, evidently a psychiatrist, who thinks the patient is complaining about a problem with his "I." In the meantime, the world continues to deteriorate: "Bigger cracks were beginning to appear in the image and tiny pieces were starting to slip out and fall slowly to the ground" (p. 407). The doctor explains that this problem is occurring because "the world is a collective figment of all our individual imaginations" (p. 408), and "everybody is starting to believe in different things and they're forming pockets of non-causality" (p. 409). The doctor, in other words, believes in the practical efficacy of logomimesis. She takes the narrator to task for being one of those people who talk about the world's "going to pieces" and thereby contribute to its actual collapse.

The doctor is not the only character who takes the coherence of word and deed so seriously. One of the main obstacles to the narrator's seeing the doctor in the first place has been a receptionist who, like some mad creature from *Alice in Wonderland*, acts in exact conformity to the literal meaning of each utterance she encounters. When the narrator asks to "see a doctor," she replies, "There goes one down the hall now. If you look quickly, you can catch a glimpse of him. See! There he goes" (p. 404). This sort of thing continues for some time before the narrator is able to make any progress at all, and even then "everything seemed to be all wrong. The whole world seemed to be slipping off sideways—all squished together and stretched out and tilted so that everything was sliding down toward the edge" (p. 405). The connection between the disastrous condition of the world and the literal-mindedness of the receptionist is explained only later by the doctor's theory.

The universal logomimesis finally infects the narrator as well. At first he just passively accepts it, as he accepts the receptionist's misreadings of his own language. But after consulting the doctor and finding that "the more she talked, the more I began to believe it, too" (p. 409), he begins to participate. Shifts in the meaning of words become alterations of his world. He walks past a public speaker in the park, who is making the usual sort of park speaker's speech, then a second "speaker," one that "woofed and tweetered" (p. 410). Since the word "speaker" can mean both a person and a mechanical device, the story's "reality" can shift from one to the other as easily as the word. Having reached home, the narrator "paused long enough to stroke the cat. He waved as I came in. 'Like—hello man,' said the cat" (p. 411). One sort of cat can turn itself instantly into another, can actually "be" both sorts at the same time in a unity sanctioned by the ambiguity of language. As the structure of this world continues to crumble, the story ends with the narrator's protest that, while it may have been true that people's perceptions of the world were altering things, "I haven't noticed anything" (p. 411).

Gerrold's story, like all logomimetic fiction, makes the structure of its fictional reality conform to patterns provided by everyday language. Instead of attempting to make the work of literature "hold the mirror up to nature" and imitate in a convincing way the world as it is, the logomimetic artist chooses to imitate structures that are already purely verbal. In doing so, he or she looks at the verbal surface only and reads the mother tongue the way Gerrold's receptionist does: no attention is paid to intended meaning. In Gerrold's story, the phrase "the world is going to pieces" is taken at face value, as if the metaphor underlying it were literally true, as if "the world" were a constructed object that could actually disintegrate into its constituent parts.

I want to insist on the *mimetic* element in such fiction. The structural principles behind fantasies like Gerrold's are not unknown to us. They are not even new. They are, on the contrary, the most familiar principles in the world, derived as they are from the commonest of our linguistic commonplaces. We have all heard the assertion hundreds of times that the world is "falling apart at the seams," but it does not occur to us (as it does to a logomimetic imagination such as Gerrold's) that we might look for the seams. Contrary to what we might assume, a story like "With a Finger in My I" is just as much the "imitation of an action" as the *Oedipus* of Sophocles. It tries just as hard consistently to conform to a structure external to itself, to a pregiven "reality." For logomimetic fiction, that reality happens to be language.

Although logomimetic fiction *imitates* language, the language imitated is not the fiction's *meaning*. I cannot urge this point strongly enough. However we want to understand the concept of "meaning," it is clear that the objects of imitation used by a fiction do not constitute such meaning. We readily accept this fact in the case of poetry that imitates the nonlinguistic world. We do not imagine that *Julius Caesar,* for example, which takes for its objects of imitation characters and actions from Roman history, has these characters and actions for its meaning. This point is particularly evident in the case of allegory, in which the meaning of the text is always different from the ostensible objects of imitation. In the case of logomimetic fiction, the meaning is probably most readily identified with the effects the fictions exercise upon the reader (most frequently—very much in general—amusement or horror) rather than with any propositional content. In this view I share the basic assumptions of critics such as Wolfgang Iser and Stanley Fish, who locate textual meaning in the experience of the reader. I will return to the issue of the "meaning" of lethetic texts in the concluding chapter.

The logomimetic text need not make explicit—as Gerrold's story happens to do—the particular linguistic structures it is imitating, providing those structures are some form of ordinary discourse. Just as our knowledge of the workings of the real

world constitutes an important part of our "literary competence" (in Jonathan Culler's terms)[5] or "horizon of expectation"
(H. R. Jauss's Gadamerian terminology)[6] when we read a mimetic work, so does our knowledge of the commonplaces of language become part of the background against which a logomimetic work is perceived. Philip Roth does not have to explain
what kind of people he is portraying in *Goodbye, Columbus:* he
expects us already to be familiar with the types and to enjoy
recognizing his imitation. If we do not possess this knowledge,
we will be less competent as readers of Roth. When we are in the
act of reading logomimetic literature, linguistic competence becomes a special sort of literary competence in that it enables us to
grasp the work's logomimetic foundation. We recognize (usually
unconsciously) the fictional structure, incredible though it is, as
somehow "right" or "perversely logical." We recognize its conformity to some linguistic form. Even if Gerrold's doctor had
never uttered the phrase "the world is going to pieces," we
would have sensed something familiar about the premise of his
story.

Logomimesis can therefore provide a kind of justification, a
sense of "rightness," to the wildest fantasy imaginable. "With a
Finger in My I" may seem crazy and wild, but it does not after all
seem so unfamiliar. Furthermore, the reader understands that
the author's playfulness is at the same time a form of high seriousness: language is being taken seriously to the degree that it
is given priority over, control over, the structure of the fictional
world. This is the "seriousness" of games, the willingness to
submit to the authority of the game's own structure. Furthermore, the reader shares the linguistic competence of the author
and therefore understands implicitly the rules of the game. The
logomimetic principle can thus provide a certain security to the
reader, even though "the world" of the fiction might be "coming
apart."

Lethetic reading thus rendered "secure" by logomimesis
therefore exhibits a certain family resemblance to Freud's "jests"

[5]See Culler's *Structuralist Poetics* (Ithaca: Cornell University Press, 1975),
113 ff.
[6]See Jauss's *Toward an Aesthetic of Reception* (Minneapolis: University of Min-
nesota Press, 1982), 22 et seq.

as described in *Jokes and Their Relation to the Unconscious.*[7] The impulse to pure verbal play that originates in childhood continues into adulthood, Freud believes, but it comes into conflict with "a factor that deserves to be described as the critical faculty of reasonableness." If "the old game of getting pleasure" from language is to continue, a method must be found of "silencing the objections raised by criticism which would not allow the pleasurable feeling to emerge." Freud suggests that a jest, as opposed to a simple joke, must have some sort of meaning:

> What distinguishes a jest from a joke is that the meaning of the sentence which escapes criticism need not be valuable or new or even good; it need merely be *permissible* to say the thing in this way, even though it is unusual, unnecessary or useless to say it in this way. In jests what stands in the foreground is the satisfaction of having made possible what was forbidden by criticism.
>
> It is, for instance, simply a jest when Schleiermacher defines *Eifersucht* [jealousy] as the *Leidenschaft* [passion] which *mit Eifer sucht* [with eagerness seeks] what *Leiden schafft* [causes pain]. [Pp. 128–29]

Everyday language in the form of the phrase "the world is falling apart" provides just such a means of silencing objections to a story in which the events reported are absolutely incredible. It is *permissible* for Gerrold to describe the disintegration of the world, because the idiom has sanctioned it. Indeed, Gerrold's procedure is not very different from that ascribed to Schleiermacher except that Schleiermacher's logomimesis results not in a story but in a definition. The structure of the words *Eifersucht* and *Leidenschaft* allows them to be analyzed in such a way as to suggest an alternative (one might almost say "literal") reading of their phonological structures. Interpreting the substantive suffixes *-sucht* and *-schaft* as the finite verbs *sucht* and *schafft* is not something we believe, but it is permitted, almost invited, by the phonology of German. It would not be improper, in fact, to consider Schleiermacher's jest a small-scale lethetic fiction.

The reader may not be certain that it is valuable or good to

---

[7]Trans. James Strachey (New York: Norton, 1963). Citations below in the text refer to this edition.

detail the process by which the world might fall to pieces, but the potential criticism that such a narration is incredible and therefore useless is blunted by the logomimetic element. Such a structure of events may not correspond to our experience of the structure of the world, but it does correspond to our experience of the structure of language. We are therefore able to "accept" what we cannot believe. A logomimetic lethetic fiction, like the joke work, involves "a choice of verbal material and conceptual situations which will allow the old play with words and thoughts to withstand the scrutiny of criticism; and with that end in view every peculiarity of vocabulary and every combination of thought-sequences must be exploited in the most ingenious possible way" (p. 130). In this way, even the fact that a statement is incredible can become a source of enjoyment: "Whatever the motive may have been which led the child to begin these games, I believe that in his later development he gives himself up to them with the consciousness that they are nonsensical, and that he finds enjoyment in the attraction of what is forbidden by reason" (pp. 125–26).

Part of the pleasure of lethetic fiction would be, if we follow this notion, the antithetical pleasure of rebellion, the joy of the forbidden. The problem with such illicit pleasures, of course, is that we are exposed to the censure of our internal psychic watchdog: "The power of criticism has increased so greatly in the later part of childhood and in the period of learning which extends over puberty that the pleasure in 'liberated nonsense' only seldom dares to show itself" (p. 126). The watchdog can be drugged to sleep, Freud asserts, by alcohol, under the influence of which "the grown man once more becomes a child, who finds pleasure in having the course of his thoughts freely at his disposal without paying regard to the compulsion of logic" (p. 127). A psychologically more complex alternative to this drugging of the critical faculty is the discovery of a means to satisfy it. We throw the watchdog a bone so that we may return to our "liberated nonsense," now safe and secure.

But who cares if the reader feels secure? Does not literature properly seek to dislodge the reader from the security of his cherished beliefs? The majority of "reader-response" critics, including Jauss, Iser, and Fish, suggest that literature becomes more interesting the more it challenges our expectations.[8] While it is surely true that some literature tries to do so, such a challenge is not the sine qua non for interesting fiction. Lethetic texts solicit the reader's disbelief, but they never do so in an attempt to challenge beliefs against which the fiction works. Quite the contrary, since lethetic texts cannot function if the reader's normal beliefs, ordinary conception of reality, are shaken, the last aim of lethetic fantasy is to alter the reader's views. Lethetic readers can function at their best only when they are secure in the knowledge that what they are reading is untrue. The lethetic text must play against a firm background of belief. Logomimesis helps keep that background firm and the reader secure. There is doubt neither about the untruth of the material presented nor about the origin of that untruth (that is, about the method by which it comes into being).

Readers might well recognize the method as akin to the process of reading in which they are engaged. When a fictional text imitates the figurative language of everyday usage, it always imitates precisely the face value of that language and never its real-life intention. In Gerrold's story, for example, the fictional premise rests on what would be in everyday circumstances a misreading of the phrase "the world is going to pieces," a misreading exactly analogous to the inappropriately literal interpretations of the receptionist. Logomimesis ignores the intention behind figurative language and treats it as if it had no connection with some actual state of affairs in the world. But of course David Gerrold, unlike the receptionist, knows very well the intended meaning of "the world is going to pieces." He simply ignores it. And the meaning he then finds in it to imitate is not a semantically incorrect one but merely one that is forgetful of the phrase's real-world intention. In other words, it is not so much a *mis*reading of the phrase as a lethetic reading.

A lethetic *text* produced by logomimesis can be properly understood to result from the application of the lethetic *mode* to a

<hr>

[8]See H. R. Jauss, *Toward an Aesthetic*, 25; Wolfgang Iser, *The Act of Reading* (Baltimore: Johns Hopkins University Press, 1978), 216–17 and elsewhere; Stanley Fish, "Literature in the Reader: Affective Stylistics," in Jane P. Tompkins, ed., *Reader-Response Criticism* (Baltimore: Johns Hopkins University Press, 1980), 88.

form of language—tropes, clichés, commonplaces—that in a sense invite us to advert to what is said rather than to what would be meant in "real" discourse. Of course the lethetic *mode* can be applied to any text at all, including texts that urgently seek belief, and such texts can then become the basis for a logomimesis resulting in a lethetic fiction. Far more common, however, is the situation in which the object of the logomimetic process, a process which is itself an act of reading, is a kind of language that can easily lose its connection to reality. No grammatical or semantic straining is required to loose the phrase "the world is going to pieces" from its everyday, figurative meaning. All we have to do is take it out of context, and the literal meaning quickly overwhelms the figurative; we become quickly aware of what these words would imply if we were putting them together this way for the first time. The norms of lexical meaning reassert themselves the moment we ignore the phrase's use in real discourse.

When a lethetic text is based on logomimesis, then, part of its invitation to the reader that he let its language remain free from the obligation to conform to the world stems from the fact that this text evidently came into being by doing the same with the language it imitates. Still, part of the invitation will have another source, namely in the fact that the events so derived are themselves incredible. If these events prove somehow to solicit belief (for example, by inviting allegorical interpretation), a logomimetic origin will not be enough to make the text lethetic. Indeed, we find a fair number of texts that are unquestionably logomimetic but are also unquestionably alethetic, texts that seek to convert the disbelief engendered by the logomimesis into belief by means of irony or allegory. We must take care to remember that, while logomimesis always results from a process of lethetic reading, it need not always produce a lethetic fiction.

The subject of logomimesis as it functions in alethetic literature requires and deserves separate study, but it will be useful for us to look briefly at an example here in order to secure the frontiers of our field of inquiry. Such a quick examination of the topic will help to show how potentially lethetic subject matter can be turned to alethetic uses, and it will provide an opportunity to continue, in a concrete context, clarifying the concept of logomimesis.

In Chapter 1 I mentioned Thomas Mann's novel *The Transposed Heads* as an example of a text that solicits the reader's disbelief. It is also an instructive example of a logomimesis rather more subtle than that of David Gerrold. I do not say that there is anything subtle about the incredible elements themselves in Mann's story—they are outrageous enough to obtrude upon the consciousness of the dullest reader. I mean only that the logomimetic character of these events will not be immediately evident to all. Mann does not do what Gerrold does: he does not cite the text whose language he is imitating. It is only upon reflection that we realize that a topos is the foundation of this fantasy.

Mann's story solicits our disbelief most centrally by presenting an exchange of heads between the two principal male characters. Schridaman and Nanda both commit the remarkable act of self-beheading, but—more incredible still—the goddess Kali offers to rejoin the heads to the bodies. Most incredible of all, when the heads are rejoined, it turns out that a mistake was made, that the Nanda head was joined to the Schridaman body and vice versa. This is certainly the sort of thing one expects of an apistic fiction, but what does it have to do with logomimesis? The answer is supplied by a realization that this action, and in fact much of the earlier action as well, arises from the lethetic reading of the German phrase *den Kopf verlieren* ("to lose one's head").

Our English idiom is almost exactly equivalent, so my reader will readily understand that the physical severing of the heads of Schridaman and Nanda is only the last step in a process of "losing their heads" over a girl named Sita. They chanced to observe Sita one day as she went to bathe in the river, and the sight of her naked body was so bewitching, so irresistibly enticing, that both fell in love with her. The complications and frustrations arising from this love triangle eventually bring about the situation in which the young men actually lose their heads in an attempt to settle what reason (which has been lost) cannot.

One of Nietzsche's joking verses from "Scherz, List und

Rache" in *Die fröhliche Wissenschaft* shows an analogous, but more explicit, logomimesis:

> *Den Kopf verloren*
>
> Sie hat jetzt Geist—wie kam's, dass sie ihn fand?
> Ein Mann verlor durch sie jüngst den Verstand.
> Sein Kopf war reich vor diesem Zeitvertreibe:
> Zum Teufel ging sein Kopf—nein! nein! zum Weibe! [#50][9]

Nietzsche's poem is also about "transposed heads," though here the figurative meaning of the idiom *den Kopf verlieren* is kept clearly in view, as it is not in Mann's story. Nietzsche is playing a verbal game with two German idioms, both with *den Kopf verlieren* and with *zum Teufel gehen,* putting them together to suggest the possibility of a "departure" of the man's head, not to the devil after all, but to the woman.

Nietzsche's verse is helpful in showing the logomimetic basis of the narrative premise Mann has taken for *The Transposed Heads.* Mann does not explicitly quote the idiom, as Nietzsche does in his title, but he has no reason to do so. David Gerrold does so because logomimesis happens to be not only the method of his story but also its theme. Nietzsche does the same because he is engaged in *Scherz:* he wants to advert to the aspect of wordplay in his poem. Mann has neither of these motivations. It is also possible—but not very likely—that Mann was not conscious of the logomimetic basis of his story. It is of course irrelevant to this analysis whether or not he was aware that his fantasy originated in a topos: it matters only that we understand the connection.

This logomimesis provides the impetus for the story and the specific justification for its incredible central scene, but Mann then moves the narrative in a direction that makes certain an alethetic reading. After the heads have been exchanged and rejoined to the wrong bodies, the story seems to reach a certain stability. The clever head of Schridaman is now joined to the

---

[9]A literal English translation: "Lost His Head: Now she has intellect—how is it that she found it? A man recently lost his reason over her. His head was well endowed before this pastime: his head went to the devil—no, no! to the woman!"

beautiful body of Nanda, while the not-so-bright head now belongs to the thin and weak body. Upon the advice of a holy man, the lovely Sita succeeds in keeping as her husband the clever-head-beautiful-body combination, thus enjoying the best of both worlds, while the less fortunate head-body combination is resigned to retire into the wilderness. Given the incredible premise of the exchangeability of heads, the situation should be stable. But it is not stable. Another marvel takes place: "In time . . . , and indeed in no long time, the Nanda-body, crowned with the honoured husband-head, became of itself, and aside from any Maya, quite a different one. Under the influence of the head and the laws of the head, it gradually became like a husband body."[10] The same process occurs with the other body, which gradually changes under the influence of the Nanda head into a beautiful Nanda body.

The second marvel absolutely negates the effect of the first. The natural order of the relation between body and head, disturbed momentarily by the miraculous exchange, is restored. It becomes clear to the reader that the supernatural separability of head and body proposed by the logomimesis has been proposed only to be decisively rejected by the rest of the story. There can be no doubt that this tale has a point to make and that this point has to do with the dominating power of the head (returned here to its status as a metaphor) over that of the body (also as metaphor). The lethetic, literal reading of the idiom *den Kopf verlieren* has been introduced, it is now clear, only to be exposed by events that authorize a figurative, alethetic reading. The "exchange" that the incredible premise makes possible is shown to be impossible after all. Even if you could transpose heads, the story tells us, you could not "transpose heads."

Mann's story makes very clear, then, that its logomimesis is not to be understood lethetically, because it does not simply let the structure of language dictate the structure of the world. Super-

---

[10]*The Transposed Heads,* trans. H. T. Lowe-Porter (New York: Vintage/Random House, 1959), 95–96; *Sämtliche Erzählungen* (Frankfurt: Fischer, 1971), 627–28. "Mit der Zeit also, und zwar in gar nicht langer Zeit, wurde der vom verehrten Gattenhaupt gekrönte Nanda-Leib auch an und für sich und von aller Maja abgesehen ein anderer, indem er sich unter dem Einfluss des Hauptes und seiner Gesetze nach und nach ins Gattenmässige wandelte."

natural events cannot for long disrupt the natural order here, and the head-body relationships obtaining at the story's beginning are precisely restored before its end. The story never "takes back" its incredible premise, of course; there is no explanation for the supernatural events, no justification as there would be if the story were "fantastic." Instead, the incredible premise is transformed into the impetus for allegory. Here we can see how lethetic and alethetic fictions work in opposite ways, when employing logomimesis. Both begin with a topos that can be understood either as figurative truth or as literal untruth, and both spin a narrative out of that topos. In the lethetic fiction, the fiction as a whole is assimilated to the literal, untrue aspect of the idiom (as in Gerrold's use of "the world is going to pieces"), while the alethetic text ultimately reasserts the figurative nature of the topos (as in Mann's *den Kopf verlieren*) and indeed of its own structure as a whole. In lethetic logomimesis, the narrative makes the figure literal and leaves it that way, while in alethetic logomimesis the figurative nature of the premise ultimately makes the whole text into a figure. It is a question of whether, in the confrontation of narrative and figure, the text "narrativizes" the figure or the trope "figuralizes" the narrative. In Mann's story, the ultimate function of the logomimesis is to direct us toward reading the whole of *The Transposed Heads* the way we ordinarily read the idiom *den Kopf verlieren*. Gerrold's story, on the other hand, uses the narrative structure to enforce an abnormal, extraordinary (but entirely plausible) literal reading of "the world is going to pieces."

Since logomimesis begins by making explicit in narrative the "literal" and incredible reading of an idiom or trope, the natural tendency for logomimetic fiction is in the direction of lethetic reading. Logomimesis naturally solicits disbelief, and that disbelief will be applied to the text as a whole unless or until the reader is given some strong signal that his disbelief is to be reinterpreted as appropriate only for the "surface" of the story. Mann, we notice, provides such a signal by introducing a second marvel that effectively cancels the first. Since the events of the story do not allow the results of the logomimetic principle to stand, the whole procedure is put "under erasure" as it were, supplying thereby the doubleness, the ambiguity necessary for alethetic reading. The erasure of the effects of "losing one's head" gives us a clue that this must not be the playful fairy tale it resembles at first. The name "Thomas Mann" on the title page will resolve any further doubts, as Mann certainly expected it would. It was, after all, a similar assumption about the seriousness of the author of the "Song of Songs" that prompted commentators on the Bible to put its explicit eroticism under erasure. This issue of the cultural factors that favor alethetic reading is an important one, and I will discuss it in detail in Part 4.

For now it is enough to indicate the connection between such assumptions about the seriousness of authors and their texts and Freud's suggestion that a psychic mechanism tends to prevent our enjoyment of "liberated nonsense." The suppression of lethetic reading is not only an individual but also a sociocultural phenomenon. Roland Barthes has made this point forcefully in the opening paragraph of *S/Z*, where he observes:

> Our literature is marked by the relentless division which the literary institution maintains between the producer and the user of a text, its owner and its client, its author and its reader. This reader is thus plunged into a sort of sloth, of intransitivity, and, in a word, of *seriousness:* instead of playing himself, instead of giving in fully to the enchantment of the signifier, to the seriousness of writing, there falls to his share no more than the poor freedom to receive or to reject the text: reading is no more than a *referendum*.[11]

For Barthes, the only texts that a reader can "desire" and take pleasure from are those that can still be written, that is, rewritten by the reader.

Lethetic texts based on logomimesis are the product of a kind of imagination that sees all language as *scriptible* ("writable" or "writerly"). Idioms and tropes are taken up in the spirit of "giv-

---

[11]*S/Z* (Paris: Seuil, 1970), 10. My translation of: "Notre littérature est marquée par le divorce impitoyable que l'institution littéraire maintient entre le fabricant et l'usager du texte, son propriétaire et son client, son auteur et son lecteur. Ce lecteur est alors plongé dans une sorte d'oisivité, d'intransitivité, et, pour tout dire, de *sérieux:* au lieu de jouer lui-même, d'acceder pleinement à l'enchantement du signifiant, à la volupté de l'écriture, il ne lui reste plus en partage que la pauvre liberté de recevoir ou de rejeter le texte: la lecture n'est plus qu'un *referendum*."

ing in fully to the enchantment of the signifier" and are rewritten. David Gerrold's "With a Finger in My I" is surely the result of discovering, and acceding to, the enchantment of the phrase "the world is going to pieces," which he rewrites by divesting it of its ordinary figurative seriousness. Freud argued that our desire to engage in such playful rearranging of the materials of language is restrained by the "critical faculty." Barthes sees the restraint in a culturally enshrined preference for passivity before the authority of the text. For both, special effort is needed to overcome psychic or cultural resistance and to reassert the right to play with language.

Freud, as I mentioned above, suggests that it is easier to return to the pleasure of "liberated nonsense" if our critical faculty can be assuaged by some "meaning." Barthes sees such a process at work in the fiction of Flaubert, who has "a way of cutting, of perforating discourse *without rendering it meaningless*" (italics in the original). Rhetorical language for Flaubert is not something exceptional, a gleaming jewel "set in the base matter of common utterance," but rather the very basis of the text as a whole, "so that this very readable discourse is *underhandedly* one of the craziest imaginable: all the logical small change is in the interstices." Flaubert, in other words, presents a text that looks *lisible* and is therefore utterly satisfying to our critical faculty and to the literary institution that insists on seriousness. Upon closer inspection, however, the logic turns out to be only decorative filler in a structure essentially composed of craziness. Barthes identifies the source of this craziness not only as rhetoric but as "the *mimesis* of language (language imitating itself)." While this mimesis is not exactly the same as logomimesis, as I have defined it, the similarity is instructive. Barthes finds the origin of Flaubert's nonsense in something akin to the logomimesis that forms the basis for many lethetic fictions.[12]

Flaubert's text is fundamentally crazy and playful because it arises from language's imitation of itself, but it is not meaningless. It has an abundance of "logical small change in the interstices." This element is essential for Barthes, though not ex-

---

[12]*The Pleasure of the Text*, trans. Richard Miller (New York: Hill and Wang, 1975), 8–9.

actly for the reason Freud would give. I mentioned above the
need for a lethetic text to have a firm background to play
against, a background that is provided in part by the "rightness"
of the language that is imitated. Barthes also sees the need for
the antithetical, *scriptible* work to have something to stand out
against:

> There are those who want a text (an art, a painting) without a
> shadow, without the "dominant ideology"; but this is to want a text
> without fecundity, without productivity, a sterile text (see the myth
> of the Woman without a Shadow). The text needs its shadow: this
> shadow is *a bit* of ideology, *a bit* of representation, *a bit* of subject:
> ghosts, pockets, traces, necessary clouds: subversion must provide
> its own chiaroscuro.[13]

For logomimetic fictions, this little bit of representation comes
from the topos, the logomimesis that stands *in loco mimesis*. It is
something we recognize as familiar and whose authority we can
accept, even when the fiction proceeds to turn it topsy-turvy and
to "forget" its serious, figurative intent.

One of Barthes's most illuminating insights about Flaubert's
success in the game of producing a text that is both crazy and
readable is also one that holds good for lethetic fiction: "This is a
very subtle and nearly untenable status for discourse; narrativity
is dismantled yet the story is still readable."[14] Barthes presents a
Flaubert who is very much like the writer of lethetic texts: he
tries to produce nonsense that has the apparent structure of
sense. But if such nonsense were to convince us that it *really were
sense,* it would fail; it would turn into allegory or irony. But if it
offered no "bit of a subject," nothing to which we could assent, it
would fail as well. The lethetic fiction must gain our assent without gaining our belief. To that end, logomimesis offers a particularly effective strategy.

[13]Ibid., 32.
[14]Ibid., 9.

Part Two /

The Lethetic Genre

CHAPTER 4 /

The Rhetoric of Unreality: Aristophanes' Birds

THE HERO OF Aristophanes' *Birds* is named Pisthetairos, or Peisthetairos, or Peithetairos—the exact form is uncertain. His name might mean "trusty companion" or "persuasive companion" or perhaps even "one who persuades companions." We will probably never know just what connotation Aristophanes sought.[1] The name is unquestionably derived from the root *peitho*, which in the active mood means "persuade, convince" but in the middle and passive shifts to "have confidence in, trust, believe." The Greek language suggests the notion that belief is the result of persuasion, so that there is no real difference between a "persuasive companion" and a "trusty" one. The noun *peitho*, "persuasion," was commonly used in connection with the theory of rhetoric to denote the object of oratory. The successful *logos* was that which persuaded the audience of the truth, justice, or desirability of the speaker's position. Pisthetairos shows himself to be a splendid rhetorician in this sense and is worthy of the title "Persuasion's companion."

I want to show in what follows that Pisthetairos's rhetorical skill underlies not just the essence of his character but indeed the entire fictional structure of which he is a part. The *Birds* is thus to be understood as radically logomimetic, for it uses the

---

[1] B. B. Rogers disagrees. See the introduction to his edition of the play, *The Birds of Aristophanes* (London: George Bell & Sons, 1906), viii–ix.

structures of ordinary language as models for its narrative. It even goes so far, in fact, as to take for its subject the process of constructing such a narrative. In other words, the *Birds* is a lethetic fiction whose story is the construction of a lethetic fiction. It is the narrative of putting together a fictional "world" (Cloudcuckooland) on the basis of structures that are purely linguistic and by manipulation of those structures in a purely linguistic way. The play thus proposes (or, in the metaphor of the fiction, "builds") a sovereign realm of language, of purest untruth, that gives absolute freedom to an unfettered rhetoricity.[2] The figures of speech need not, in such a realm, justify themselves by representing something: they need only play and interact and draw attention to themselves. They are free—as birds.

If we care to believe the birds themselves—that is, the chorus of birds in the play—they *are* birds. The first parabasis makes a splendid argument in favor of the central importance of birds in the history of the universe and the life of mankind, and one of the principal cadences occurs on the following lines (ll. 719–22):[3]

> You call a bird everything having to do with omens:
> A voice/rumor/oracle is one of your birds; you call a sneeze a bird,
> A sign a bird, a sound a bird, a servant a bird, an ass a bird.
> Are we not then manifestly your prophetic Apollo?

> ornin te nomizete panth' hosaper peri manteias diakrinei:
> pheme g' humin ornis esti, ptarmon t' ornitha kaleite,
> xumbolon ornin, phonen ornin, therapont' ornin, onon ornin.
> ar' ou phaneros hemeis humin esmen manteios Apollon?

The passage takes off from the fact that the Greek word *ornis* was used to mean an omen, "without direct reference to birds," according to Liddell and Scott. But it goes far beyond this (ap-

---

[2]I mean this word in Paul de Man's sense but especially as developed in my essay "Kafka's Rhetorical Moment," *PMLA* 78 (Winter 1983). For de Man's definition of rhetoricity, see *Blindness and Insight* (New York: Oxford University Press, 1971), 136; and also *Allegories of Reading* (New Haven: Yale University Press, 1979), especially the first chapter.

[3]References to the *Birds* are to Rogers's edition, though I do not always follow his readings. Important deviations from his text are noted.

parently nearly "petrified") metaphor to develop a virtual equation of "birds" and "words." The term *pheme* can mean "oracle," which fits easily into the announced context of birds and prophecy, but it also can mean "voice" and "rumor" and indeed any "talk" or "speech" in general. This association leads in two directions, to concepts traditionally linked with omens, such as sneezes, and to the broader area of the symbol (*xumbolon*). All signs are called "birds" (according to the birds) and thus all language (*phone*). Everything that carries meaning is a bird, so apparently everything that carries *anything* is a bird, too, thus servants and asses. B. B. Rogers confesses to the suspicion that "the allusion to a *therapon* and an *onos* is merely a comic winding up of the various objects which might be considered 'birds',"[4] though there has been much scholarly speculation about possible connections between birds or omens and servants and asses. There may be no connection whatever beyond the notion that the word *ornis* is interchangeable with any other word, since words are in effect birds. The attention of the audience is thus shifted from the *signatum* (the concepts of "servant" and "ass") to the *signans* (the linguistic structures *therapon* and *onos*). A transformation of the entire universe into birds such as that suggested in the parabasis is to a large extent carried out in the plot: all the characters who are not birds to begin with either become birds or desire urgently to become birds or at the very least are willing to become part of the avian empire.

The passage develops from a logomimesis, an elaboration and literalization of a rhetorical figure: the metonymic substitution of "bird" for "omen." The chorus of birds takes so seriously the power of language that it does not distinguish between "calling" something by another thing's name and the one thing *being* the other. The comic effect is substantial, of course, but the joke is not on the birds, who emerge absolutely victorious at the end of the play, or on the humans who use such imprecise language. The joke is on language itself, whose rhetoricity creates situations in which a fellow cannot tell his ass from a bird in the air— cannot *tell* the difference. We may see a difference or know one, but we cannot tell it, speak it. The position of the birds in the

[4]Rogers, *The Birds of Aristophanes*, 98 n.

chorus is that a difference that cannot be told cannot matter. The result of the rhetorical power of language to metamorphose everything into an *ornis* is that *ornithes* supplant the gods. "Manifestly," the birds claim, "we are your prophetic Apollo." What need is there for Apollo himself if the birds can replace him? The answer of the play is that there is no need at all.

The circumstances in which these lines about the power of birds and words are uttered both support and effectively dismantle the concept being put forth: it is, after all, just so much birdsong. The situation presented is so outrageous, with such a throng of imperialistic birds strutting back and forth, planning to build a city in the sky, that the audience cannot believe the fiction to be a representation of anything in the world. Literary critics have tried to discover ways to read the play alethetically, to convert their disbelief into the discovery of underlying meaning, but the most acute readers of Aristophanes have come to find this procedure unproductive.[5] The play is a fantasy that is an allegory of nothing. The reader remains incredulous, he forgets the world (which clearly has no connection to this text) and attends to the word. The power that the birds claim for themselves is a power derived from *language,* but also a power *over* language—and nothing else, as long as we disbelieve. The rhetoric of the *Birds* is a rhetoric of persuasion, a peitho, based on a rhetoric of tropes, in which tropes (birds) try to convince us that tropes (both words and birds) have tropologic power—that is, the logomimesis keeps turning back on itself, increasing its power through feedback. Pisthetairos exercises this power better than anyone else and is the chief spokesman for the "tropocentric" position, a position that can only be successfully defended inside the magic circle of a lethetic fiction. The avian rhetorician is convincing only as long as we do not believe. The "persuasive companion" is persuasive only as long as he is *not* a credible (*pistos*) representation.

When Pisthetairos first announces his great plan for a city in the sky, he asks for the trust of the birds: "I see a great scheme for the birds, and the power [*dunamis*] to bring it off, if you'll

[5]See, for instance, Gilbert Norwood, *Greek Comedy,* 2d ed. (New York: Hill and Wang, 1963), chap. 6, and Cedric Whitman, *Aristophanes and the Comic Hero* (Cambridge: Harvard University Press, 1964), chap. 5.

trust me [*ei pithoisthe moi*]" (ll. 163–64). But this trust does not require that he be believed by the audience, which stands outside the circle; it requires only that he persuade the birds of the play, who are inside it. Even some characters themselves, we should note, do not actually believe Pisthetairos: Tereus the Hoopoe, the first of the birds to be converted to Pisthetairos's scheme, is thoroughly persuaded of the value of this happy idea, but he is also thoroughly incredulous. When the chorus asks Tereus, "What are the words he [Pisthetairos] speaks," the Hoopoe replies, "Incredible things, beyong hearing [*apista kai pera kluein*]" (ll. 415–16).[6] His enthusiasm for the grand scheme is bound up with its incredibility, and there is no better way to express that enthusiasm than by stressing that the plan is not to be believed: "He speaks of some great bliss neither sayable nor believable [*legei megan tin' olbon oute lekton oute piston*]" (ll. 421–22). As it turns out (and as Tereus well knows), the plan is neither beyond hearing (*pera kluein*) nor past telling (*oute lekton*): its power consists entirely in Pisthetairos's ability to speak of it persuasively. But it *is* incredible (*apista, oute piston*), and it has power over the listener/reader precisely because he or she is willing to let disbelief function in the lethetic mode, turning attention away from the world, which the text ignores, to the word, which it celebrates.

The paradox of Pisthetairos's success at speaking the unspeakable is the paradox of all self-referential, logomimetic language, which does not worry about the connection, or lack of it, between speech and the world. Since the reader through his disbelief has, like the Hoopoe, been willing to accept such a disjunction of word and world, Pisthetairos's oratory concerning the power of words (that is, birds) is highly persuasive. For this reason attempts at alethetic readings of the *Birds* are unsatisfactory and in a real sense destructive of the play's effect. To seek connections, though hidden ones, between the text and reality is an activity that can only undermine the text's most crucial as-

[6]Rogers puts a comma between *pera* and *kluein*, explaining that *pera kluein* is neither "good Greek nor good sense" (note to v. 416, p. 52). But *pera legein* is attested in Sophocles, according to Liddell and Scott, and therefore it is hard to believe that a precisely analogous expression would be bad Greek. That it is not good sense says nothing against it, given the context.

sumption. The issue is not whether one allegorical interpretation or another is correct: it is rather that the very idea of allegorical interpretation is incompatible with the idea of
Aristophanes' fiction. A correct alethetic reading, if we could
find one, would stand in opposition to the rhetoric it claimed to
clarify.

There is no reason to be surprised, then, that Pisthetairos
himself shares the disbelief of his audience and of the Hoopoe in
the "truth" of his city in the air. It would be inconsistent for him
to believe in the marvelous things he has created, since it is the
nature of the marvelous to engender disbelief. When a mes-
senger informs him that the city's wall has been constructed by
the birds in practically no time, even Pisthetairos is made to
marvel: "Do you marvel [*thaumazeis*] that the building was done
so quickly?" asks the chorus (ll. 1164–65), and he replies, "In
truth it seems to me like lies [*isa gar alethos phainetai moi
pseudesin*]" (l. 1167). Dudley Fitts's translation, "Why, it's a lie
come true!"[7] brilliantly captures the comic juxtaposition of *alethos* and *pseudesin* but obscures the basic issue: the untruths have
not been transformed into truth. Pisthetairos acknowledges that,
considered in terms of a correspondence between representation and reality—that is, "in truth"—these marvels are lies.
Pisthetairos is not a poet on the model of Aristotle's Homer, who
knows how to "lie as one ought" and can make the incredible
disappear. On the contrary, he thrusts the untruth in front of
the audience's eyes. His is not the rhetoric of the *eikos,* which
seeks to persuade the audience of the appropriateness of its
representation: his is the rhetoric of the lethetic mode, which
seeks to persuade us to forget, to loose the surly bonds of earth,
to let his winged words carry us away.

In commenting on the excellences of the *Birds,* Gilbert Norwood suggests that the only possible flaw to be found in the play
would arise from our belief in it: "to enjoy the wildest story we
must entertain a spurious momentary belief in it; and if we do,"
we find ourselves misunderstanding Aristophanes.[8] Norwood is

[7]*Aristophanes: Four Comedies* (New York: Harcourt, Brace & World, 1957), 217.
[8]*Greek Comedy,* 242. The rest of the quotation, though not exactly relevant to
my argument, is worth recording: "and if we do, the Basileia passage might seem
more suited to Shelley's *Prometheus Unbound* than to Aristophanic drollery. But

surely right to suppose that a "spurious momentary belief" would be detrimental to our enjoyment of the *Birds,* though my reasons for thinking so are quite different from his. But why in the same breath does he insist that such belief is essential to "enjoy the wildest story"? If such belief is indeed "spurious," that is, "illegitimate, invalid, false," then it hardly seems necessary. Aristophanes goes out of his way to make sure that the chances for such spurious moments of belief are minimized, and we have no reason to assume (aside from those reasons advanced by Aristotelian notions of representation) that we cannot do entirely without them. Norwood, acute critic that he is, is sensitive to the necessity of disbelief to the success of the *Birds,* but he cannot rid himself of the received idea that poetry cannot function without belief. The result is that his position is quite self-contradictory and stands a testimony to the power both of Aristophanes and of Aristotle.

In spite of the never-ending attempts to find ways to read the *Birds* in the alethetic mode, critics like Norwood and, more recently, Cedric Whitman have argued effectively against allegorizing the play. Norwood is blunt:

> In the *Birds* [Aristophanes'] purpose, for anyone not obsessed with research-mongering, is almost too obvious to state: it was the working out of a glorious comic fancy. . . . We should hardly be justified even in asserting that it satirizes the irresponsible day-dreams of man (whether Greek or barbarian) in his weaker moments. No one at all is derided: this is a fairy-tale gloriously funny and gloriously told.[9]

Dudley Fitts agrees that

> the [satirical] attack this time is of less importance than the creation of a comic dream, the dream of Cloudcuckooland the Beautiful, that ideal commonwealth in the skies. Elaborate political reconstructions of the dream have been made—classical scholarship is ingenious and tireless—but they seem, in all their complexity, pas-

---

we have no business to harbour memories of Shelley and other more orthodox writers on the divine government; this passage is only another proof of the un-Hebraic lightness wherewith Athenians could on occasion take their religion."
[9]Ibid., 241.

times better suited to the academies of Cloudcuckooland itself than to the enrichment of our understanding.[10]

The most sophisticated and stimulating reading of the play to date is that of Cedric Whitman, who goes beyond the nonetheless important assertion of the primacy of the "comic fancy" or "comic dream." Whitman realizes that the play is a logomimesis, that it is built on the notion of the power of speech. Whitman remarks that

> when we speak this language [the language of absurdity], we play with words and give them a primacy over their meanings which inverts our usual sense of reality. The *Birds* plays with language in a way far beyond any of the other comedies, and the sense of reality undergoes considerable change by consequence. . . . The word is all, it creates consciousness, and its enormous vitality stubbornly resists fact. A word becomes an image or metaphor, and the image or metaphor lives in the mind, independent of reason and far more compelling. . . . Images and metaphors are dream substance and make dream worlds, and every world is an absurdity, a verbal nothing.[11]

Whitman provides evidence from the writings of Gorgias that such a view of the "priority of language" over reality existed among the ancient Greeks and that thus to interpret Aristophanes does not "do historical violence, by introducing modern ideas of relativism, subjectivism, and the question of the relation between reality and language."[12]

As the argument I have made so far would indicate, I am in general agreement with Whitman's approach. Brilliantly insightful though it is, however, I think his reading is a little misleading in one area. That Aristophanes plays with words and "gives them a primacy over their meanings" is beyond dispute: Whitman's analysis of the *Birds* would alone be enough to make it so. But that such wordplay "inverts our usual sense of reality" remains a highly doubtful contention. The distinction, the lack of correspondence, between language and reality is the essence of

---

[10]*Four Comedies*, 159.
[11]*Comic Hero*, 172–73.
[12]Ibid., 173.

disbelief, and the *Birds* goes out of its way to be sure of its audience's disbelief. The issue is not "reality" but power, not whether words have the ability to make new and separate worlds (what M. H. Abrams has called "heterocosms"),[13] but whether the word has the power to function independently of the world, to take our attention away from reality in a head-to-head contest. "Speech," says Whitman, "assists and directs the 'subjective restructuring of the world,' and thus occupies a position of power analogous to, if not identifiable with, divinity itself." Such a statement seems less applicable to Aristophanes than to the romantic view of the function of literature as analyzed by A-brams.[14] This position assumes that the reader's belief is essential if the heterocosm, the "subjective restructuring of the world," is to be accepted. Aristophanes quite clearly does not want our belief, our agreement that his play is a representation of a world that is "probable" if indeed also "impossible." There is no restructuring of the world, subjective or otherwise, in the play. The world goes its own way, untouched, unrestructured.

This disagreement notwithstanding, Whitman's discussion of the *Birds* in *Aristophanes and the Comic Hero* remains one of the most acute readings of a lethetic text that I know of. Whitman understands, though he does not formulate that understanding as I would, that the fiction is founded upon logomimesis. He notes that the opening of the play is based on what he calls a "dramatized metaphor," the Greek slang phrase *es korakas elthein*, "to go to the crows" (equivalent to the English "go to the dogs"). "The metaphor in hand may be no more than simple slang, but to stage two characters who pace out the actual steps of 'going to the birds' has the unmistakable effect of putting language itself in the controlling position."[15] It is an operation one finds frequently in lethetic fictions, what I would call the transformation of topos into atopos, of rhetorical commonplace into the outrageous. It is useful to recall that Liddell and Scott even propose "paradox" as one of the meanings of *atopos*. The rhetoric of the *Birds* is composed of a use of tropes that goes against expectation, *para ten doxan*, by rendering the com-

---

[13]*The Mirror and the Lamp* (New York: Oxford University Press, 1953), 272 ff.
[14]Ibid., 278, for instance.
[15]*Comic Hero*, 175.

monplace "out of place" (*atopos* = "without place"). Its suasion
(peitho) works neither through nor toward the *doxa* of the audience, as is the case with ordinary rhetoric, but exactly counter
to it.

The *Birds'* rhetoric is, for all its persuasiveness, highly disinterested. The transformation of topos into atopos takes language that we assume to be connected to the world from its
normal place, severs cleanly its bonds to reality, and lets it float
splendidly in the air. It does not wish to convince us that we, too,
should "go to the crows": it is not utopian propaganda. The city
of Cloudcuckooland is not utopia but atopia, and there is no way
for us to reach it except on the wings of sovereign speech. But
that, after all, is what the peitho of Pisthetairos tells us all along,
that language can do the impossible and incredible. That it can
does not, however, make the impossible and incredible any more
possible or credible than they were before. Reality is unaffected
by the power of speech, though opinions may be changed by it.
Aristophanes shows over and over again how language can be
both omnipotent and totally ineffectual at the same time. And
from time to time he lets us glimpse the fact that, were we not
sure of the ineffectuality, the omnipotence would be neither
exhilarating nor entertaining. It would be horrifying.

The metamorphosis of topos into atopos takes place under
circumstances that are carefully fenced off from the situations to
be encountered in the "real" world that conforms to doxa. And
indeed one of the most certain methods a text can use to establish the magic circle that surrounds a lethetic fiction is to display
such metamorphoses, to show us its logomimesis. Such a display
reminds us that incredulity is called for, if only to keep us safe
from the power such transformations represent. It would be, at
the very least, extremely uncomfortable and unsettling to live in
a world in which a fundamental principle of the universe, "spin"
(*dinos*), important enough to be worthy of worship as a god,
turns out to be a big pot (*dinos*). That this happens in the *Clouds*
is both very funny and potentially very disquieting, funny to us
who stand safely outside the circle but a cause of real discomfi-
ture for poor Strepsiades. We may laugh to watch Pisthetairos
reveal and then realize his plan to turn the *polos* ("celestial
sphere") of the birds into a *polis* ("city"), but we do so secure in

the knowledge that the world in which we actually live does not permit such things.

It is for this reason that I must disagree with critics such as Dudley Fitts who insist that *"The Birds* is not a play of escape."[16] Whitman also contends that the play ought not to be seen as "an escapist manifesto."[17] Both Fitts and Whitman are of course attempting to defend Aristophanes against a charge that critics are fond of leveling against works they disapprove of, since the word "escapist" is always meant in the most disparaging sense possible. But just because the charge of escapism that critics make is silly we ought not to dismiss the concept it misuses. The *Birds* does rely to some degree on the need to escape, not from Athens, but from the ambiguities of language that make Cloud-cuckooland possible, into the privileged safety enjoyed by the audience of a fiction. Our incredulity allows us to escape the consequences of living in a logomimetic universe. It is a wonderful place to visit, but we can be glad that we do not have to live there. Those who do have to live there are figures of terror. By encouraging us to retain our disbelief, the lethetic fiction can present what is terrifying, can let us both take part in and escape from it at the same time. I will discuss lethetic horror in detail in Chapter 6. For now, I want just to suggest that a literary work may be both "escapist" and valuable without contradiction.

For the birds in the play, the transformation of the polos into a polis is literally a change from topos to atopia. Pisthetairos explains to the Hoopoe, who is not quite sure what is meant by *polos,* since it is an unusual word, even for a Greek, that it means simply topos: the birds' "place" (l. 180). The birds give up their real place, the polos, for an imaginary polis that exists only through the power of the trope. This transformation is paralleled by another, the change of the birds themselves from speechless barbarians to masters of language and of the marvels that language can generate. Thus they move from being themselves *aloga* ("dumb animals") to having power over *aloga* ("inexplicable things"). And as the birds become the rulers of atopia, we find that the gods of Olympus are reduced to aloga, barbar-

[16]*Four Comedies,* 159.
[17]*Comic Hero,* 168.

ians unable to utter coherent speech. Pisthetairos changes, too, not simply by becoming himself a winged creature, but by becoming more secure in his mastery over language. This mastery involves not only the making of speeches but also the interpretation of the utterances of others.

At crucial points in the play, the most important form of rhetoric is the rhetoric of reading, which is based on such interpretation. The opening scene of the play is a scene of reading in which Pisthetairos and his companion Euelpides try to interpret the croaking and cawing of a couple of birds. They have purchased these two, a crow and a jackdaw, as guides to help them find the man-turned-bird Tereus, from whom they wish to learn about the various cities he has flown over. They want to find a better spot than Athens to which to "retire." Tereus, having been a man, can be expected to speak Greek, but to find him the two Athenians must follow the advice of aloga, the crow and jackdaw. Doing so presents considerable difficulties, not because the birds fail to find their way to Tereus, but because the men are unable to understand what their calls and gestures mean. Euelpides keeps asking Pisthetairos what his bird has to say: "What does your crow say about the road?" (l. 23). Of course the crow has nothing at all to *say*, dumb creature that it is. Though it has wings to fly, it has no winged words. The men are in no better condition themselves: they are able to speak, but they have not yet developed their skills to the point where they can take wing. Euelpides describes their departure from Athens as "winging away from our homeland on both feet [*aneptomesth' ek tes patridos amphoin podoin*]" (l. 35). The speechless birds and the wingless men are trying to fly on their feet, but Aristophanes suggests they will only succeed when they learn to take off on the metrical "feet" of poetic speech. Until then there is no way for them to "find the way," and they are faced with an *aporia*, a lack of passage. "We're ready and willing to go to the crows," says Euelpides, "and yet we are not capable of finding the way [*epeita me 'xeurein dunasthai ten hodon*]" (l. 29). The dunamis (power, capability) that is lacking will be supplied by Pisthetairos's rhetoric, his power over language, including the power to read the language of others. This is the power to make "feet" into wings.

The birds' ability to speak and Pisthetairos's to understand are perfectly linked in the play, by the logic of juxtaposition, if not by cause and effect. We learn later that Tereus has "taught language [*edidaxa ten phonen*]" to the birds, who had formerly been "barbarians" (ll. 199–200). But before Pisthetairos "sees" his grand scheme, the only birds in the play (excepting the man-bird Tereus and his servant) are such speechless barbarian birds, the crow and jackdaw, whose mouths are good only for biting (ll. 25–26). The revelation of the birds' ability to speak comes after Pisthetairos has demonstrated his ability to speak by convincing the Hoopoe of the magnificence of his plan. Thus, although we are told that Tereus taught the birds language long since, what we witness is a dramatic change from barbarian birds to fully articulate, civilized (*civis = polis*) creatures deserving a city to house their civilization. The *aporia* that results first from the Athenians' losing their way, then from the unacceptability of the Hoopoe's suggestions for a better hometown, is made to vanish through the sudden acquisition by both man and bird of an awesome power of speech. The dunamis that had been lacking is supplied by Pisthetairos's logos. The birds of the chorus urge him to share with them the wonderful thing he has, "some power greater than my stupid wits can detect [*dunamin tina meizo paraleipomenen hup' emes phrenos axunetou*]" (ll. 455–56). The power to change a polos into a polis is more than sufficient to make the birds into gods.

Inside the magic circle of the lethetic fantasy, rhetoric is not only the result of an aporia but its solution.[18] The gap between trope and persuasion ceases to exist when it is no longer necessary to concern ourselves with the relation of language to the world. When the entire universe of discourse is discourse, tropes become arguments—and very persuasive arguments at that. Here is a situation in which the figural nature of language cannot mislead us, where the undecidability between dinos/spin and dinos/pot may be transformed from a problem into the solution to all problems. If there is no more difference between the sky and a city than an iota, no more difference between birds and the power of speech than the literalization of a metonymy, then

---

[18]I refer here to Paul de Man's argument, culminating on p. 131 of *Allegories of Reading*, that rhetoric exists as "the aporia between trope and persuasion."

those who control the tropes control everything. And the birds, through Pisthetairos, control the tropes.

Who, then, would not want wings? As it turns out later, everyone does, and one schemer after another comes to Pisthetairos seeking to be winged. The last of the wing-wishing rascals is an informer, and to him Pisthetairos tells straight out the nature of the birds' power: "everyone can fly with words [*pantes tois logois anapterountai*]" (ll. 1438–39). The verb *anapetomai*, which occurs a number of times in the scene with the informer, was used in the very first scene to describe how Pisthetairos and Euelpides "flew away from Athens on both feet." Even irony—and Euelpides' *aneptomesth'* is surely ironic—is subject to the logomimesis that drives the play forward. By substituting *logois* for *podoin*, words for feet, Pisthetairos does not so much transform the figure as point to the force behind it, for it is only words that make figures possible. The topos is driven to atopia by the obvious paradox of Pisthetairos's procedure, for the power (dunamis) he finds in words is released by ignoring the significance (*dunamis* = "force, meaning") of the figures he uses. The fictional, fabulous structure of Cloudcuckooland is raised into place by a *dunamis adunate*, an impossible power that is also a powerless power.

Pisthetairos is not consistent in his logomimesis. Why should he be? He does not always literalize his tropes, and when it suits him, as it does at the end of the scene with the informer, he can unexpectedly use a figure as a figure. Disgusted with the lack of success his rhetoric has had with the informer—"I wanted to turn you, winging you with honest words, to lawful work [*anapterosas boulomai chrestois logois trepsai pros ergon nomimon*]" (ll. 1448–49)—he exchanges his verbal wings for Corcyraean wings (*Korkuraia ptera* = "Corcyraean whip") and scourges the informer from the stage (ll. 1461 ff.). This informer has been treated to a most thorough lesson in the "vertiginous possibilities of referential aberration"[19] inherent in rhetoric. The radical suspension of logic that Pisthetairos engenders remains under his control, and he uses tropes however it pleases him. In practice, that is, he makes the decisions not only about what he says

[19]*Allegories of Reading*, 10.

but also about what the things he says mean. His authority resides not so much in his ability to bring forth various tropes and topoi as in his absolute right to read himself. We do not know from one moment to the next whether we are dealing with the literal or the figurative level of language: we must wait for Pisthetairos to tell us. And he is always ready to tell us, ready with readings that operate in the context of the lethetic fiction but whose atopia makes them ineligible for acceptance in the world we live in.

Though Tereus the Hoopoe claims credit for teaching the birds to speak, Pistehtairos was the one who brought them the real power of speech by showing the power of reading. The reason the birds did not recognize their rightful place of sovereignty was that they were "unlearned and not curious, and you haven't pored over Aesop [*oud' Aisopon pepatekas*]" (l. 471). The interpretation of *apologoi* is obviously one of Pisthetairos's specialties, and by sharing his skill with the birds he brings them a gift as valuable as the one Prometheus gave mankind or more so. The contrast between Prometheus and Pisthetairos is made evident when the former appears near the end of the play to share some information and advice. We are made to realize that Prometheus' gift of fire to men, valuable though it was, was as nothing compared with Pisthetairos's gift to the birds. Prometheus received only trouble for his pains, but Pisthetairos is about to win away from Zeus sovereignty (*Basileia*) over the entire universe. Prometheus comes to make sure that, when the gods come to make terms, Pisthetairos insists upon having Basileia as his bride. He also announces that the barbarian gods, the Triballians, are pressuring Zeus to make peace with the birds. The existence of these barbarian gods surprises Pisthetairos, as it does us. "Are there actually some other gods, barbarians, above you?" he asks (ll. 1525–26). And indeed, when the divine delegation arrives, it consists of Poseidon, Heracles, and a barbarian Triballian god.

Why, in this final dialogue scene in the play, does Aristophanes contrive the appearance of a barbarian god of whose existence we had hitherto been unaware? Whitman does not try to explain, perhaps feeling that those who do try may well belong in the academies of Cloudcuckooland. Heinz Hofmann, in

Mythos und Komödie, his monograph on the *Birds,* resorts to the principle of political representation: "With regard to the Triballian, his participation is motivated solely by the democratic principle, which accordingly presupposes the presence of barbarian gods on Olympus. The spread of foreign cults in Athens certainly played a role in all this, as they increased toward the end of the fifth century and engendered bitter enmity." Hofmann argues further that the references to the barbarians' being "above" has nothing to do with superior position but refers only to their geographical location "up north" in Thrace, the source of such foreign cults. "The principal function of the Triballian god is therefore to exhibit the disadvantages of the democratic principle," we are told, in that he affords a comic contrast to the other members of the delegation, whose sociopolitical roles are more traditional.[20]

This pronouncement is very learned and ingenious, but I think an explanation of the Triballian's presence can be found closer at hand, by considering the structure of the play rather than the religious history of Athens. In any case, the Aristophanes with whom we are familiar did not hesitate to satirize his enemies head-on: if he had wanted to express his displeasure with foreign cults or with the democratic principle, he would have been clear about it. At issue in the play is not the democratic principle but the power of speech, and in the final scene is dramatized the Olympians' abdication of authority over language. Since the opening scene shows the birds as barbarians and Pisthetairos as an unsuccessful reader, it is fitting that the closing scene should show the gods, whom the birds have supplanted, as barbarians and Pisthetairos as a successful reader. The play as a whole thus presents a symmetrical reversal of the roles of birds and gods, and the Triballian is a key figure in making that symmetry clear. Poseidon's lament, "O democracy, what will you bring us to, if the gods elect such a one!" (ll. 1570–71), is more an indictment of his fellow gods than of the democratic principle, for in electing the barbarian to be a member of the embassy, they have in effect given up. And in the

---

[20]*Mythos und Komödie: Untersuchungen zu den "Vögeln" des Aristophanes* (Hildesheim: Georg Olms, 1976), 133–34.

remainder of the scene Poseidon acquiesces to the "votes" of Heracles and the Triballian without much protest. The difficulty with these ballots among the ambassadors is not the principle but the incomprehensibility of the barbarian's words.

The purpose of making the democratic principle part of the action here is not to satirize it so much as to create a situation in which the decision about the future of the universe is made in effect by an *alogon*, a dumb brute. The Triballian speaks "all but unintelligible Thracian"[21] or what Fitts calls "a murky language rather like that of Muta and Juva in *Finnegans Wake*."[22] Much learning has gone into the deciphering of this gibberish, so much indeed that Whitman can claim that "the Triballian's speech is clear enough except for 1615, *nabaisatreu*, and this has been most plausibly explained as *ne Belsourdon*, 'Yes, by Zeus Campestris.'"[23] Perhaps it is clear to linguistic scholars such as Joshua Whatmough (who offered the explanation given above), but it seems unlikely that it was intended to be clear to the audience. It certainly is not clear to the other characters, who interpret it in contradictory ways. One is tempted to agree with Fitts that "much needless ingenuity has been expended by Professors attempting to reduce it to sense,"[24] for to see it as "sense" *would* be a reduction of one of Aristophanes' most brilliant jokes. Two preliminary ballots prepare for the ultimate confrontation between Pisthetairos and the delegation over the restoration of Basileia to the birds. In the first, Poseidon and Heracles agree that "the scepter" should be returned to the birds, the Triballian voting his *nabaisatreu*, which Pisthetairos (or Heracles—the speech assignments in this scene are not agreed upon) interprets to mean assent. In the second, Heracles reiterates his vote and elicits *saunaka baktarikrousa* from the Triballian, which Heracles insists means an affirmative. Poseidon goes along. Then Pisthetairos, as if it were an afterthought, mentions the requirement that Basileia be given to him in marriage. Poseidon, who finds this condition nonnegotiable, prepares to leave, reminding the reluctant, starving Heracles that giving up Basileia would be

[21]*Comic Hero*, 196.
[22]*Four Comedies*, 250.
[23]*Comic Hero*, 321, n. 90.
[24]*Four Comedies*, 250.

in effect disinheriting himself. When Pisthetairos answers with the precedent in Athenian law that a bastard—such as Heracles—cannot inherit, Heracles votes to give up Basileia. Poseidon votes against it, and that, says Pisthetairos, "leaves everything up to the Triballian" (l. 1677).

With supreme authority over the entire universe at stake, the matter is to be decided by a barbarian who can say nothing more intelligible than *kalani korauna kai megala basilinau ornito paradidomi.* One word of this, the last, is ordinary Greek, and it means "give back." But the rest of the utterance (except for the *kai*) is not ordinary, not exactly Greek. It might mean "I give back the beautiful [*kalani*] and great [*megala*] lady Basileia [*korauna Basilinau*] to the birds [*ornito*]," or perhaps we should read *basilin au ornito paradidomi*, that is, "I *do not* give Basileia back to the birds." Poseidon thinks it speaks not about Basileia but rather about *badizein*, "to depart," and that the Triballian is recommending that the delegation "depart like the swallows [*badizein hosper hai chelidones*]" (l. 1681). Here we have unlimited possibilities for "referential aberration," the ambiguity of normal language driven to extreme, such that the "confusion can only be cleared up by the intervention of an extra-textual intention."[25] The extratextual intention that prevails is provided by Pisthetairos:[26] "In that case he means 'give her back to the swallows! [*oukoun paradounai tais chelidosin legei*]" (l. 1682). Though this interpretation is perhaps the most farfetched of all, it prevails. Poseidon is overcome and gives in, the vote having gone two to one against him.

The issue is thus decided by the gods' linguistic abdication, dramatized by means of the Triballian, and Pisthetairos's linguistic aggressiveness, particularly his forceful reading of his own and everyone else's speech. (We ought to note that the play's final choricon, which directly follows this scene and introduces the exodos, wherein Pisthetairos's apotheosis is made manifest, is also centrally concerned with the irresponsible abandonment of authority over language to "barbarians," that is, to

[25]*Allegories of Reading,* 10.
[26]Some editors, including Rogers, assign this speech to Heracles, but the logic of the play makes Pisthetairos the more likely choice. Whitman (*Comic Hero,* 196) apparently agrees.

sophists such as Gorgias and his son Philip. This choricon, like the others and unlike the play as a whole, is satirical: but it descants on a theme treated lethetically in the previous scene.) Pisthetairos's victory and subsequent elevation to godhood are the direct result of his and the birds' seizure of power over language. The "grand scheme" is shown to have been not so much the idea of transforming the birds' polos into a polis as the principle, or dunamis, that underlies such transformations. The capitulation of the Olympians is shown finally to be the result of aphasia as much as hunger.

The exodos is properly described as "the most astounding victory in Aristophanes, perhaps all comedy,"[27] perhaps, actually, in all of literature. It is also surely the most incredible. The fast-talking, punning old Athenian is transformed into a divinity whose splendor outshines sun and stars (l. 1709 ff.), and the final words of the play hail him as the "highest of gods [*daimonon hupertatos*]" (l. 1765). Here is the ultimate lethetic fantasy, rigorously consequential in its own terms: if we choose to ignore the world and attend to the word, there is nothing to prevent our doing anything that language can do, and the best talker is the highest divinity. The apotheosis of rhetoric that Pisthetairos's victory represents lies latent in every logomimetic fiction. In the *Birds* it is made dazzlingly manifest.

This apotheosis of rhetoric—a rhetoric that is both persuasion and tropology at once—is made possible by the lethetic mode but is undermined by it as well. The power of language can only become a "reality" when reality is forgotten. The glorious victory of Pisthetairos and the birds, exhilarating and curiously moving though it is, has no relevance to the world in which we must make our lives. This is not a criticism of the play, of course, for the play assumes the unconnectedness of word and world as its very foundation. The power of speech is presented as a dunamis adunate, and that contradiction is the play's "rhetorical moment," that which generates the power of the fiction. Both power and powerlessness are essential features of language, and one increases in direct proportion with the other, so that the most powerful language conceivable is also inevitably the most

---

[27]*Comic Hero*, 196.

"impossible," the most persuasive speech the most outrageously figurative.

The reader will understand, I hope, that I do not intend to suggest that the *Birds* was meant as, or is only useful as, an object lesson in the philosophy of language. The play is surely one of literature's clearest examples of a lethetic fantasy, and that designation means, among other things, that it is not interested in teaching anything. But part of its effectiveness as a lethetic fantasy arises from the fact that it is rigorously logomimetic, that its subject matter is taken not from the world but from itself. It dramatizes the very assumptions that guide its composition, displaying the absolute victory of the logomimetic imagination in the person of Pisthetairos. In the act of turning its attention away from the world and toward language, it finds nothing more appropriate to speak about than the turning away from the world and toward language (that is, the construction of an atopia called Cloudcuckooland). The play, mirroring the gesture of its hero, makes itself powerful by reading itself. Any further reading, even and especially if it is a lethetic reading such as that offered here, will disclose the logomimesis. Only attempts at alethetic reading will miss the point, for in seeking the connection between the text and the world they will cover up or ignore the text's central concern with the rhetoric of unreality.

CHAPTER 5 /

Incredible Joinings:
Syllepsis in Lewis Carroll,
Oscar Wilde, and Robert Nye

STRUCTURALIST POETIC THEORY, especially as practiced by Todorov and Genette, has focused on how narrative structures function analogously to linguistic structures. In his *Grammaire du "Décaméron,"*[1] for example, Todorov undertakes to analyze the "syntax" of narrative and to show how elements in stories function like parts of speech in sentences. In the section of *Figures III*[2] called "Discours du récit," Genette discusses features of Proust's *A la recherche du temps perdu* in terms of "voice" and "mood" directly comparable to the grammatical categories so named. This is, of course, part of the structuralist program to found a poetics that would be a science of literature as linguistics is a science of language. The analogy between the structure of narrative and the structure of the sentence has been both provocative and productive but has never been—was never intended to be—more than an analogy in illustration of certain notions of literary structure. No claim was ever made that poetic content bore any such relation to linguistic structures.

And yet there is reason to think that such a claim might be made. The discussion earlier of logomimesis, as well as the foregoing discussion of the *Birds,* has shown how fictional content

[1]*Grammaire du "Décaméron"* (The Hague: Mouton, 1969).
[2]*Figures III* (Paris: Seuil, 1972).

can indeed be derived from linguistic microstructures, particularly tropes, and that some kinds of poetic actions are nothing
more than the logomimesis of the gestures effected by such
tropes. I want now to illustrate this notion further by showing
how we can understand the origin of an important class of lethetic fictions as residing in a figure properly, if not entirely con-
ventionally, designated by the classical term "syllepsis."

Even if one wanted to use the term "syllepsis" in a conventional sense, one would have to be cautious. There are two currently accepted ways of understanding the term, both of them
with fine classical pedigrees supporting their claims to legitimacy
and neither in obvious contradiction to the other.[3] The *Oxford
English Dictionary* gives both meanings in its definition: "A figure
by which a word, or a particular form or inflexion of a word, is
made to refer to two or more other words in the same sentence,
while properly applying to or agreeing with only one of them
. . . or applying to them in different senses. . . . Cf. *Zeugma*." In
other words, syllepsis might be either *grammatical* or *semantic*. An
example of the first sort is George Puttenham's line, "My Ladie
laughs for joy, and I for woe," wherein "laughs" serves as predicate for both "Ladie" and "I," in spite of the fact the the locution
"I laughs" is ungrammatical. Syllepsis of the second sort is employed in Pope's *Rape of the Lock* ii, ll. 105–109:

> Whether the nymph shall break Diana's law,
> Or some frail china-jar receive a flaw;
> Or stain her honour or a new brocade,

[3]The concept of syllepsis has recently been taken in another direction by
Michael Riffaterre (for example, in "La syllepse intertextuelle," *Poétique* 40
[1979], 496–501). For Riffaterre, the "intertextual" syllepsis in which he is interested "consiste à prendre un même mot dans deux sens différents à la fois, sa
signification contextuelle et sa *signification intertextuelle*. La signification contextuelle, c'est le sens que demande la fonction du mot dans la phrase. La
signification intertextuelle, c'est un autre sens possible (dans le dictionaire, du
moins, c'est à dire dans l'abstrait), que le contexte élimine, ou négativise, parce
qu'il lui est grammaticalement et sémantiquement incompatible" (p. 496). Obviously, this type of syllepsis must be understood as a feature of *every* text. My
conception of syllepsis is much more limited, involving only that relatively small
number of texts in which language "puts together" what we believe reality keeps
apart. Ultimately, *all* literature is sylleptic for Riffaterre. Only certain lethetic
texts are sylleptic in my view. It should be clear that my notion of syllepsis and
Riffaterre's differ so widely that they can hardly even be said to disagree. They
speak to entirely different concerns.

Forget her prayers, or miss a masquerade;
Or lose her heart, or necklace, at a ball. . . .

Here the literal ("stain . . . brocade" and "lose . . . necklace") and figurative ("stain her honour" and "lose her heart") uses of the verbs "stain" and "lose" confront each other in the double objects each is given. Some authorities (for example, Lausberg and Plett)[4] refer to this figure as "zeugma," while others (for example, Huntington Brown)[5] warn against doing so. In this area of rhetorical terminology a certain amount of disagreement seems virtually permanent.[6] For my purposes it is enough to note that there is a substantial weight of authority behind calling this figure, particularly in its semantic form, syllepsis.

Syllepsis of this kind may be understood as *making explicit* the semantic duplicity of certain linguistic forms that unite concepts assumed to be separate "in reality" *and*, at the same time, *proposing equivalence* between the two concepts thus set forth. It unmasks duplicity but, in the same gesture, asserts unity by accepting the authority of language in preference to that of "reality." This acceptance may be ironic, as it surely is in the lines of Pope quoted above, but it is unreserved: the "nymph" (though not the poet describing her) is presented by the trope as one who would find no difference of consequence between staining her honor and staining her garment. The effectiveness of the trope depends on the confrontation of two incompatible semantic structures, one posited by language, the other by "reality" (that is, doxa, or common sense, or reason, or what have you). In Pope's lines the confrontation corresponds to that between the values of the satirist, who stands with "reason," and the object of his satire. Syllepsis of this kind is rightly considered, along with irony, to be one of the figures of *thought*, for at stake are structures not just of language (as in the case of grammatical syllepsis) but of concepts.

There is a close relation between semantic syllepsis and pun-

[4]Heinrich Lausberg, *Elemente der literarischen Rhetorik*, 3d ed. (Munich: Max Hueber, 1967); and Heinrich F. Plett, *Textwissenschaft und Textanalyse* (Heidelberg: Quelle & Meyer, 1975).

[5]See Brown's article on syllepsis in the *Princeton Encyclopedia of Poetry and Poetics* (Princeton: Princeton University Press, 1965).

[6]For example, Jacques Dubois et al., *Allgemeine Rhetorik* (Munich: Quelle & Meyer, 1974), treat syllepsis as a purely grammatical figure.

ning, since puns also exploit semantic ambiguities. But the pun does not, as syllepsis always does, make the ambiguity into a confrontation. The sentence "She was doing some filing" is ambiguous, and if we imagine a secretary sitting in front of some filing cabinets holding a nailfile, we can think of it as making a pun. But it is not a syllepsis until both meanings of "filing" are made specific, as in "She was filing her nails and my letters," in which the locutionary structure itself implies that filing letters and filing nails are instances of the same activity. I should probably note in passing that such confrontations become even more dramatic if semantic and grammatical syllepsis are combined, as in "The soldiers were filing their nails and past." Even in such cases, however, it is the semantic and not the grammatical confrontation that takes precedence and that gives the trope its peculiar force.

That force arises at least in part from the application of the reader's (or listener's) disbelief: if the reader of Pope believed that there was indeed no difference between staining one's honor and staining a dress, the point of his witty lines would be lost. It is only because we do not believe in the equivalence of filing nails with filing papers that the trope works. We are confronted with two powerful structuring principles, our own belief and our own language—that which we assume to be true and that which we disbelieve but whose validity is vouched for powerfully by this linguistic "evidence." Our pleasure in the trope arises from our recognition of the incompatibility of the two structuring principles, an incompatibility that we know to be quite harmless because there is no need to resolve it. We do not feel obliged to discover "real" reasons why filing nails and filing papers might be the same. In other words, syllepsis is a figure that asks to be read lethetically. The alethetic approach is not prevented—it never can be—but it is discouraged: it almost always proves to be more trouble than it is worth. What would be gained by discovering a nonlinguistic similarity between filing nails and filing papers?

This element of disbelief, which makes syllepsis so especially interesting for my purposes, has been recognized by one of the earliest authorities to mention the trope. Herodian, writing in the second century after Christ, defines syllepsis as "the inclusive reference of a predicate to a compound subject where the predicate states a proposition true of only one part of the subject and untrue of the other part." An example would be the line from *Iliad* 9.5, "The north wind and the west wind that blow from Thrace," which is true only of the north wind.[7] This is obviously not what anyone today would call syllepsis, but it shows us the antiquity of the notion that syllepsis is a "putting together" of the true and the untrue. Even though Herodian's figure is probably "of little but historical interest," as Huntington Brown says,[8] it serves to remind us that the element of disbelief, of untruth, is central to the development of thinking about this trope.

We might expect to find syllepsis prominently employed in texts that themselves solicit disbelief, and our expectation is not disappointed. One of our most prominent writers of incredible fictions, Lewis Carroll, is also one of the great practitioners of syllepsis. The refrain that runs throughout "The Hunting of the Snark" offers several examples:

> They sought it with thimbles, they sought it
> with care;
> They pursued it with forks and hope;
> They threatened its life with a railway-share;
> They charmed it with smiles and soap.

Some rhetoricians might argue that there are really not several syllepses here but only one. All would agree that "with forks and hope" is a semantic syllepsis as defined above, where "with" is used in two different senses with respect to its two objects (in the first sense, "by means of"; in the second, "in a manner characterized by"). The phrase "with smiles and soap" is ambiguous and could be read as meaning "They charmed it using smiles and soap" or "They charmed it using soap while smiling." Technically speaking, the first reading would involve no syllepsis, since "with" would be understood to mean "by means of" in both cases. Technically speaking once again, there is no syllepsis at all in "They sought it with thimbles, they sought it with care" since,

---

[7]S.v. "Syllepsis," *Princeton Encyclopedia of Poetry and Poetics.*
[8]Ibid.

though "with" is used in two different senses, the word is used twice, not once. There is parallelism but no syllepsis.

Carroll's verse gallops blithely and wittily over all such technical distinctions. An initial "naive" reading of the quatrain does not find any difference in effect between the "genuine" syllepsis, "with forks and hope," and the nonsyllepsis, "with thimbles . . . with care," and for very good reason. Since the real issue in syllepsis is a confrontation of two semantic systems, the precise locutionary form in which that confrontation is presented is not important. Syllepsis is a figure of thought, not of grammar or syntax. As long as the reader/listener perceives a situation in which the linguistic system puts together that which he or she believes is "really" separate and distinct, he or she will experience what we might call a "sylleptic" effect.

To approach this point in another way, let us suppose that Oscar Wilde, not Alexander Pope, had written the line about staining honor and dresses. We might have heard a character in one of his plays exclaim, "After my rendezvous with Jack I feared that my dress was stained. To my relief it was merely my honor." From the point of view of traditional rhetoric, there is no syllepsis at all here, since we do not have "a word . . . made to refer to two other words in the same sentence." But the joke works just as well in this version as in Pope's because the same confrontation is staged between the same two semantic structures, though that confrontation is provoked in a slightly different way by this particular verbal form.

I am proposing that, just as irony is a figure of thought that does not depend on a specific verbal formulation to achieve its ironic effect, so is syllepsis a figure of thought capable of achieving a sylleptic effect by several alternative locutionary strategies. The relation between syllepsis and irony is even deeper, for both rely on a structure of expectation (belief) against which the trope works and without which it would fail altogether. But unlike irony, which forces the reader to reinterpret the utterance before him in such a way as to bring it into conformity with his belief (He says "Beautiful weather," but I know it's snowing, so he must really mean "Terrible weather"), syllepsis allows each semantic structure to go its own way. This statement means nothing more than that irony is alethic, syllepsis lethetic.

The ironic mode, as we all know, characterizes a large number of the alethetic fictions of our tradition, and an author's entire oeuvre can be dominated by this one mode. One thinks of Thomas Mann in this connection almost at once. Another, far smaller, class of fictions, lethetic fictions in this case, could properly be called sylleptic. But before examining some examples of sylleptic fiction, I should first indicate how a narrative—as opposed to a specific phrase—might properly be described as involving syllepsis.

Here again Lewis Carroll provides the most instructive example. Here is the last stanza of the "Gardener's Song" from *Sylvie and Bruno:*

> He thought he saw an Argument
> That proved he was the Pope:
> He looked again, and found it was
> A Bar of Mottled Soap.
> "A fact so dread," he faintly said,
> "Extinguishes all hope!"

All nine stanzas follow the same pattern: "He thought he saw an [X] / That [did something]: / He looked again and found it was / A [Y]. [Two lines quoting the character's reaction]." He thinks he sees an elephant, but it turns out to be a letter; a supposed banker's clerk is revealed to be a hippopotamus; and so on. The last stanza is especially interesting because the mistake involves a special sort of confusion. To "see" an argument is a very different matter from "seeing" a bar of soap, for in the first case "see" does not mean "to perceive with the eye" but "to grasp, understand, intuit." It is troublesome enough, of course, to mistake a postage stamp for an albatross, but at least these two items are both concrete objects. To mistake such a concrete object for an abstraction such as an argument is far worse. It is the last straw. It extinguishes all hope.

Carroll's poem works its way to a climax that is an alternative formulation of the syllepsis "He saw an argument and a bar of soap." But the spirit of this syllepsis pervades the entire work, in which the poet "takes seriously" the equation proposed by the trope between the literal and metaphorical meanings of "to see."

If one "sees" both arguments and objects, then one could mistake the one for the other; and if this kind of mistake is possible, it follows that all sorts of other, equally outrageous and disquieting mistakes are likely. Syllepsis is a "putting together," and once things are put together, it becomes difficult to tell them apart. Carroll's poem is completely and rigorously sylleptic in its point of view, driving the topos of "seeing an argument" to the atopia of mistaking almost anything for almost anything else. Though the poem in fact ends with the verse that gives the clue to the locution that forms the basis for the logomimesis, the nonsense universe based upon it is already fully set up when the poem opens.

This is all wonderfully amusing to us, of course. It is no skin off the reader's nose if the absolute rule of a particular trope has such distressing consequences, because the reader does not believe it. His universe is not ordered on such principles, and he is prepared to live by his belief that seeing arguments and seeing soap are two different sorts of actions. The poor character, however, who is stuck inside the poem, has nothing to be amused about. One of the great comic strokes of the poem is that the hero, characterized throughout as close to despair, succumbs in the end; within the confines of the atopia he inhabits, he has indeed nothing to hope for. This syllepsis is not just a verbal quirk for him; it is the fundamental law of nature—for him. For us it is an occasion for high mirth, thanks to our disbelief.

The "Gardener's Song" is sylleptic, then, not only or even primarily because it can be shown to develop from a figure that traditional rhetoric would call syllepsis but chiefly because its narrative operates sylleptically by "putting together" that which only language can put together. Since syllepsis is a figure of thought, the confrontation between language proposing sameness where belief would insist upon difference, that thought alone is enough to demonstrate the working of the figure. No particular locutionary form makes *Buddenbrooks* ironic, and in the same way no special verbal pattern makes Carroll's poem sylleptic. The poem plays with the *idea* of "seeing," taking seriously the semantic unity proposed by the same word being used for two different things (perceiving and understanding). Because this unity flies in the face of our belief, the narrative based on it is also incredible.

/ 88

A sylleptic narrative is based on the assumption of certain unifications that we believe only language can produce, but it need not either explicitly provide a typical rhetorical syllepsis or specify the unifications at issue as long as the results of such a "putting together" are dramatized. Oscar Wilde, for example, never gives us a line like "He was Earnest in name and by nature." He does, both in the first act and at the final curtain of *The Importance of Being Earnest,* explicitly connect the notions of having a certain name and being of a certain nature. More important, his play sets forth an atopia in which verbal labels readily replace "genuine" characteristics and in which the characters are perfectly willing to accept such replacement. We do not find examples of traditional rhetorical syllepsis on every page of the play; indeed we have a hard time finding any at all; but for all that, the play is sylleptic, and indeed also lethetic, to its very core.

Earnest is in fact a superb example of a lethetic fiction. It is a literary structure that rivets our attention upon itself and allows us to forget the world we accept as the "real" one without making the least pretense to asserting its own "reality." On the contrary, it actively solicits our disbelief not only by aggressively using fantastic coincidences to tie the plot together but also, as we will see, by having its characters readily accept signifiers in place of signifieds (for example, the words "Certainly, mamma" in place of actual compliance and so forth). There is nothing supernatural in the play, but it is incredible all the same. It may therefore serve to highlight the distinction made earlier between lethetic texts and either fantastic or marvelous ones, as Todorov defines them. There is nothing supernatural about Gwendolyn's fixation upon the forms of language, but it is incredible nonetheless that she would drop Jack in an instant if his name turned out not to be Ernest. It is quite on a par with the incredulity elicited by Carroll's "Gardener's Song": we do not believe that people easily mistake bars of soap for arguments, though there is nothing supernatural about such mistakes.

The energy that drives the plot forward is generated to no small degree by Gwendolyn's infatuation with the name of Ernest, a name that Jack just happens to have assumed. "My ideal has always been to love some one of the name of Ernest," she confesses, going on to explain that "there is something in that name that inspires absolute confidence" and that it is "the only really safe name" (pp. 61–62).[9] Gwendolyn is not so naive as to believe that a man might actually be earnest, but of course if such a man existed one might properly say that he would inspire absolute confidence. Being a modern and sophisticated girl, Gwendolyn has given up such hopes. She has replaced them, however, with an "ideal" based entirely upon the verbal tag "Ernest" and has transferred to it all the confidence that one would properly owe to the characteristic. This is an entirely unexpected, indeed incredible, strategy, but it is entertaining rather than simply foolish because it has the untrustworthy but potent authority of language behind it. The audience does not believe that the quality of earnestness is replaceable by the name of Ernest, but the fact that Gwendolyn accepts such replacement is given a comprehensible (though not credible) motivation.

Gwendolyn has replaced all faith in human qualities by faith in verbal surfaces. Intentions are irrelevant. When Jack/Ernest attempts to propose marriage to her, she insists on his making the explicit verbal gesture, even though she already knows both his intentions and her own:

Gwendolyn. I adore you. But you haven't proposed to me yet. Nothing has been said at all about marriage. The subject has not even been touched.
Jack. Well . . . may I propose to you now?
Gwendolyn. I think it would be an admirable opportunity. And to spare you any possible disappointment, Mr. Worthing, I think it only fair to tell you quite frankly beforehand that I am fully determined to accept you.
Jack. Gwendolyn!
Gwendolyn. Yes, Mr. Worthing, what have you got to say to me?
Jack. You know what I have got to say to you.
Gwendolyn. Yes, but you don't say it.
Jack. Gwendolyn, will you marry me?
Gwendolyn. Of course I will darling. How long you have been about it! [Pp. 62–63]

When she later proclaims to Cecily that "in matters of grave importance, style, not sincerity is the vital thing" (p. 114), she is

[9]*The Plays of Oscar Wilde* (New York: Modern Library, n.d.). Citations below in the text refer to this edition.

speaking of one of her own must fundamental principles. She is, in style, a model of filial obedience: when her mother tells her to come with her into the next room, she replies, "Certainly, mamma," in the most courteous fashion (p. 60). That this acquiescence to her mother's wishes is purely verbal, that Gwendolyn in fact remains right where she is, is in perfect conformity to this principle.

Gwendolyn, then, is dead earnest about one thing, and that thing is the verbal surface. She may have "the gravest doubts" about the credibility of Jack's explanation of why he has deceived her, but "I intend to crush them." In the next breath she is ready to say that this explanation "seems to me to have the stamp of truth upon it" (p. 114). She is able to manage the conventional verbal surface quite independently of the real state of affairs in the world, and if the required verbal convention directly contradicts her own commonsense notions of the way things really are, it bothers her not a whit. She is therefore able to tell Jack, without the least trace of embarrassment, "If you are not too long, I will wait here for you all my life." She knows that a properly romantic young lady is supposed to tell her beloved that, if he must leave, she is prepared to "wait for him all her life." She also knows that in practice such an idea is absurd, that the sentiment can only be validated, as it were, by never having to be put into practice. Just as she prompts Jack earlier to the proper performance of his verbal duties in proposing, she prompts him here to his duty in not holding her to her (conventional and insincere) word. She thereby acknowledges her insincerity, but that acknowledgment is not bothersome to her or to anyone else because insincerity is taken for granted. Or, to state the matter in another way, Gwendolyn is *always* sincere— whether she means it or not.

Gwendolyn is not unique among the play's characters in these qualities. Over and over again we find that the persons of Wilde's comedy are more earnest about language than they are about anything else. The logomimesis indicated by the title is doubled, for not only does the action turn upon the sylleptic equation of names and qualities, but earnestness proves to be a crucially important issue after all. Everybody participates in the rigorous game of taking speech seriously. Even Lane, the man-servant, takes part:

Algernon. I hope tomorrow will be a fine day, Lane.
Lane. It never is, sir.
Algernon. Lane, you're a perfect pessimist.
Lane. I do my best to give satisfaction, sir.

And poor Canon Chasuble finds that living in world of such serious folk requires caution. One may not speak metaphorically and say, "Were I fortunate enough to be Miss Prism's pupil, I would hang upon her lips," without eliciting glares of disapproval. The use of metaphor is a risky business for everyone in the play, particaulrly in the vicinity of Lady Bracknell, as earnest a literal reader as one could hope to find. When Algernon confesses inadvertently that his fictional friend Bunbury "was quite exploded," she wonders if he was "the victim of a revolutionary outrage" (p. 117). Such glib acceptance of the face value of language is also responsible for her reaction to the circumstances of Jack's birth. First of all, when Jack says that he has "lost" both parents, her reply ("That seems like carelessness") addresses the form and not the meaning of his statement. Then, when he goes on to relate that he knows nothing about the circumstances of his birth and knows only that he was "found" in a handbag in a cloakroom at Victoria Station, Lady Bracknell makes the substitution of "found" for "born" the basis for a trope that she, at least, takes quite seriously: "You can hardly imagine that I and Lord Bracknell would dream of allowing our only daughter—a girl brought up with the utmost care—to marry into a cloakroom, and form an alliance with a parcel?" (p. 68). She keeps to this line throughout the play, reminding everyone later on that "until yesterday I had no idea that there were any families or persons whose origin was a Terminus" (p. 118). She had asked about Jack's parents and had been told about handbags and railway stations, and that substitution is linguistically, if not socially, quite acceptable to her.

The preference for linguistic forms over meaning, intention, or "reality" is as marked in Lady Bracknell as in her daughter. Only language makes it possible for a man to be descended from a handbag, and only language makes it possible for a woman, Lady Dumbleton, to have been "thirty-five ever since she arrived at the age of forty, which was many years ago now" (p. 123). In either case, the verbal form has social consequences quite independent of reality. Everyone knows that Lady Dumbleton is not thirty-five, but her saying that she is creates a linguistic and social fact that has far greater importance for Lady Bracknell, her daughter, and indeed the other characters in the play than the importance of being genuine, sincere, "earnest." It was necessary for the Snark hunters to say something three times to make it true, but for Wilde's characters, once is enough—and even if that still does not quite make it "true," what does it matter? Truth is irrelevant. And if truth is to have any importance at all, it had better find a way to conform to language.

Earnest's plot keeps scurrying in efforts to let the "truth" somehow conform to someone's text. The master text is of course the name "Ernest" itself, which we learn later not only Gwendolyn but Cecily as well is prepared to insist upon. Cecily in her own way has gone further than her counterpart, for she has actually produced a text, in the form of her diary, to which Algy discovers he conforms by happy accident—or at least gives the appearance of conforming—by announcing himself as Jack's ne'er-do-well brother Ernest. Like Gwendolyn, Cecily has a particular attachment to this name ("It had always been a girlish dream of mine to love some one whose name was Ernest" [p. 96]) and has spun out a completely documented fantasy based upon it. When Algernon/Ernest confesses his love for Cecily and asks her to marry him, she replies with the unexpected information that they have already been engaged for the last three months:

Algernon. But how did we become engaged?
Cecily. Well, ever since dear Uncle Jack first confessed to us that he had a younger brother who was very wicked and bad, you of course have formed the chief topic of conversation between myself and Miss Prism. And of course a man who is much talked about is always attractive. One feels there must be something in him after all. I daresay it was foolish of me, but I fell in love with you, Ernest.
[Pp. 94–95]

Cecily has fallen in love, as she readily admits, with a "topic of conversation" rather than with any actual person, but the under-

lying syllepsis that makes the plot (im)possible sanctions the substitution of discourse for "reality." Cecily quite prefers the text
she has written in her diary to the life she has been actually
leading, and now she finds herself in the happy position of being
able to insist that "reality" (in the form of Algernon) shape itself
to fit. For Cecily, then, Algernon's function is to "be" the Ernest
of her book.

The syllepsis of person and history touched upon here is a
favorite topic, as one might expect, of logomimetic literature.
Thomas Mann plays on the notion in the last volume of his
Joseph tetralogy, where even Joseph himself has trouble at times
distinguishing the life he is leading from the narrative that life is
shaping. But the most extreme atopia to come out of this topic is,
I think, the little story of Hans Daiber called "Es steht
geschrieben" ("It Is Written").[10] The hero of Daiber's tale, Karl
Kornemann, arrives in town to take a new job, happens past a
bookshop window, looks in, and finds to his surprise a volume
with his picture on the cover. It is a photo of him as he is at that
moment, and when he adjusts his tie, the tie in the picture is
adjusted as well. Karl buys a copy of this book and opens it to
find the very words that begin the story "Es steht geschrieben."
He closes the book in confusion, then reopens it to read that he
was reading. He is horrified. He tries to get rid of the book,
finally throwing it into a pond in the park. But as the book sinks
to the bottom, Karl finds himself suddenly unable to breathe,
and he falls unconscious as he attempts to retrieve the volume
from the water. A park attendant takes him to the hospital. He
recovers quickly. "After the medical examination he went up to
a bookcase, threw the medical books out, and climbed onto the
highest shelf" (p. 16). The story ends with this complete oblitera-
tion of distinction between man and book.

Daiber intends nothing more by this than to provide a little
verbal entertainment, but it is interesting to see how the story
develops out of a change in the relationship of control between
man and book. At first, Karl appears to be in charge of the
situation, to actually "write" his book, as the book changes in

[10]In the collection *Argumente für Lazarus* (Munich: Langen/Müller, 1966),
15–16.

response to what he does. After he starts to read his story, however, the book begins to take control, so that what the book does—to "drown," for example—becomes inscribed in the living experience of the hero. He ceases to "write" and can only "read." At the end of the story, the only action that the man can initiate is the attempt to "be" his book. In the story of Cecily and her Ernest, however, Cecily remains fully in charge of the writing process, so that her text remains in conformity with the greater text of an archetypal romantic love story. Cecily manages her fantasy love affair so that it proceeds just as it "ought," with the required temporary breakup to demonstrate its earnestness: "It would hardly have been a really serious engagement if it hadn't been broken off at least once" (p. 96). Here again, the pure verbal surface of "earnestness" is accepted as the substitute for the genuine article.

Algernon's only role in this, his own love story, is to make sure that he adheres to the script. He may not change the name of the hero, for instance, from "Ernest" to "Algernon" without toppling the entire structure. Algernon has in fact blundered into the leading role in Cecily's drama by his ruse, but he finds that he likes the role and wants to keep it. So he, like Jack, finds himself suddenly taken with the urgent desire to become christened with the name of Ernest. Jack and Algy want to write themselves into the fantasy constructed by Gwendolyn and Cecily, just as everyone in Athens wants to take part in Pisthetairos's rhetorical triumph by becoming birds. The importance of being Ernest in Wilde's play is directly comparable to the importance of being a bird in Aristophanes's, because in both cases it is a matter of submitting to an uncompromising linguistic authority. In Wilde's play the source of this linguistic power seems at times to be primarily erotic—the sexual attractiveness of the two young ladies—while Aristophanes makes Pisthetairos's sexual rejuvenation consequent to his rhetorical dominance. But even in *Earnest* it is the powerless power of rhetoric that makes the whole mechanism go. The allure of the girls and the social pretensions of Lady Bracknell are not in themselves adequate motivation for the syllepsis on which the play builds.

Indeed one is not sure how attractive the girls would be for

Jack and Algernon if they were not so rhetorically determined.
Jack calls Gwendolyn "a sensible, intellectual girl" in the most
admiring sort of way, though the only demonstration of her
intellect we have seen is her insistence on the priority of verbal
forms. He also describes Cecily as "not a silly, romantic girl, I am
glad to say. She has a capital appetite, goes for long walks, and
pays no attention at all to her lessons" (p. 71). If we wonder how
it is that paying no attention to one's lessons constitutes proof
that one is not silly, we find our question answered later by
Cecily herself. When Miss Prism prods her to the "intellectual
pleasures" of German grammar, Cecily complains, "But I don't
like German. It isn't at all a becoming language. I know perfectly
well that I look quite plain after my German lesson" (p. 76).
Cecily's concern with the effect that the sound of German might
have on her is echoed in Miss Prism's worry that the chapter in
her political economy book on the subject of the "fall of the
rupee" would be "somewhat too sensational" for a young lady.
Miss Prism is evidently thinking sylleptically, substituting a literal for a metaphorical meaning of "fall" and fearing the effects of
such language upon the tender soul of her pupil. Ignoring the
matter of the rupee's "fall" is for Miss Prism a way of preserving
Cecily's innocence, and ignoring her German lessons is for
Cecily a way of preserving her sexual attractiveness. In both
cases it is a matter of avoiding the destructive power of
language.

The power that Cecily fears in German grammar is the same
power that she and the rest of the play's characters bow to
throughout the comedy: the authority of the naked signifier, the
pure verbal surface. Lady Bracknell has already given the explanation of how this power works in the field of foreign languages:
"French songs I cannot possibly allow. People always seem to
think that they are improper, and either look shocked, which is
vulgar, or laugh, which is worse. But German sounds a thoroughly respectable language, and indeed, I believe it is so"
(p. 60). What Lady Bracknell approves of about German, its
respectable "sound," is of course just what Cecily cannot toler-
ate. To "sound" respectable, whether one is so or not, is not
likely to enhance the attractiveness of a young lady. In Cecily's
system of values, attractiveness is explicitly connected with the
appearance of being "wicked and bad." The other young people

hold similar views, even Jack, the most "serious" of all of them. He is embarrassed "to be forced to speak the truth. It is the first time in my life that I have ever been reduced to such a painful position, and I am really quite inexperienced in doing anything of the kind" (p. 107). And later: "Gwendolyn, it is a terrible thing for a man to find out suddenly that all his life he has been speaking nothing but the truth. Can you forgive me?" But of course it is really only the verbal form of wickedness, not wickedness itself, that is valued.

Gwendolyn, Cecily, and the rest are devoted to the verbal surface that they are so well able to manage. But what makes it manageable is that is has no fixed connection to the nonlinguistic world save through accident. Language that is not simply a string of signifiers to play with would be dangerous, shocking, and improper. Lady Bracknell makes this point in one of the few examples of rhetorical syllepsis in the play. She expresses her displeasure at hearing the sounds of an argument: "I dislike arguments of any kind. They are always vulgar, and often convincing" (p. 128). It is easy to see why she would dislike *vulgar* arguments (that is, altercations), but only reflection upon the basis for the atopia in which these characters live gives a clue as to why she should also dislike *convincing* arguments (in this case, "courses of reasoning"). Convincing and credible language would tear down the foundation of Lady Bracknell's world, and she is candid enough to admit it. This, after all, is a world in which smoking counts as an "occupation" (p. 65) and hair may be described as curling "naturally . . . with a little help from others" (p. 96). Convincing arguments could be only a threat to inhabitants of such a world, which is after all not so distant from that world of Lewis Carroll's Gardener, in which arguments may become indistinguishable from bars of soap.

Wilde's play uses syllepsis as a basic strategy in exploring the very topic announced in the title: "being Earnest." It would be foolish to deny, of course, that there is a powerful element of irony at work here as well or that the play's success depends upon our willingness to acknowledge the importance of not being earnest. But this ironic element returns us to the issue of lethetic reading, for lethetic literature, above all, reminds us of the importance, at times, of forsaking the serious. Wilde's irony is not spurring us to ever-more-complex hermeneutic strategies in the hopes of finding "the truth" behind this apparent non-sense; it insists, rather, that this really is nonsense. But it became nonsense by being very "earnest"—not about the world we live in, to be sure, but about the language we use. The characters in the play do precisely what we in the audience must not do if we are to enjoy the performance: they accept the word as a per-fectly good substitute for the world. They believe. We enjoy the sylleptic point of view that underlies this atopia because we do not share it.

The syllepsis upon which *Earnest* is founded is, for all its seem-ingly limitless mirth, severely limited. Like most sylleptic narra-tives, it is prepared to accept only one kind of incredible linguis-tic unification, in this case the substitution of signifiers for their signifieds. Actually, most of the syllepses of fantasy are even more specific than this. We are familiar, for example, with sto-ries about werewolves, vampires, and similar creatures that man-age to be both human and animal at the same time, or both alive and dead at the same time. Though one cannot point to a partic-ular sylleptic locution as the origin of such tales, they are genu-inely (if often rather simplemindedly) sylleptic because they posit as unified what we believe to be in reality separate. Science fiction makes use of all sorts of sylleptic premises: one of the more frequent among them proposes the unification of man and machine, either by the anthropomorphization of the me-chanical (robots) or by the mechanization of persons (cyborgs). Another favorite syllepsis plays on the idea of being "in two places at once" by having a character live quite literally "in an-other world" while at the same time inhabiting this one. A varia-tion on this theme has the character slip back and forth between two time periods so easily that the boundary between them seems to vanish. A prize-winning story a number of years ago, Richard McKenna's "The Secret Place," joins these two ideas: the "secret place" in which the heroine spends much of her time turns out to be not another world at all but this world in the far distant past.[11]

---

[11]Anthologized in Aldiss and Harrison, eds., *Nebula Award Stories Number Two* (New York: Pocket Books, 1967). Citations below in the text refer to this edition.

What makes McKenna's story particularly interesting is that the syllepsis of "this world / other world" operates structurally as well as thematically. The real action of the tale concerns not the adventures of the heroine in her Miocene wonderland but rather the narrator's discovery of what Helen's secret place "really" is. The girl who participates in the marvelous adventure really does not know how deeply marvelous it is; only the narrator, a scientist engaged in geological mapping, is able to disclose its wonder. Helen, the narrator's secretary, explains to him how she and her brother used to play fairy-tale games in the desert. She eventually goes so far as to let him participate in her fantasies, to run with her in the make-believe forests and across imaginary streams. "I played Helen's game, but I never lost sight of my own [i.e., geological map making]. Every night I sketched in on my map whatever I had learned that day of the fairyland topography. Its geomorphology was remarkably consistent" (p. 8). Later on, as the scientific project on which the narrator is working draws to a close, the information is combined in the form of geohistorical maps that he is given to examine. "But when I came to the bottom map, of the prevolcanic Miocene landscape, the hair on my neck stood up. *I had made that map myself. It was Helen's fairyland. The topography was point by point the same*" (p. 13). The syllepsis of this world and the other world in which Helen has lived comfortably for so long now engulfs the narrator and threatens to overcome him. Science and scientific methods have led directly into the land of atopia. A point of view predicated upon credibility has produced evidence of the incredible.

This syllepsis of science and the occult—a technique, by the way, that has a tradition in science fiction long predating McKenna—occasions a conflict that the scientist is not able to resolve. The narrator marries Helen, but he makes a career of denying what Helen represents. "I am a professor myself now, graying a bit at the temples. I am as positivistic a scientist as you will find anywhere in the Mississippi drainage basin. When I tell a seminar student 'That assertion is operationally meaningless,' I can make it sound downright obscene. The students blush and hate me, but it is for their own good. Science is the only safe game, and it's only safe if it's kept pure" (p. 15). But this rigorous separation of safe, pure science from Helen's wonderland is constantly threatened and not only because the story has shown how the scientific method might produce evidence of the incredible. Helen and the narrator have a son, the living syllepsis of science (the narrator) and the occult (Helen). In spite of every effort, the boy, Owen, will not allow his maternal heritage to be repressed: "He learned to read on the modern sane and sterile children's books. We haven't a fairy tale in the house—but I have a science library. And Owen makes fairy tales out of science" (p. 15).

McKenna's story, then, makes the sylleptic process part of its narrative structure. It does so in a limited way, of course, a way that would be familiar to readers of Lovecraft and other, earlier fantasy writers; but it does it all the same with considerable art. But this sylleptic narrative process need not be as clearly bounded as it is in "The Secret Place" and in most fantasy and science fiction or as it is in *The Importance of Being Earnest*. There are no inherent limitations on the ability of language to put together what "reality" keeps apart. Language is capable of finding ways to unite everything with everything else. This fact is hardly news, either to linguists or to literary critics, but it shows the potential for limitless verbal play in the sylleptic strategy. And one recent novel goes far toward exploiting this very idea of unlimited syllepsis: Robert Nye's *Merlin*.

Curiously enough, Nye's novel really belongs in the tradition of Oscar Wilde, though on first glance there is little about *Merlin* that would remind one of the verbal pyrotechnics of *Earnest*. The connection is more indirect, mediated by the implacable idiosyncrasy of Ronald Firbank. Nye acknowledges his book's debt to Firbank by dedicating the volume to his (and Gertrude Stein's and Thomas Malory's) memory. Readers may be more familiar with Stein and Malory than with Firbank, whose eccentric novels (for example, *Valmouth*, 1919, and *Concerning the Eccentricities of Cardinal Pirelli*, 1926) are deliberately artificial and fantastic—and not to everyone's taste. Firbank's artifice and fragile brilliance places him directly in the tradition of Wilde, as Charles Osborne has noted.[12] He shares with Wilde, and with

[12]*Penguin Companion to English Literature* (New York: McGraw-Hill, 1971), 183.

Gertrude Stein, an interest in the manipulation of language without much regard for serious meaning, a love for elaborate and unconventional verbal structures that are not really about anything. By his dedication, Nye is placing *Merlin* within this tradition. It is, I think, an apt gesture, for *Merlin* is nothing more than a verbal castle in the air, an Arthurian Cloudcuckooland that is serious only about the capacity of language to make everything seem a transformation of something else.

Because Merlin is a magician—that is, one who effects transformations—his story is to a considerable degree the story of endless metamorphoses and of Merlin's capacity for effecting and participating in them. But it is also the story of the way in which Merlin was himself changed into a story, and it is for this reason akin to a large-scale version of Daiber's "It Is Written." Its larger scale, however, and the background of events and characters familiar to us from Malory do not make Nye's tale any more credible than Daiber's. The larger scale serves in fact as Nye's opportunity to pile one fantasy on top of the last, to interweave so many strains of myth that the reader is forced to recognize early in his reading that an elaborate game is being set up. First of all, the novel begins in a very un-Arthurian fashion with a ribald version of the harrowing of hell, in which Christ appears as a dancing girl attended by an ape. The girl makes the devil drunk and leads the dead souls out of hell while Satan lies in a stupor on the infernal floor. Upon awakening, Lucifer decides to retaliate by producing an Antichrist. He will beget upon the body of a virgin of his choice—a virgin rather more ripe than the other Virgin is reported to have been—his own son, Merlin.

This new addition is not designed to bolster the credibility of material of which its first publisher, Caxton, was more than a little suspicious. Nye is waving good-bye to credibility and is releasing his readers, as early in the narration as he possibly can, from the burden of alethetic reading. Those who like to look for allegory in the Arthurian legends—religious allegory, for example—will find themselves frustrated by the author's strategy of making almost every conceivable allegory part of the fantasy. Whether we are looking for religion, philosophy, alchemy, or even literary criticism, all of it is here, surfeit of it, included in the explicit verbal surface. We are not allowed to look for Christian parallels, for example, because Christian parallels are thrown in our faces in profusion. Our efforts to discover the meaning behind the text are countered by the promiscuous semiosis in which it engages. It cannot mean *something* as long as it seems to mean *everything*.

The desire for impossible unions, both sexual and semiotic, impels the plot of *Merlin*. If we were to try to find the rhetorical basis for Nye's fantasy, the topos from which his atopia is engendered, the most likely candidate would have to be the phrase "the sword in the stone." This is not a rhetorical syllepsis in the strict sense, of course, but it is, as an image, as sylleptic as could be. We do not believe that real swords will go into real stones, though the powerless power of language can make it happen in a wink. Nye's novel is a great conjurer's trick of putting the sword into the stone (putting impossible things together) over and over again. As Merlin observes about the story of his life, "the same event goes on happening."[13] And at the beginning of that story, during the act of conceiving Merlin, the devil remarks, apropos of nothing, "'All the same, my dears . . .' 'All the same what?' demands my uncle Beelzebub, crowned head of the diptera. 'All the same,' says my father" (p. 16).

And in one way or another everything in the world of the book does prove the same. But since everything is different at the outset, no little effort is involved in making it the same, and even after great expenditure of labor some of the difference remains. Lucifer wants his union with the virgin Vivien to the "the same" as that of the Holy Spirit with the Virgin Mary, but he also wants it to be the opposite. As it happens, since the baby Merlin is baptized at his birth by Sister Mary Contradiction, the man Merlin becomes a genuine syllepsis of heaven and hell. He is both the son of God and the son of Satan, both Christ and Lucifer. He is a living affront to the law of noncontradiction. That is his charm.

The charm of Merlin, which he works upon all the matter of his own history, is to effect this same syllepsis upon everything he touches, and to do it over and over again, making great

[13]*Merlin* (Toronto: Bantam, 1981), 175. Citations below in the text refer to this edition.

chains of equivalence until the end of the chain actually joins its beginning to form a circle. The scene of Merlin's conception is endlessly repeated in new guises. The chapter that is thematically climactic in the novel occurs when Merlin views the first fulfillment of Uther's desire for Igrayne and learns how strong his voyeuristic tendencies are. Merlin has given Uther the shape of Igrayne's husband, Gorlois, so that the king can act out a sexual fantasy that Merlin has placed in his mind. It is a scene of both sexual and semiotic lust, Igrayne and Uther supplying the sex while Merlin and the narrator seduce the reader to unnatural acts of semiosis. "Her body is firm and white as marble. Under the whip it has grown like marble inflamed. . . . His prick is long and hard, like a little sword. . . . And the man and the woman roll locked together across the bed, Igrayne's body bucking to take the thrust of him. . . . Nineve sees a sword thrust into a stone, a lance thrust bleeding into a golden cup" (pp. 146–48). Nineve is "seeing" sylleptically, seeing/observing and seeing/understanding at the same time. She observes nothing more than Uther swiving Igrayne as hard as he can, but she understands this union as equivalent to the lance entering the cup or the sword entering the stone. But of course Nineve *is* a syllepsis herself, since she is "really" the shape-shifted Merlin, and he is watching the diabolical insemination of a lady who reminds him very much of his mother, Vivien. In other words, he is watching a repetition of his own conception.

He will watch it again, when Arthur conceives a passion for Morgan le Fay and Merlin conjures her to his pleasure in the king's secret chamber at Camelot. Arthur and Mordred are thus repetitions of Merlin himself, who is the devil's son. Merlin is forever watching versions of himself performing the intercourse that will produce further versions of himself. In fact, he is even able to watch that "first" satanic copulation between Vivien and Lucifer. His crystal prison in the forest of Broceliande takes him out of time, though also out of action: *"How come I am watching at my own conception?* Answer: *What else is there to do in a crystal cave!"* (p. 24). And that is not the end of the matter, since Lucifer is identified with the author of the book ("I write *all* the books," he says [p. 69], and "It is my father's pride to imagine that *he* is writing this book with the aid of his lieutenants," says Merlin [p.

84]). The author is on the one hand Robert Nye but on the other Sir Thomas Malory, from whom Nye has inherited the matter of the story and who was imprisoned, like Merlin, when he wrote the *Morte d'Arthur*. The devil, Malory, Merlin, Arthur, Mordred, Uther, and Nye himself are all "the same," all imprisoned in the voyeuristic act of watching themselves engender themselves.

Nor have we yet reached the end. Because Merlin is a shape shifter and has had occasion to appear in many nonhuman as well as human forms, he identifies himself with everything he has appeared or could appear to be:

> I was in many shapes before I was Merlin. I have been a drop of light in the air. I have been a shield in the thick of the battle. I have been enchanted for a year in the foam of the sea. I have been a string of a harp. . . . I have been Balin who killed his brother Balan. I have been Balan who killed his brother Balin. I have been a sword in the stone. I have been in a stone that floated on water. I have been a stag that flees. I was the invisible chess player who checkmated Sir Perceval at Mount Dolorosus. I am Mercurius the alchemist. I am Merlin, the devil's son. [P. 9]

All these things he was in the days of his freedom he still is in the eternity of his imprisonment:

> I am a man turned inside-out. Once I was adept. Once I was able to be in anything I wished. A free shape-shifter.
> Now the tables are turned and I am imprisoned in the shapes. Many. So that if I say I am shut in a tree which is one side green leaves and the other side flames, then that is true. And if I say that at one and the same time I am being held prisoner in a spiral castle made of glass, and that castle situate in a spinning island bounded by a metal wall and the island held fast in the sea by a great magnet—that is true also. And if I say she has locked me under the earth in a rock tomb—no change. [P. 12]

The free Merlin could "be in anything," and the imprisoned Merlin is trapped in everything. The narrative of Merlin's biography presents the trapped version as audience and commentator for the adventures of the free version. Freedom and imprisonment are "the same" for the necromancer, as long as the self is the same as the self. Merlin is the vessel (a form of grail) in which the alchemist changes everything into everything else: "'Alchemy is metaphors,' you say. 'The alchemist works on himself. His *prima materia* is *him*. He labors to transmute the base matter of his dreams into gold'" (p. 223).

Merlin transmutes his dreams into the dreams of others, and these others (Uther and Arthur in particular) try to make the fantasies into a script to be acted out. If Merlin is the syllepsis of man and book, the book-of-Merlin is a source of scenarios according to which others may order their lives in an *imitatio Merlini* (= *diaboli*). Uther's first fornication with Igrayne is the result of just such a process: Merlin suggests that Gorlois carries a whip for the purpose of chastising his naked wife. Uther "goes pale with desire as I speak the words in his ear, and I sense some fantasy picture flash across a secret chamber in his skull" (p. 133). Uther is excited, and Merlin no less so: "I am thrilled by my own power to create the erotic fantasy in Uther's head. . . . Perhaps it is the source of the magic I know already. . . . The real world acts out the dream, or its necessarily imperfect copy" (p. 134).

For this reason not only all the characters and objects in the novel must be seen as "the same" (that is, as Merlin) but all its actions as well. All of Merlin's adventures are Merlin's dreams acted out by avatars of Merlin on a stage set with trees, brooks, castles, and so forth inspirited by Merlin. Merlin is the retort in which the transformations take place and the philosopher's stone that makes them happen. Merlin is both the stone and the vessel. Merlin is the grail.

It is no surprise, of course, that a fiction as thoroughly sylleptic as Nye's can and indeed *must* accept both versions of the grail tradition at once, both that in which the grail is the vessel used at the last supper and that in which it is a holy and magical stone. Merlin tells Uther the first version, in which the grail cup was brought to England by Joseph of Arimathea but was somehow lost before it reached its intended sanctuary in Glastonbury (p. 124). But in the form of the tale's commentator, he says, "I am the spirit of the stone. The Grail stone,' that is. King Alexander found this stone at the entrance to Paradise. It is a cure for the world" (p. 13). The stone contains the spirit, and the cup contains the liquid, so the grail must be the perfect container. Everything that contains anything, or might contain something, is a grail. The woods where Merlin rides with Nimue "are a sun-filled Grail" (p. 227); the snow that falls on England makes "all the land a snow-filled Grail" (p. 100); and Friar Blaise, a cleric whose "nature is not chaste," is described as having "palms made for the cupping of his own seed. . . . Pearlpale grails" (p. 73). This sequence leads us right back to Merlin, ever cupping his own seed by watching himself engender himself. Merlin is the grail.

"I am a man shut up in a maze of himself," he says (p. 129), which statement is quite literally true in his case. He is imprisoned in a glass castle where everything he sees is a reflection of himself, and that castle (or that cup, or that stone) is the story of Merlin that Merlin has become. The devil his father is able to have Merlin confined in this prison because Merlin falls in love with his own story as it is embodied in the person of Nimue. She too is a shape shifter, appearing to Merlin in various forms:

> One moment my mother the virgin Vivien sits by the fire. She nurses me at her breast and sings me to sleep.
> Then when I awake the Lady Igrayne is beside me. She runs like a lapwing on tiptoe, but naked, in one silver slipper.
> Or else most disturbing of all the little Queen Morgan le Fay, her black-as-hell gown, dancing in the firelight. . . . You change all the time as you move in and out of the shadows. [P. 222]

But to Beelzebub her appearance is quite different: "Her face is like a looking glass. He is looking at himself!" (p. 220). It is at Nimue's request that Merlin builds the Grail Castle that will serve as his prison, though he knows that it will mean his "death" (that is, the end of his story). Of course, Merlin the mage cannot die; he can only come to an end and begin again—like any book.

Nye has achieved what might seem a utopia of formalism, the ultimate coherent fiction in which there is nothing that does not play its essential role in the whole. There is in this novel "no free note," to use the phrase of that other son of the devil, Adrian Leverkühn. The total coherence that Mann's musician strives for (with the help of his venereal Lucifer) is brought to perfection by *Merlin*. But I think it is clear that Nye's intentions are to give us not utopia but atopia. This coherence is so complete, so perfect, that we cannot credit it. Everyone is Merlin. Everything is a grail. All grails are Merlins. We cannot take this coherence any more seriously than the coherence of arguments with bars of soap. Needless to say, given the limitless range of Nye's syllepsis, we find that his Merlin can be understood to unite an argument that he is the Pope—well, not the Pope himself, perhaps, but the papal nuncio—with a bar of soap. Sir Gawain finds his version of the Grail Castle (death) by slipping on a bar of soap. What spirit inhabits that fatal bar of soap? Do we take this seriously? Is this not a version of the Sleeve Job?

I have not as yet mentioned the Sleeve Job, because it provides the last best argument that this ultimate syllepsis, this total coherence, this formalist never-never land, is served up in the expectation that we will not believe it. As we are being told the story of Merlin, we are promised, teased, and threatened with the story of Sir Gawain and the Sleeve Job, a tale that the demon Astarot wants to tell Lucifer. Finally, when Merlin is in the process of building the Grail Castle that will imprison him—at the end of the novel therefore—Astarot has his chance. He explains that Sir Gawain met a damsel in the forest of Broceliande who was so impressed with Gawain's knightly behavior (he refrained from raping her) that she offered to reward him with a unique and forbidden perversion called the Sleeve Job. Gawain has never heard of the Sleeve Job but imagines that it must be absolutely exquisite, since it is forbidden. Instead of accepting her very tempting offer on the spot, Gawain offers to marry the lady and to receive from her "the promised and forbidden Sleeve Job on their wedding night," which by custom cannot occur until seven years of betrothal have passed. After this long and frustrating delay, the wedding night arrives, and Gawain reminds his new bride of her vow. She had forgotten. She resists, but finally she agrees to deliver the long-awaited Sleeve Job:

> "'Go into the bathroom and lather yourself. I want you stark naked and covered from top to toe with soap. . . . Then come back to me here, and you shall have the Sleeve Job. . . .' And Sir Gawain does just as the young enchantress has told him. . . . He is running

to his love! Naked! Soapy! All ready! The Sleeve Job! THE SLEEVE
JOB! Now! But what's this? Running, Sir Gawain's right foot alights
on a little tiny insignificant cake of soap. . . . He slips! He
skids! . . ."

"But Sir Gawain?" says my father.

"Brained himself on the iron bed," says Uncle Astarot.

"But the Sleeve Job?" says my uncle Beelzebub.

"Ah yes, the Sleeve Job," says my uncle Astarot. "Well, Sir
Gawain being dead, he never did find out what the Sleeve Job is."

"So how can this be the end of it all?" screams my father.

My uncle the count Astarot holds up his right hand in blessing.

"I didn't say it was the end of it all," he says, choosing his words
with care. "There was and shall be no end of it all. Ever. World
without end, remember?" He grins from ear to ear and crosses
himself with his tail. "Begin," he says. "Again," he says. "Begin
again," he says. "This is just the end of the story," he explains. [Pp.
235–38]

And it is also the end of the novel.

Sir Gawain may not have lived to have the Sleeve Job practiced
upon him, but Lucifer and the reader have certainly had it practiced upon them. Near the beginning of the narrative, in the
middle of a mock-sermon by Beelzebub possessing the person of
Friar Blaise, the Friar is made to say, "My child, if this great con
of the devil's is conceded, why, what then? Does the world come
to a stop? Time turn itself inside-out? Solomon in all his wisdom
achieve the Sleeve Job? No" (p. 40). But indeed Merlin's self-
imprisonment in the Grail Castle makes him into "a man turned
inside-out," and narrative time is turned inside-out by Astarot's
trick. The whole story is one enormous Sleeve Job, turning back
upon itself, not as part of a self-conscious formalism but as part
of a huge dirty joke in which the joke is on Merlin, Lucifer, and
the reader.

By ending his novel with the story of Sir Gawain and the
Sleeve Job, Nye has prevented all but the most determined attempts at alethetic reading. Here is a vivid demonstration of how
the formalist aesthetic can be driven beyond all bounds of credibility—not to mention propriety—by a joyously excessive rigor.
Three decades of literary criticism have asked for the Sleeve Job,

and it is little wonder that someone has finally obliged. And though this fantastic playing with correspondences, this un-limited syllepsis, could be read as a parodistic critique of formal-ism, I really do not think it has any other goal than to celebrate "Merlin's merry muse." That at least is the implication of Nye's choice for the epigraph on his title page of this line from Geof-frey of Monmouth's *Vita Merlini:* "Fatidici vatis rabiem musam-que jocasam Merlini cantare paro" ("I prepare to sing the mad-ness and the merry muse of the prophetic seer Merlin"). A *musa jocosa* unquestionably inspires Nye's book from beginning to end.

If it is proper to talk about an "ironic tone" taking hold of a work and suffusing it, it is equally correct to speak of the syllep-tic spirit of Robert Nye's *Merlin.* Lewis Carroll and (at times) Oscar Wilde may seem closer to the rhetorical roots of syllepsis, because we can often identify sylleptic figures that the fictional atopia then imitates. But Nye is, if anything, more rigorous in his application of the sylleptic idea: language joins that which we believe belongs apart. Once we understand this notion, it is easy to see why we must regard *Merlin* (and indeed all sylleptic narra-tive) as fundamentally logomimetic. The structure of Merlin's world does not correspond to that of our real, everyday world, in which we believe, but to another incredible structure achieva-ble only in speech. Language, as Nimue appropriately observes, is the perfect alchemist's material. A story world made ex-clusively of infinitely transmutable material can model itself only on the limitless transmutability of metaphor.

In Nye's work no less than in Carroll's, the incredible flights of fancy are given a kind of authority and justification by linguistic structures, familiar patterns of speech making unfamiliar pat-terns of thought acceptable. Since conventional literary lan-guage has made familiar to us talk of skin that is "white as marble" and erections like swords, the fancy that makes the coupling of Igrayne and Uther equivalent to the Arthurian "sword in the stone" seems to have its feet on the ground. Every-day language gives the marvelous an anchor in the familiar and thereby makes it "right." Nye's syllepsis does not come from nowhere and baffle us; it comes from the commonest of commonplaces, whence it attains the reader's assent. Nye, Wilde, and Carroll, though each was working in a different way and toward a different end, all found in syllepsis a method for connecting the reader's world with the atopia of fantasy.

CHAPTER 6 /

Incredible Sunderings:
Dialepsis in Christian Morgenstern,
Nicolai Gogol, and Edgar Allan Poe

SUETONIUS REPORTS in his *Iulius* (20.2) that Caesar
was able to intimidate Bibulus, his fellow consul for the year 59
B.C., to such a degree that Bibulus remained at home and left
Caesar to govern Rome by himself. Caesar had so effectively
seized total control of the government that "some citizens, when
they were supposed to sign something as witnesses, would as a
joke write the date not [in the usual form as] 'in the consulate of
Caesar and Bibulus' but rather as 'in the consulate of Julius and
Caesar'" (*ut nonnulli urbanorum cum quid per iocum testandi gratia
signarent non Caesare et Bibulo sed Iulio et Caesare consulibus actum
scriberent*).

The joke depends on a confrontation between the structure of
language and the structure of what we believe is reality. The
conventional Latin designation for a particular year requires two
names, those of the two consuls governing; but the political real-
ities of the year 59 B.C. were such that in fact only one man was
governing. Language is able to resolve the difficulty by making
use of the fact that a single person may have several names, in
effect thereby dividing the person. The individual person Julius
Caesar is easily split into two verbal objects, "Julius" and
"Caesar," which language may then treat as completely independent entities. We do something similar in English when we say
"between a rock and a hard place" or "six of one, half a dozen of

the other." From the point of view of language, every separate word is a separate "thing."

Classical rhetoric did not give a name to this relatively unusual turn of speech. If it had, it might well have noted the relation between this trope and syllepsis. As we have seen, syllepsis works on the capability of language to put together what we believe reality keeps apart. The "Julius and Caesar" figure works in an analogous but opposite way: here language divides what, we would insist, reality keeps together. If the first figure is a "taking together" (syllepsis), the second is clearly a "taking apart" (*dialepsis*). We may speak of this sort of locution, then, both conveniently and properly, as dialepsis.

Many of us will have become familiar with the possibilities of dialepsis from one of the enduring witticisms of childhood, in which a disagreement between two children is to be settled by a vote, one child claiming a majority of three to one because of the votes of "me, myself, and I." Three different words are asserted to imply three different "persons." The child proposing this dialepsis of the single self into three is not likely to be successful—without being able to prevail by other means—because children learn very early the vast differences between the structure of language and the structure of the world. But if the child were successful, if his or her playmates accepted the propriety of this mystic division, there would be no more dialepsis. Like syllepsis, dialepsis comes into being only when the structure proposed by language conflicts with what we believe is the structure of reality. If the structure of language is accepted as mirroring the world, the trope ceases to be a lethetic figure and may indeed cease to be a figure at all.

One might investigate the trope at greater length, but here again, as with syllepsis, my central concern is not with the trope, narrowly conceived, but with the possibilities for lethetic narrative that it suggests. Dialepsis is evidently also a figure of thought, a concept that can be used as the foundation for structures more complex than an individual phrase. Many writers of fantasy have built upon this foundation, perhaps none, however, more consistently and characteristically than Christian Morgenstern. Like Lewis Carroll, Morgenstern is best known for his "nonsense" verse; but whereas Carroll tends to base his logomimesis on syllepsis, Morgenstern more often chooses dialepsis.

Morgenstern's nonsense universe is characterized by a never-ending confrontation between the structure of language and the structure of the world, with language always victorious—within the atopia of the fiction. Ordinarily the poems show us the results of such a victory by language, but from time to time the confrontation itself is dramatized. A good example for my purpose is "Der Werwolf" ("The Werewolf"). The poem[1] tells how a werewolf comes one night to the grave of a village schoolteacher with the request that the dead teacher arise and "decline me" (*beuge mich*). The teacher does so: *der Werwolf, des Weswolfs, dem Wemwolf, den Wenwolf.* But when the werewolf requests that he go on to decline also the plural, the teacher confesses that he cannot. There are plenty of *Wölfe*, he explains, but *wer* exists only in the singular. The werewolf's eyes fill with tears at the thought of his wife and child, whose existence is threatened by this news, but "because he was no scholar, he departed with thanks and humility" (pp. 66–67).

Because the German word *Werwolf* gives the appearance of being a composite of the interrogative pronoun *wer* with the ordinary noun *Wolf*, Morgenstern's schoolteacher is able to produce a nonsense paradigm for all four cases of the singular. But indeed the interrogative pronoun in German happens to be declinable only in the singular; one uses singular forms no matter how many people one is inquiring about. He cannot continue his silly-scholarly exercise into the plural, so he simply declares that the plural does not exist. This is wonderfully clever fun so far, but now Morgenstern adds the brilliant touch. In a world that contains werewolves and speaking corpses, the issue of what language will and will not allow holds life-and-death interest. If by the incredible (but linguistically justified) logic of the teacher the word *Werwolf* can only exist in the singular, the "object" werewolf—whose existence is after all purely a figment of speech—must be similarly limited. This werewolf must be the only werewolf; the wife and child cannot be.

[1]I cite Morgenstern from the *Galgenlieder* (Berlin: Bruno Cassirer, 1921). Page numbers in my text refer to this edition.

The poor werewolf has suffered from the effects of a process quite the same as that practiced upon Julius Caesar in the ancient Roman joke. His name has been taken apart and used in a way that we do not consider "really" legitimate. Paradoxically, this dialepsis results in the fantastic assertion not that the werewolf is two creatures but rather that his species cannot contain more than one member. The (incredible) separation of *Wer* from *Wolf* creates a conflict between the two parts of the werewolf's name that the teacher can resolve only by leaving the pieces sundered: "Zwar Wölfe gäb's in grosser Schar, doch 'Wer' gäb's nur im Singular." His inability to put the pieces back together leaves the werewolf bereft of plurality.

"Der Werwolf" presents a dialepsis of language upon itself, the results of which threaten to restructure the atopic world of the poem. Morgenstern's dialepsis is usually more direct, however, as in his famous poem about the picket fence ("Der Lattenzaun"):

> Es war einmal ein Lattenzaun,
> mit Zwischenraum, hindurchzuschaun.
>
> Ein Architekt, der dieses sah,
> stand eines Abends plötzlich da—
>
> und nahm den Zwischenraum heraus
> und baute draus ein grosses Haus.
>
> Der Zaun indessen stand ganz dumm,
> mit Latten ohne was herum.
>
> Ein Anblick grässlich und gemein.
> Drum zog ihn der Senat auch ein.
>
> Der Architekt jedoch entfloh
> nach Afri-od-Ameriko. [P. 33][2]

[2]A rough English translation: "There was once a picket fence with spaces to look through. An architect who saw it stood suddenly by it one evening—and took the spaces out and built a big house out of them. Meanwhile the fence stood there stupidly with pickets with nothing around them. A disgusting and vulgar sight. So the city council called it in. But the architect absconded to Afri-or-Ameriko."

What is only threatened in the poem of the werewolf is put into practice here: the world is rebuilt on the basis of language's ability to give separate names to things which have no independent existence. Although we do not believe that Zwischenraum can exist apart from the objects around it, the noun *Zwischenraum* has all the capabilities that other nouns have. The verbal picket fence can be disassembled into "pickets" and "spaces," and the spaces can be taken away and used as materials to build something else.

Morgenstern's brilliance does not reside entirely or even chiefly in creating this sort of dialeptic atopia. What makes these poems glitter is the rigor with which the principles are applied. That the architect can build himself a house from the stolen Zwischenraum is amusing; but that the reader's attention is then directed back to the fence and the problem of its lack of intervening spaces is an inspired stroke. If Zwischenraum is a substance capable of being used to build houses, its absence must be understood as denuding the fence of something. The remaining pickets are described in terms that suggest vulgar nakedness—a lack of clothing—or horrifying bareness, as if they were a skeleton deprived of the flesh that would properly cover them: "Ein Anblick grässlich und gemein." The shocked city government has to intervene, presumably to protect the public from such a disgraceful display of "Latten ohne was herum."

The chief focus for the poem, in fact, is not the Zwischenraum itself or the house that is built from it but the terrible results of that loss. That the architect has actually managed to "make something out of nothing" is marvelous, but no more so than what we find in countless fairy tales and fantasies, and Morgenstern simply mentions it, as it were, in passing. The architect is treated not as the hero of a marvelous adventure but as a criminal who has committed an outrageous act of defacement. The poem presents him as someone who has done something terrible to the fence rather than as someone who has done something wonderful with "space." He runs off to a foreign country—in fact to a verbal amalgam of all the foreign countries traditionally sought by European outcasts. The little story is thus made symmetrical by the architect's having to pay with his absence for his act of making absence (Zwischenraum) absent.

Symmetry is important to this poem, because the dialepsis
upon which it is constructed originates in an inappropriate (that
is, incredible) imposition of symmetry. Since it is obviously possible to remove pickets from a fence leaving nothing but space,
the poem assumes that one ought to be able also to remove the
spaces until there is nothing left but pickets, "Latten ohne was
herum." If we can separate pickets from spaces, why not spaces
from pickets? This is an important point, because the dialepsis
comes into being only when the second incredible separation is
proposed.[3] There is nothing incredible or even unusual in sepa-
rating things from certain spaces, and there would be no dialepsis if the architect had taken the pickets away to build a house
leaving nothing but bare space on the fence. It is not the separation itself that engenders the dialepsis but rather the fact that
the "wrong" element has suffered removal. We are prepared to
believe that pickets can exist apart from spaces: it is the idea of
"Räume ohne was herum" that we do not credit and that makes
the poem work.

Similarly, another of the *Galgenlieder* describes the unhappy
adventures of a sigh that goes skating one night ("Der Seufzer"
[p. 21]:

> Ein Seufzer lief Schlittschuh auf nächtlichem Eis
> und träumte von Liebe und Freude.
> Es war an dem Stadtwall, und schneeweiss
> glänzten die Stadtwallgebäude.
>
> Der Seufzer dacht' an ein Maidelein
> und blieb erglühend stehen.
> Da schmolz die Eisbahn unter ihm ein—
> und er sank—und ward nimmer gesehen.[4]

The separation of a sigh from a person is nothing unusual as
long as we assume that the person only is capable of indepen-

---

[3]Compare the locution "doughnut holes," which catches our attention by presenting an apparent dialepsis (Is the bakery selling empty spaces?) that is exploded by the realization that these "holes" are not in fact the holes themselves
but rather the dough removed in order to make the holes.

[4]In literal English: "A sigh went skating on nocturnal ice and dreamed of love
and joy. It was near the city dike, and the city-dike buildings gleamed white as
snow. The sigh thought about a maiden and stopped, burning with passion. So
the ice underneath him melted—and he sank—and was never seen again."

dent existence. We can easily imagine a person without a sigh, but we have difficulty imagining a sigh without a person. We have no difficulty *speaking* of it, however: our language works perfectly well no matter what noun we make object of the preposition "without."

Once language has spoken the phrase "sigh without a person" or "spaces without pickets," there is nothing to stop its pushing the process further. Sighs and spaces that are capable of taking over the quality of independent existence from persons and pickets may take over additional qualities as well. Thus the architect is able to build a house out of the Zwischenraum he has stolen, something one could indeed do with pickets. And the sigh takes on the human characteristics of going ice skating and burning with passion. Indeed, there is no way to picture the scene described by Morgenstern without giving the sigh at least a quasi-human shape. But "Der Seufzer," even more forcefully than "Der Werwolf," demonstrates the destructive as well as the creative potential of logomimesis. If the sigh gains its independent existence by rhetoric, so does it die by rhetoric as well. It is not by accident that Morgenstern gives the sigh this peculiar combination of human traits—ice skating and lovesickness—since precisely this combination turns out to be fatally dangerous in the atopia ruled by language. When one is in love, one burns with passion (erglüht), and the logomimetic principle transforms that metaphorical heat into energy sufficient to melt ice. The same process that made the invisible sigh into a fictionally visible form transforms it into something that "ward nimmer gesehen." Again, Morgenstern works with *symmetrical* nonsense.

He also works with nonsense that is on or near the borders of what was known in Poe's day as "German" horror. "Der Werwolf," "Der Lattenzaun," and "Der Seufzer" are all delightful poems, but they all contain a more or less heavy whiff of the tomb. "Der Lattenzaun" is the lightest in tone of all of them, since no one dies in the poem or starts off dead. Yet even here there is a macabre cast to the playfulness, with the central action described as a criminal act resulting in an "Anblick grässlich und gemein." In short, there is ample reason for these particular nonsense verses to be called *Galgenlieder* ("Gallows Songs"). In a few, this vein of gallows humor reaches such a degree of purity that the horrifying and the comic blend into an inseparable image, at once attractive in its logomimetic power and repellent in its grimness. "Das Knie" is such a poem.

This poem does little more than assert that a knee makes its lonely way through the world:

Ein Knie geht einsam durch die Welt.
Es ist ein Knie, sonst nichts!
Es ist kein Baum! Es ist kein Zelt!
Es ist ein Knie, sonst nichts.

Im Kriege ward einmal ein Mann
erschossen um und um.
Das Knie allein blieb unverletzt—
Als wär's ein Heiligtum.

Seitdem geht's einsam durch die Welt.
Es ist ein Knie, sonst nichts.
Es ist kein Baum, es ist kein Zelt.
Es ist ein Knie, sonst nichts. [P. 20][5]

Because it is a lethetic fiction, the poem ignores the question of how a knee could accomplish this independent, if lonely, existence, but it offers instead an explanation of how the knee came to be alone. It is simply all that is left after a steady process of effacement of a human body by gunfire. It is no longer connected to the human world at all, save perhaps by the fact that it retains the ability to move through the world. It is just another object, like a tree or a tent.

Morgenstern here presents in the sparest possible terms that form of dialepsis that is most prevalent in lethetic literature, the separation of one part of the body from the rest of the person. This notion has been the origin of countless marvelous tales, sometimes comic, more often horrifying. Several of these will be the subject of detailed discussion below.

The knee of the *Galgenlieder* is of special interest because Mor-

[5]"A knee goes lonely through the world. It's just a knee, that's all! It's not a tree! It's not a tent! It's just a knee, that's all. Once in the war a man was all shot up. His knee alone remained unwounded, as if it were a shrine. Since then it goes lonely through the world. It's just a knee, that's all. It's not a tree, it's not a tent. It's just a knee, that's all."

genstern has so balanced the humor and horror of his fantastic image. The notion of a man being slowly shot away until nothing but his knee is left ("as if it were a shrine") is surely horrifying. But we cannot help finding it funny that a knee, a part of the body not ordinarily thought particularly handsome or noble, is the one thing left unharmed. A knee in isolation is not exactly a dignified idea, and it is made sillier still by the addition of some unspecified form of locomotion. In fact, the first stanza, read in isolation, would probably seem uncomplicatedly humorous. But after presenting the ghastly history recounted in the second stanza, Morgenstern is able to repeat the first quatrain almost word for word with an entirely new effect. What seemed just silly and amusing at first is now disquietingly complex. We are not sure how to react.

Another dialeptic fiction that renders its readers uncertain about how to react is Gogol's "The Nose." It is this story in particular that contributes so much to Gogol's reputation of being "controversial, puzzling, and elusive."[6] It would not be amiss to think of it as the Russian equivalent of the *Birds,* so extensive is the literature seeking, without success, to reduce it to sense, to find some clear and firm line to take about its meaning. "The narrative has been subjected to numerous interpretations: sociological, metaphysical, psychological, and psychoanalytical. Castration anxiety . . . has also been mentioned. . . . In spite of [all this] . . . , it may simply be that Gogol intended only to provide a nonsensical jest, as Pushkin suggested."[7]

One thing we may take as certain, however: that Gogol's tale is a towering example of the dialeptic imagination at work. Gogol has separated the inseparable and has granted independence to something we know to be absolutely dependent. Like Morgenstern, Gogol enforces an inappropriate symmetry in his nonsense world. The nose of collegiate assessor Kovalyov gets the uniform, the status, the high social position to which a noseless Kovalyov aspires. Just as the spaces in Morgenstern's "Der Lattenzaun" obtain more dignity than the pickets (the spaces are made into a house, while the pickets just stand there nakedly), so

[6]Fruma Gottschalk, ed., *The Nose* (Letchworth: Prideaux Press, 1972), 9.
[7]Ibid.

does the nose have greater dignity than its former owner. When Kovalyov confronts his nose in the cathedral, he stammers, coughs, and speaks in incoherent fragments: "I don't know how best to put it, sir, but it strikes me as very peculiar. . . . Don't you know where you belong? And where do I find you? In church, of all places!" When after a great deal more of this hemming and hawing, Kovalyov finally comes out with it ("Don't you realize you are *my own nose!*"), the nose replies with perfect aplomb and more than a little condescension, "My dear fellow, you are mistaken. I am a person in my own right. Furthermore, I don't see that we can have anything in common. Judging from your uniform buttons, I should say you're from another government department."[8]

This dialepsis of Kovalyov's body is also somehow a division of his identity, of his self. In fact, the whole story can be understood as a logomimesis on the idea of being apart from one's self: a certain level of excitement can make a man "beside himself," as Kovalyov is described later in the story (p. 61). Russian has an analogous expression, *vnye syebya* (literally "outside oneself"), that Gogol uses here,[9] undoubtedly intending it to be both literally and metaphorically true for Kovalyov. The collegiate assessor is locked out of the social "place" that he believes is the rightful place of his true self. The nose becomes the insider: "Judging by its uniform, its hat, and its whole appearance, it must be a state councillor" (p. 49). Such a one can only look down his nose at the likes of Kovalyov.

The person who first discovers Kovalyov's nose, the barber Ivan Yakovlevich, suffers from a similar logomimetic loss of "himself": the narrator reports that "his surname has got lost and all that his shop-front signboard shows is a gentleman with a lathered cheek and the inscription 'We also let blood' " (p. 42). If a man can be vnye syebya, "outside himself," and if a man can lose part of his verbal self, his name, then a man might very well also lose a part of his physical self. In another symmetry, the barber who loses part of his own self discovers the lost part of

[8]*Diary of a Madman and Other Stories*, trans. Ronald Wilks (Harmondsworth: Penguin, 1972), 50. Citations below in the text refer to this edition.
[9]Gottschalk, ed., *The Nose*, 33.

someone else's dialeptically severed self. He instantly recognizes Kovalyov's nose, which he finds in a breakfast roll. It is from these humble beginnings that the nose rises practically instantaneously to the heights of "state councillor."

At least one of the best critics of Gogol has already indicated that "The Nose" is a story that puts language in total charge. Donald Fanger, referring to Roland Barthes's notion of irony as "the question posed by language to language" that "expands the language rather than narrowing it," calls such expansion "the principal achievement of 'The Nose,' which forces the reader to contemplate nothing less than the autonomy of the word (as he tries to picture the nose frowning, praying, hurrying, decked out in a resplendent uniform)."[10] Fanger understands Gogol to be pushing his dialeptic premise as far as it will go. It is not enough to assert that a person's nose could exist apart from the person; Gogol pushes forward by substituting the word "nose" for "person" in all sorts of sentences, making "nose" the subject of a variety of verbs ordinarily requiring a human subject ("pray," "wear," "reply," "frown," and so forth). The "autonomy of the word" is forced upon the reader's attention because sentences such as "The nose's face was completely hidden by the high collar and it was praying with an expression of profound piety" (p. 49) cannot occur in the phenomenal world or even in the imagination. All one can do with them is *say* them.

Fanger sees "more than downright nonsense" in the creation of such an autonomy of the word. Though he does not disagree with the position that "The Nose" is as a whole a nonsensical fiction ("too much of the text escapes" every interpretation that tries to make sense of it,[11] Fanger would see it as a nonsensical fiction that over and over again provokes the reader to an inevitably unsuccessful attempt at alethetic reading. "The temptation to read meanings into the story arises from the fact that fragments of meaning can be read out of it."[12] Sometimes the story seems to be aiming at pure satire, shooting down the familiar targets of social pretension and self-delusion. Sometimes it

---

[10]*The Creation of Nikolai Gogol* (Cambridge: Harvard University Press, 1979), 121.
[11]Ibid., 120.
[12]Ibid., 121.

looks like an allegory of the person who finds himself "out of place" in ordinary society. The large number of such familiar and conventional elements might, in another context, be clues to a convincing interpretation of the story's meaning. The combination, however, "mocks a serious attitude toward the plot (the accepted notion of significant form)" and "mocks ordinary assumptions about intentionality (the very notion of language as the carrier of messages)."[13] The story as a whole becomes "a trap for the unwary."

If Fanger is right, "The Nose" may be not a genuinely lethetic text but rather one that has the (alethetic) intention of mocking intentionality. An element of satire has come in the back door, though the target is not Kovalyov or his social pretensions but rather the reader's own urge to alethetic reading. To that end it does not, like the *Birds*, try to prevent alethetic reading; it rather quickens our desire for meaning only to frustrate it. The story's atopia, its autonomous realm of language, becomes a trap. What we would have, then, is not exactly a lethetic fiction, as I have defined it, but something more like an antialethetic fiction. Lethetic fictions are never "traps for the unwary," because they do not even occasionally ask to be read allegorically. Gogol's story, as Fanger reads it, solicits disbelief *as a whole*, while various of its *parts* lure us down false trails of allegory, trails that would seem to lead to belief in the whole. It uses the overall form of a lethetic text for the alethetic purpose of exposing the process of alethetic reading.

Fanger's position may be taken as a demonstration of the irresistible power that alethetic reading exerts upon literary criticism. Even "The Nose," one of the most outrageously incredible tales in the canon of modern literature, becomes a message about the nonexistence of messages. This conversion is perfectly legitimate, of course, and I do not wish to appear to object to Fanger's procedure. His job is to read Gogol, which he does admirably—and alethetically. But one does not have to object to Fanger's reading to suppose that the option of seeing "The Nose" as a lethetic text still remains open. Let us suppose that we are not in the least tempted to read meanings into the story; let us suppose that we are willing to let the autonomous realm of

13Ibid., 122.

language go its own way; and let us suppose that the story is not a trap that threatens to confine us but a magic "word" that offers to liberate us. In that case, "The Nose" could remain a dialeptic fantasy with no messages to deliver.

The story is disquieting enough, even understood as a lethetic fiction. The comic tone that prevails cannot entirely wipe out the potential for horror (or, at the very least, the grotesque) in the central image of dismemberment. "We also let blood," says the barber's sign. The threat of violence remains palpable throughout the tale, as when the nose's appearance on Nevsky Prospect causes "such a crush outside that the police had to be called" (p. 66). Like Morgenstern's "Das Knie," Gogol's story with a light touch presents material that is by nature extremely unpleasant and that could be downright frightening. In fact, the story seems at times both funny and frightening at the same time, funny because it is so outrageous in its fantasy, frightening because the subject of that fantasy is dismemberment.

Freud has apparently provided once and for all an explanation for the powerful and deeply ambivalent reactions elicited by these fantasies of dismemberment in his essay on "The 'Uncanny.'" Our sense of horror arises not out of shock that such violence has been done to someone else but rather out of fear that something analogous could happen to us. Freud argues that "it is the threat of being castrated in especial which excites a peculiarly violent and obscure emotion, and that this emotion is what first gives the idea of losing other organs its intense colouring."[14] "Dismembered limbs, a severed head, a hand cut off at the wrist, feet which dance by themselves—all these have something peculiarly uncanny about them, especially when as in the last instance, they prove able to move of themselves in addition. As we already know, this kind of uncanniness springs from its association with the castration-complex" (p. 151). This fear of castration is a familiar one to us, Freud asserts, but we repress it. The uncanny emotion arises when this familiar but repressed feeling is reawakened in us by a stimulus that reminds us, in spite of ourselves, of this infantile anxiety.

It is important, however—particularly so in this context—to

---

[14]Benjamin Nelson, ed., *On Creativity and the Unconscious* (New York: Harper & Row, 1958), 138. Citations below in the text refer to this edition.

recall that Freud set up a number of significant hedges around his argument about the repression-compulsion and the uncanny. It is clear that Freud is aware of the existence of a special class of fictions that solicit disbelief and of special conditions that attach to the reading of these (in my terminology lethetic) fictions:

> The story-teller has this license among others, that he can select his world of representation so that it either coincides with the realities we are familiar with or departs from them in what particulars he pleases. We accept his ruling in every case. In fairy-tales, for instance, the world of reality is left behind from the very start, and the animistic system of beliefs is frankly adopted. Wish-fulfilments, secret powers, omnipotence of thoughts, animation of lifeless objects, all the elements so common in fairy-stories, can exert no uncanny influence here; for, as we have learnt, that feeling cannot arise unless there is a conflict of judgment whether things which have been "surmounted" and are regarded as incredible are not, after all, possible; and this problem is excluded from the beginning by the setting of the story. [P. 150]

Like Todorov's "fantastic," Freud's uncanny requires a hesitation between a natural and a supernatural view of events reported. The uncanny feeling will not arise unless we are prompted to wonder if something we have always thought to be impossible might yet happen.

But this is precisely what cannot happen in the case of lethetic fictions like Gogol's "Nose" and Morgenstern's "Das Knie." Because such fictions make not the slightest attempt to obtain belief for their impossible premises, there is never any question of our supposing that it might somehow be possible for a knee or a nose to wander through the world independent of a person. The thought *is* potentially horrible, but its horror cannot touch us because the boundary of our disbelief protects us from it. The horror is there, but it is, as it were, on the other side of a glass wall, like a python in a herpetarium. The python is, in itself, frightening; but the situation in which the python is presented is reassuring.

Our ambivalence about the horror in "The Nose" and "Das Knie" works along similar lines. It is not the shock of the uncanny or the pleasant hesitation of the fantastic; it is the assured safety of lethetic fiction, wherein the most terrible things may be displayed without arousing anxiety. We can laugh at what happens behind the glass wall because we know it will not happen to us. Morgenstern's and Gogol's nonsense is not uncanny because it is not problematic. We *know* that we are not in danger of being reduced to anything resembling ambulatory knees and noses, since such things are not possible in the world we inhabit.

If the reader believed that the structure of language could shape the structure of the world, he would indeed suffer from Freud's uncanny and worse. But such belief is radically excluded by narratives that are lethetic: the reader always remains at home in a world that operates in familiar—often boringly familiar—ways. The question then arises as to whether it is possible for lethetic texts to be frightening. If the reader is always safe, the actions of the fiction can have no direct effect upon him. How could a story that we do not believe frighten us? Can there be such a thing as a lethetic horror story?

The question is answered for us in the tales of that master of lethetic horror Edgar Allan Poe. For though there is no question that Poe's stories achieve their frightening effects on large numbers of readers, it appears highly doubtful that (whatever Poe himself may have thought) large numbers of these readers actually believe what they read. The only open question in this regard is whether these obviously apistic fictions are to be understood simply as highly successful entertainment or as allegories of something "deeper."

As I have emphasized from the beginning, there is no argument that will definitively preclude the alethetic reading of any text. Allegorizing readings of the *Birds* will probably never cease, no matter what Cedric Whitman or I may say, because the assumption behind alethetic reading—that fiction, no matter how outlandish, conceals some hidden kernel of truth—is an article of hermeneutic faith not refutable by human discourse. The question before us always must be, therefore, whether the text in question is genuinely enriched by allegorical interpretation. A comic fantasy like the *Birds* seems to me to achieve its aims without the aid of alethetic reading. The same obviously cannot be said for *The Faerie Queene* or for the fantastic tales of Borges: such texts are impoverished by failure to read alethetically. Are the tales of Poe more like the *Birds* or *The Faerie Queene* in this respect? It is my contention, for reasons that will become evident in what follows, that they are more like the *Birds*. I contend further that many of Poe's tales are in fact lethetic horror stories based upon dialepsis.

It is occasionally necessary to remind ourselves, as J. L. Austin has helped us to do, that language can do other things than correspond to the facts, can have other goals than to convey the truth. A work of fiction, like any other utterance, may perform one or more of several actions, none of which may involve communication of the truth. The *Birds,* the Münchhausen stories, and numerous other tall tales have no other purpose than to amuse us. They have their effect and thus succeed by making us laugh. Other fictions make it their legitimate business to do nothing more than make us cry. An example that happens to be prominent at the time I am writing is the film *E.T.,* which no adult believes but which nevertheless elicits tears from all but the most cynical. We are glad it makes us cry; that is what we want it to do, and we expect nothing more. One can "discover" no end of deeper truths in such fiction (the "Christian" interpretation of *E.T.* is currently making the rounds), but they are genuinely irrelevant. We go to the *Birds* to laugh and to *E.T.* to cry, and all the hidden messages in the world will not add anything to their success.

And we go to Edgar Allan Poe to be frightened. Few people can succeed in frightening us as well as he, and even fewer really care if he does anything else. The interesting and important question for literary criticism ought to be not "What meaning can we extract from these texts?" but rather "How do these texts succeed so well in doing what everyone acknowledges they do?" How and why, in other words, do Poe's tales achieve the remarkable effect of frightening us *withoug producing genuine anxiety?* If Aristotle was confronted with the problem of how and why people derived pleasure from watching tragedies, we are confronted with the analogous question of how and why people derive pleasure from being frightened by Poe. The questions are similar, though I make no pretentions to equality with Aristotle, nor do I imagine that my answers will be as useful as his. My answers are, in any case, very different.

One key to understanding Poe's success at composing lethetic horror stories comes from an unlikely source: the epigraph to one of the less famous tales, "The Man That Was Used Up." This is one of Poe's humorous fictions, one that obviously wishes only to provoke laughter and does not expect to frighten anyone. In going to this tale I follow the recommendation of William Carlos Williams, who suggests that "to understand what Poe is driving at in his tales, we should read first not the popular, perfect . . . but the less striking tales."[15] The story itself is of some interest, but the epigraph from Corneille gives us a clue about the working of Poe's imagination. The French original reads, "Pleurez, pleurez, mes yeux, et fondez-vous en eau!/La moitié de ma vie a mis l'autre au tombeau" (*Le Cid,* III, iii), and Poe gives this English version: "Weep, weep, my eyes! It is no time to laugh/For half myself has buried the other half." The translation is rather free, and the contrast it makes with the original is instructive. The second line of Corneille's couplet speaks of "half my life" putting the other half in the tomb, whereas Poe speaks of "half myself." Now, the other changes that Poe makes (that is, the replacement of *fondez-vous en eau* with "It is no time to laugh") are apparently occasioned by the need to make a rhyme, but the substitution of "self" for "life" is required neither by rhyme nor by reason. Poe presumably made the change because he preferred his version to Corneille's original.

Poe's preference is for a more boldly dialeptic formulation. Corneille's figure, by adverting to the "life" of Chimène, does not directly involve Chimène's physical person. She is in fact speaking of two other people, her lover and her father. Poe's version, on the other hand, unmistakably implies a division of the body into two independent halves. That Poe had such a division in mind is borne out by the text of his story: General Smith, the used-up person of the title, has suffered a fate almost identical to that of the soldier in Morgenstern's "Das Knie." He

---

[15] "Edgar Allan Poe" in William L. Howarth, ed., *Twentieth Century Interpretations of Poe's Tales* (Englewood Cliffs: Prentice-Hall, 1971), 37.

has been so shot up in the Indian wars that there is nothing left of him but an "exceedingly odd-looking bundle of something"[16] that the narrator unwittingly kicks out of his way upon entering the General's quarters. The story is a logomimesis on the text of Corneille as translated by Poe, for the General has literally buried half of his physical substance. All that remains of him is one leg, one arm, one eye, and portions of his head and torso—in short, half of his "self."

Poe's version of the couplet by Corneille could easily serve as the epigraph for a number of his other stories as well, for the dialepsis that divides a living body into two is one of the characteristic features of Poe's fiction. Another of the "Extravaganzas," the "Article for Blackwood: A Predicament,"[17] seeks to entertain us with the narrative of a lady whose head is cut off by the hand of a clock. We need not trouble ourselves with the method by which Poe contrives to have his heroine, the Signora Psyche Zenobia, stuck in the face of a tower clock. What is interesting for us is the principle of dialepsis as it is applied in this absurd situation. As the clock hand slowly cuts through the neck, the pressure forces one of Zenobia's eyes out of its socket. Its behavior, once released, is peculiar:

> The loss of the eye was not so much as the insolent air of independence and contempt with which it regarded me after it was out. There it lay in the gutter just under my nose, and the airs it gave itself would have been ridiculous had they not been disgusting. Such a winking and blinking were never before seen. This behavior on the part of my eye on the gutter was not only irritating on account of its manifest insolence and shameful ingratitude, but was also exceedingly inconvenient on account of the sympathy which always exists between two eyes of the same head, however far apart. I was forced, in a manner, to wink and to blink, whether I would or no, in exact concert with the scoundrelly thing that lay just under my nose. [*E&C*, pp. 268–69]

The point of view in these lines is dialeptic in a way familiar to us from the *Galgenlieder*. The ejected eye acts like a prisoner that

---

[16]Julian Symons, ed., *Edgar Allan Poe: Selected Tales* (Oxford: Oxford University Press, 1980), 59. This edition is cited below in the text as *ST*.

[17]Edgar Allan Poe, *Extravaganza and Caprice* (New York: Scribner's, 1914). This edition is cited below in the text as *E&C*.

has been liberated from unnatural bondage, an eye-without-a-person now somehow superior to the person-without-an-eye. It has a genuine independent existence, attested by its ability to wink and blink of its own volition, and a paradoxical (and inconvenient) power over the person to whom it was formerly attached. Whereas formerly the Psyche Zenobia could wink her eye, now her eye in effect winks her. Poe, like Morgenstern, lets the newly independent entity take over, along with independence, additional qualities from its formerly inseparable partner. Zenobia is released from the power of her lost eye only when the second eye drops out. "In falling it took the same direction (possibly a concerted plot) as its fellow" (*E&C*, p. 269).

The clock hand finally cuts through the neck, with the result that the heroine finds herself in two places at once:

> I will candidly confess that my feelings were now of the most singular—nay, of the most mysterious, the most perplexing and incomprehensible character. My senses were here and there at one and the same moment. With my head I imagined, at one time, that I, the head, was the real Signora Psyche Zenobia—at another I felt convinced that myself, the body, was the proper identity. To clear my ideas upon this topic I felt in my pocket for my snuff-box, but, upon getting it, and endeavouring to apply a pinch of its grateful contents in the ordinary manner, I became immediately aware of my peculiar deficiency, and threw the box at once down to my head. [*E&C*, p. 270]

The potential dialepsis in the contrast between "I" and "myself" is actualized logomimetically by severance of the self into "I, the head" and "myself, the body." The "self" is uncertain as to where its proper lodging should be, now that it has the unaccustomed and unwelcome luxury of choice. This uncertainty and confusion is such that the head delivers a speech (difficult for the body to hear, lacking ears) expressing astonishment "at my wishing to remain alive under such circumstances" (*E&C*, p. 270). Half of Zenobia's "self" would evidently be better off if it could bury the other half and could thus end all the perplexity and confusion. It would also bring to a close the most outrageous identity crisis in all of literature.

A crisis of a different sort provides the material for another of the extravaganzas, "Loss of Breath." Poe's hero and narrator makes sure we understand the logomimetic origin of the story: "I discovered that *I had lost my breath.* The phrases 'I am out of breath,' 'I have lost my breath,' etc. are often enough repeated in common conversation; but it had never occurred to me that the terrible accident of which I speak could *bona fide* and actually happen!" (*E&C,* p. 92). The story treats "breath" not as an activity in which a person engages—in which he must engage, in fact—but as an object separable from that person. It is a "thing" that one can actually "lose" in the sense of "mislay." Indeed, the hero takes the first opportunity to conduct a search for his lost breath: "It was possible, I thought that, concealed in some obscure corner, or lurking in some closet or drawer, might be found the lost object of my inquiry. It might have a vapory—it might even have a tangible form" (*E&C,* p. 94). He is not able to find his missing breath, but what he does find confirms and extends the dialepsis. Among the items he uncovers are "two pairs of hips" and "an eye" (*E&C,* p. 95).

Poe's literary atopia is one in which things threaten to "come apart" at any moment at the behest of language, and when they in fact do so, it comes as no great surprise. "Never Bet the Devil Your Head" uses, to demonstrate the impossible power of rhetoric put into action, the form of a cautionary tale about the dangers of swearing. Mr. Dammit claims he can leap over a stile and "cut a pigeon-wing over it in the air" (*E&C,* p. 159), and he is so sure he can do it that he says he will bet the devil his head that he can. No reader of Poe can have the slightest doubt about the outcome: Mr. Dammit's verbal flourish is made to come true, and Mr. Dammit is made to come apart at the neck. "He did not long survive his terrible loss," not for the reasons we might suppose, but because "the homeopathists did not give him little enough physic, and what little they did give him he hesitated to take" (*E&C,* pp. 165–66). Poe thus makes absolutely certain that we will not be tempted to find his story credible, for belief would turn this lethetic and dialeptic game into the moralizing cautionary tale it masquerades as being.

Not everyone will find such grotesque scenes as amusing as Poe seems to have thought they were, but few will find them frightening. This dialepsis, like that in "A Predicament" and "The Man That Was Used Up," is put forward in such a way as to seem silly and harmless rather than terrifying. But others of Poe's dialeptic tales, like "The Tell-Tale Heart" or "The Masque of the Red Death," are among the world's masterpieces of horror. What is the difference between the grotesque "extravaganzas" and the genuinely chilling "serious" tales?

One thing should be clear: the difference is *not* one of belief. There is no more reason for us to believe the supernatural events of the tales of terror than those of the humorous pieces, particularly since Poe gives no greater "justification" for, say, the appearance of an autonomous suit of clothes "untenanted by any tangible form" in "Red Death" than for the survival of the decapitated Signora. Nor can we attribute the difference in effect to a difference in belief on the part of the narrator or characters in the stories. The characters and narrators are as uniform in their belief as are readers in their disbelief. Zenobia has no doubts about the reality of what is happening to her, and the narrator of "The Man That Was Used Up" shows not the slightest trace of incredulity at General Smith's condition.

But there is a crucial difference between the narrators of the tales of terror and those of the comic grotesques: in the former, the narrators themselves find the events terrifying, while in the latter they treat horrifying occurences as if they were merely an inconvenience or a puzzle to be solved. Zenobia expresses "extreme horror" at first when she discovers the clock hand descending upon her neck; but this turns quickly into amusement, impatience, surprise, even happiness. Likewise the narrator of "The Man That Was Used Up" was initially frightened enough that he "shouted with terror, and made off, at a tangent, into the farthest extremity of the room." But then curiosity takes over, and he is content to sit in an armchair to await "the solution of the wonder." When he learns that the "bundle" is the General—when he has, therefore, "a full comprehension of the mystery which had troubled me so long"—he can depart calmly (*ST*, pp. 60–61).

The narrators in the tales of terror describe events that are really no different in kind from those presented in the comic extravaganzas, but they find these events horrifying. Their horror works to orchestrate ours. We must realize that a different point of view could make the supernaturally chilling climax of

"The Masque of the Red Death" seem just as humorous as the dialeptic nonsense of "The Man That Was Used Up." Considered apart from the context in which Poe presents it, the notion of an autonomous costume is not especially frightening. It is in fact the same sort of fancy that has been treated comically in animated cartoons for children, and it is not very different from the sort of dialepsis that Morgenstern finds amusing. Where Morgenstern gave us "Latten ohne was herum," Poe gives us "Kleider ohne was darin." The "untenanted cerements" of Poe's tale are dialeptically separated from any wearer, as Morgenstern's sigh is separated from any sigher. As the Cheshire Cat fades away, leaving only its smile behind, so has the inhabitant of these garments faded away. Poe also works on the principle of symmetry that is to be found in nonsense poetry: if a man may walk around without clothes, why may not clothes walk around without a man?

The supernatural climax of the "Red Death"—the very moment that is both most horrifying and most incredible—is based on a dialepsis that is not especially frightening in itself. What makes it terrifying are elements that are not at all supernatural and incredible: the costume that contains no person is a particularly grisly and naturalistic portrayal of one who has died of the Red Death, a disease that has devastated the country depicted in the story; the figure appears (or is first glimpsed) just at midnight, and it moves "with a slow and solemn movement, as if more fully to sustain its *role*" (*ST*, p. 140). These and other details that set up an expectation of horror are entirely responsible for the distinctly uncomic effect of the supernatural conclusion. When those accompanying details are presented in a light vein, as they are in "Loss of Breath" and the other extravaganzas, dialepsis—even such a very gruesome one as is experienced by Psyche Zenobia—holds no terror. If the very same supernatural revelation that concludes the "Red Death" were combined with a different set of elements (suppose it were a Mickey Mouse costume, for example), we can be sure that the effect would have been different as well.

It is useful to keep these considerations in mind when trying to understand the workings of a story that is both gruesome and dialeptic, as is "The Tell-Tale Heart." It is easy to suppose that the horror we feel in reading this masterful tale is the direct result of our distress at the notion of a heart with a life of its own. Freud's "uncanny" emotion would appear to be altogether at home here. But while we could very well assume that uncanny feelings afflict the murderous narrator, we cannot ascribe them to ourselves as readers. The narrator believes that a heart has a life of its own and beats loudly long after the body it once animated is gone, but we do not. Freud made clear that belief is an essential element in his uncanny, so that concept will not help to explain *the reader's* reaction to the events of "The Tell-Tale Heart."

Our horror is orchestrated by the vividly described emotions of the narrator. It is his terror at the sound of the heartbeat to which we react, his graphic description of the murder and the events leading up to it. In fact, it would not be far from the mark to say that it is the narrator's dialeptic imagination, not the dialepsis itself, which so engages our emotions. We observe that imagination at work right at the beginning of the tale, when we hear about the old man's eye, "a pale blue eye with a film over it. Whenever it fell upon me, my blood ran cold; and so by degrees—very gradually—I made up my mind to take the life of the old man, and thus rid myself of the eye forever!" (*ST*, p. 186). Only the eye is found offensive, considered apart from the person. As for the person himself: "I loved the old man" (*ST*, p. 186). Indeed the narrator cannot do violence to the old man as long as his eye is closed, "for it was not the old man who vexed me, but his Evil Eye" (*ST*, p. 186).

A powerful emotion of horror at the thought of an independently existing body part permeates the story long before the old man's body is actually carved up. This horror is not the reader's—not at first, at any rate—but the narrator's alone. He has separated the eye psychologically from the rest of the old man; it is an object of terror in its own right, a deathly thing that "resembled the eye of a vulture" (*ST*, p. 186). We may very well think that the narrator is mad, but there is a logic to the structure of his madness. Once it is believed, as the narrator believes, that the eye has a life of its own apart from its possessor, then something akin to Freud's uncanny must enter into his feelings about it. I do not say we have to assume that the narrator fears

/ 133

castration; we need assume only that Freud was right in thinking that belief in "actual" dialepsis would make one feel threatened. There can be no doubt that the narrator's deep fear of the "vulture" eye is connected to an anxiety that he might somehow be torn apart (as by a vulture).

The atmosphere of "The Tell-Tale Heart" is suffused with the narrator's terror of the eye and with his vision of it as an independent object. Just before the murder takes place, the story fixes our attention upon the eye when the narrator opens his lantern

> until, at length, a single dim ray, like the thread of the spider, shot out from the crevice and fell upon the vulture eye.
> It was open—wide, wide open—and I grew furious as I gazed upon it. It saw it with perfect distinctness—all a dull blue, with a hideous veil over it that chilled the very marrow in my bones; but I could see nothing else of the old man's face or person: for I had directed the ray as if by instinct, precisely upon the damned spot. [*ST*, p. 188]

This is a horrifying scene, but it is instructive to remember that nothing has yet happened of a horrifying nature. We simply share the irrational fear of the narrator, though we know that his fear is irrational and probably think him mad.

In making this point, I by no means wish to deny that our knowledge of his murderous intention contributes to the excitement of the scene. I want to suggest only that the special character of Poe's terror arises here not from the impending murder— countless literary hacks have used and will continue to use the threat of murder as a cheap way to create excitement—but from the dialeptic vision that provokes it. Poe counts on the fact that his narrator's anxiety will be infectious despite any antipathy the reader feels toward a murdering madman. The reader does not believe any of it anyway, and he does not have to do so. More correctly, he had better not. If he believed the text, understood it as the transcript of the confession of an actual murderer, he would find its effect muddied by all the complex feelings one normally has about actual events. He could not *enjoy* its terror— not without at the very least a certain ambivalence and guilt. He would very possibly be subject to the anxiety that accompanies the uncanny emotion.

If all these things are true, however—if the dialeptic imagery of severed body parts with a life of their own and of autonomous costumes and of lost breath is not in itself frightening; if it does not excite in us something like Freud's uncanny anxiety; and if we are kept distant from the events anyway by our disbelief— what accounts for the shudder we feel in reading Poe, the shudder without which Poe's stories would probably cease to interest us? I have spoken of the role of accompanying details that orchestrate our feelings in the "Red Death" and of how the narrator's own terror in "The Tell-Tale Heart" infects us. I now want to make this notion more precise with what will seem to many an odious comparison: Poe's narrators provide in the tales of terror a verbal equivalent of cinematic background music or a television "laugh-track." Just as background music orchestrates our reactions to film images that might otherwise be emotionally neutral, and just as a laugh track stimulates laughter in response to material that might otherwise not seem especially humorous, so does Poe's running commentary of horror prompt us to the appropriate feelings of fictional terror. It is hard not to join in the amusement or distress of others, even when we know that the distress is not genuine or that the jokes are not funny. Poe exploits this fact fully in all his stories. We should note that, when he is trying to amuse us, as in "The Man That Was Used Up" and "A Predicament," he tries to provide the equivalent of a laugh track by causing us to laugh first at material that is not supernatural. The silly gibberish poetry quoted by Zenobia at every opportunity serves the orchestrating function, as do the mindless conversations about the General in "The Man That Was Used Up." This comic commentary, like the horrifying commentary in the tales of terror, gives the stories their particular emotional coloring.

Poe's dialeptic tales, then, are either humorous or horrifying, depending not on the dialeptic images themselves but on the character of the narration in which they are embedded. The incredible "taking apart" of the world by language is not inherently distressing, though certain dialeptic images unquestionably lend themselves to lethetic horror. But even such images—the severed head that keeps living, for example—can be treated humorously by a writer determined to do so. We may question Poe's success at provoking laughter in the story of Psyche Zenobia, but we are certain that he does not provoke terror. Poe presents only these two alternatives in his dialeptic fiction. The incredible taking apart of our familiar reality results in stories that are either funny or horrifying but never tragically sad and moving, never quietly contemplative, never inciting to action or anger. In fact, when we look at all of logomimetic fiction, whether dialeptic, sylleptic, or sui generis (like the *Birds*), there seems to be a predominance of either humorous or frightening works. All of the sylleptic works I have examined in detail are comic, and all the dialeptic works are comic or terrifying. One is led to wonder whether these are the only possibilities for lethetic fiction, and if so, why.

It will probably be most productive to investigate this question from the other side, as it were, by considering the sorts of things that we would expect lethetic fictions, on the basis of the theory, *not* to be able to do. In the first place, it is obvious that lethetic fictions cannot be expected to have any effect on the reader that would result from his belief. We will never experience feelings of recognition, for example, when reading this genre of literature except for our recognition of the familiar language upon which logomimetic fiction is based. The situations depicted are necessarily always unfamiliar and out of this world. Logomimesis gives us never "what oft was thought, but ne'er so well expressed" but rather just the opposite, what is often expressed by everyday language but is never really "thought" seriously.

The distance placed between the reader and a lethetic fiction also frequently precludes processes of identification with the characters except at those times when they distance themselves from the action in which they participate. We sympathize with some of the narrators in Poe's tales of terror ("The Fall of the House of Usher" is a good example) when they express what is essentially our horror and disbelief at what is happening, as we can sympathize with Pisthetairos's confession that "it all seems like lies" to him. But when Pisthetairos is constructing his verbal atopia, or Gwendolyn hers, or Merlin his, we do not feel close to them. We feel no human concern regarding Merlin's fate in Nye's version of the story, and we are not troubled in the least that he is confined in a crystal prison.

Lethetic fictions, because they produce distance through dis-belief, are more amenable to aesthetic goals of amusement or horror than to pity and compassion. Before I go any further, however, I hasten to point out that it is by no means impossible for lethetic fictions to be moving: it is just perhaps a little harder. There is no doubt that some of the best science fiction is able to affect our human sympathies in spite of an openly incredible premise. Arthur Clarke's *Childhood's End,* one of the classics of science fantasy, has profoundly moved a generation of readers in the beautiful, spectacular, and sad description of the mar-velous departure of the telepathic children from the earth. The reader cannot sympathize with the children, who have become something alien, but we sympathize deeply with the adults who are left behind. The scene of children leaving home, leaving their parents behind forever and in the process hurting them, is so nearly universal that we recognize it and react to it even when some of its components are incredible. We are similarly moved by the incredible, magical conclusion of John Varley's "The Per-sistence of Vision," when the narrator's sight and hearing—at-tributes that have isolated him from the only community to which he has ever wanted to belong, the deaf-blind community of Keller—are taken away by the "healing" touch of a girl. Here again, we respond not to the incredible event but to the human act of love of which it is a component.

It is important to realize that in these cases (as in the directly analogous case of the film *E.T.*), the incredible elements in the stories play no significant role in their capacity to move us. The separation of a boy from his beloved friend or of parents from children, a girl's reaching out to dispel a man's loneliness—these are familiar event structures that can move us powerfully *even* when certain elements in those structures are incredible and tend to make us keep our distance. It would probably be proper to say that we are moved in such cases in spite of such incredible elements, in spite of the fact that, instead of being separated from his dog or from his father, a boy is being parted from a creature from another planet. We find ourselves similarly moved by a conversation between a boy and the stuffed bear he calls Pooh when it becomes clear that the boy is on the verge of growing out of his world of make-believe. We do not believe in the conversation itself, but we certainly believe in the powerful, ambivalent emotions that accompany the loss of childhood.

Coleridge surely had something similar in mind when he spoke of the "dramatic truth" of the "Ancient Mariner" and of its engendering "such emotions as would naturally accompany such [imaginary] situations, supposing them real." I wish to argue, however, that no "suspension of disbelief" is required. We can share the mariner's terror at the death of his shipmates and his even greater terror at their sudden reanimation by seraphic spirits. The fact that we do not believe in seraphic spirits is irrelevant where the issue of our belief in the mariner's horror is concerned. Coleridge apparently assumed that incredulity, once excited, would necessarily apply to every aspect of a work of fiction *unless it could be temporarily put out of action,* "suspended." I contend, on the other hand, that readers have no difficulty in believing one thing and disbelieving something else at the same time. We do not have to put our disbelief into suspension any more than any other attitude. Do we "suspend" our feelings of tension and foreboding during the Porter scene in *Macbeth?* Do we "suspend" our amusement at Falstaff when Hotspur is on stage? We do not, just as we do not for a moment abandon our disbelief in the conversational abilities of stuffed bears at those moments when part of such conversations moves us. In these cases our attention is directed, not to the incredible elements themselves, but to other, recognizably human event structures of which they are a part. We might want to speak of such instances as alethetic moments within lethetic structures.

When the fiction does focus our attention on its logomimesis, on the very things that solicit our disbelief, the reader is necessarily kept at a distance, and the emotion most likely to be aroused is that of surprise. This surprise may be the intellectual surprise of amusement or the more emotional shock of horror, but it is inevitably something perceived at a distance, through a glass—a Carrollian looking-glass or a narcissistic glass castle in the forest of Broceliande. Whether the surprise is comic or terrifying, it is enjoyable only because it is separated from us by its incredibility. If we thought these fantasies real, they would, as Samuel Johnson pointed out in another context,[18] "please no more." Lethetic fictions balance our desire for the excitement of surprise, of the world being turned upside down, with our need to feel safe.

Lethetic fictions are therefore not the sort of art that urges us to practical action. They do not say to us, like Rilke's ancient statue, "You must change your life [*Du musst dein Leben ändern*]." The distancing effect of the incredulity they solicit has nothing in common with Brecht's *Verfremdungseffekt,* which seeks to remind the audience of the fictionality of the play so that they can better understand it as a rhetorical structure intended to teach them and convince them of the need for action. Brecht's "alienation effect" aims, at other words, at an alethetic goal. As Brecht discovered to his chagrin, it is not so easy to harness disbelief in this way. The audiences of *The Threepenny Opera* were quite happy to accept Brecht's invitation not to believe the play, but quite often they took it as an invitation to treat the performance as a lethetic fiction, as something surprising, stimulating and amusing, leaving them safe and secure in the world they were familiar with. The play's remarkable success in the heart of capitalism (it ran for years to delighted audiences in New York) is in large part due to its unintended reception as a lethetic fiction.

What we do not believe can surprise us, but it does not require us to do anything about it. In particular, it does not force us to worry about those things we have found to be so far out of the ordinary. Brecht wants his audience to worry, but Aristophanes, Carroll, Morgenstern, Nye, and Poe do not. They allow us the luxury of reacting to the extraordinary, of being surprised and even shocked, without having to suffer the consequences that normally attend such experiences in real life. If lethetic fiction tends to specialize in the shocking—the shock of the comic or of the horrific—it is because this is what it can do better than any other genre.

[18]*Preface to Shakespeare.*

Part Three /

THE LETHETIC MODE

CHAPTER 7 /

The Oblivious Reader:
Lucian and Edgar Allan Poe

I WILL NOW return to a matter that I mentioned in the opening chapters but put off treating in detail: the lethetic *mode* of reading. When we read lethetic texts as they seek to be read, we are of course reading in the lethetic mode, but the mode is not applicable only to such texts. We may, in principle, read anything as if we did not believe it, no matter what the author appears to want from us. There is nothing to prevent us from imagining any text to be nothing but a set of signifiers controlled only by the basic conventions of the language (that is, *langue*) it uses. When we do so, we employ the lethetic mode in a special way, a way clearly different from that which we use when we read the *Birds* or "The Hunting of the Snark" or the *Galgenlieder*. When we read Morgenstern lethetically, we are doing no more than what he has signaled he wants us to do. We read with the grain, so to speak. But one may read lethetically against the grain, engaging in a special form of lethetic reading I will call "oblivious" reading.

This sort of oblivious reading must be distinguished from simple misunderstanding and from parodic falsification. An oblivious reading is not the same as a naive misunderstanding, an incorrect supposition that the author wants disbelief. It is rather a deliberate ignoring of what the author's intention may be. The oblivious reader knows that the text intends to tell the truth, but he goes right ahead and acts as if that intention were irrelevant. In parodic falsification, on the other hand, the reader presents his version of the text at hand in such a way as to show it up, to make clear that its intention to tell the truth has been unsuccessful. Parody of this sort is hardly oblivious reading: it takes the truthful intention of its object seriously, keeps it firmly in mind, and seeks to disclose and perhaps correct the text's errors.

A particularly interesting text to illustrate these distinctions is Lucian's *True History (Alethes historia)*, written some time about the middle of the second century after Christ. Here we have a fiction that attempts (naively, in my view) to falsify by parody what Lucian understands as the lies of Aristophanes and other poets but ends by being the object of a significant number of oblivious readings.

The rigor of Aristophanes' forgetfulness of the world in the *Birds* has been more often than not misunderstood, since it has been assumed that he must have meant his play either as alethetic (that is, as incredible but ironic and allegorical) or credible. No third alternative was imagined. And since the play makes it very hard to find irony and allegory as its goal, particularly when we consider the absolute victory of the hero, there have always been people who supposed that it must, somehow, have been meant to be convincing (in Aristotle's sense of *eikos*) and thus believable. We find this attitude given vivid expression by Lucian in his *True History*. Aristophanes is by no means the sole or even the chief target of Lucian's displeasure, but the *Birds* does play a minor role, affording us the opportunity of a convenient contrast. For among the wonders that Lucian reports having seen on his journey is the city of the birds: "We were surprised to find here the city of Cloudcuckooland, but we could not land because of the adverse wind. I learned the King was called Koronos [that is, Crookbeak] the Kottuphionos. And I thought of Aristophanes the poet, a wise and veracious [*alethous*] man whose writings were unjustifiably disbelieved" (A 29).[1]

[1] I use the Greek text of Julius Sommerbrodt, *Lucianus* (Berlin: Weidmann, 1893), vol. 2. For the reader's convenience I cite by book (A or B) and paragraph number rather than by page. Because there is little point in reproducing a great

The attitude expressed by these lines, which fairly drip with irony, is that the *Birds* is a mendacious document whose untruth and incredibility deserve the exposure and censure of satire. Such satire is the announced goal of the *True History*, as we hear in the opening paragraphs of the introduction: "[The following pages] are intended to have an attraction independent of any originality of subject, any happiness of general design, any verisimilitude in the piling up of fictions. This attraction is the veiled reference underlying all the details of my narrative; they parody the cock-and-bull stories of ancient poets, historians, and philosophers; I have only refrained from adding a key because I could rely on you to recognize as you read" (A 2).[2] Lucian gives a number of examples of such "cock-and-bull stories," but the most important and influential of all mendacious storytellers is "the Homeric Odysseus, entertaining Alcinous's court with his prisoned winds, his men one-eyed or wild or cannibal, his beasts with many heads, and his metamorphosed comrades; the Phaeacians were simple folk, and he fooled them to the top of their bent" (A 3).

The concluding paragraph of the introduction bears quoting in its entirety:

> When I come across a writer of this sort, I do not much mind his lying; the practice is much too well established for that, even with professed philosophers; I am only surprised at his expecting to escape detection. Now I am myself vain enough to cherish the hope of bequeathing something to posterity; I see no reason for resigning my right to that inventive freedom which others enjoy; and, as I have no truth to put on record, having lived a very humdrum life, I fall back on falsehood—but falsehood of a more consistent variety; for I now make the only true statement you are to expect—that I am a liar. This confession is, I consider, a full defense against all imputations. My subject is, then, what I have

---

deal of transliterated Greek, I will give the original, in the text, only of those words and phrases to which I pay special attention. The translation of this passage is mine.

[2]This and the translations from the *True History* that follow are from the English edition of Lucian by H. W. Fowler and F. G. Fowler, *The Works of Lucian of Samosata* (Oxford: Clarendon Press, 1905), 2:136 ff.

never seen, experienced, nor been told, what neither exists nor could conceivably do so. I humbly solicit my readers' incredulity. [A 4]

Lucian is no rustic Phaeacian to be taken in by even the most skilled liars, such as Homer and Odysseus: he recognizes untruth when he sees it and is not prepared to let it escape. Neither Lucian nor the critical tradition to which he and we belong supposed that there could be a mode of poetic utterance that was founded on the assumption of "escaping detection" (*lesein*) but that expects the true world rather than the untrue world thus to escape our attention. Lucian assumes that, if a poet produces conflicts between his words and the world, the poet must suppose his audience will somehow be induced to overlook or ignore (*lesein*) these conflicts. Aristotle makes exactly that assumption in his discussion of the marvelous in the *Poetics*. Aristophanes in the *Birds* assumes that his audience will overlook or ignore the world itself while at the same time remembering the *un*truth of his poem.

Lucian solicits his readers' incredulity openly and explicitly, as every apistic mode of utterance does, though usually covertly and implicitly. Homer and Odysseus (in Aristotle's view) solicit belief and hope by various devices to have what Aristotle called the *aloga* ("irrationalities") he says are necessary to the marvelous escape detection; Homer and Odysseus do not speak in the apistic mode. Lucian is right to satirize Homer/Odysseus if we assume they worked according to Aristotle's principles, for they have failed to convince at least one reader, namely Lucian. Lucian is right to satirize Aristophanes also if we make the same assumption—an assumption I have tried to show is completely unjustified in the case of the *Birds*. Aristophanes lied as consistently as Lucian says *he* wishes to, and more consistently, really, since he takes as his subject the construction of a fiction.

Lucian, therefore, may be understood to read Aristophanes as if he were an Aristotelian Homer, and he evidently feels he is doing a service to humanity by exposing the lies he finds in the ancient poets. His attitude is made even more explicit in his dialogue *The Liar* (*Philopseudes*, that is, "The Lover of Lies"): he is angry.

It makes me quite angry: what satisfaction can there be to men of their good qualities in deceiving themselves and their neighbors? There are instances among the ancients [the same instances cited in the *True History*] . . . : here are men of world-wide celebrity, perpetuating their mendacity in black and white; not content with deceiving their hearers, they must send their lies down to posterity, under the protection of the most admirable verse.[3]

The example at hand in *The Liar* is a certain Eucrates and his friends, all of whom are full of the most outrageous humbug about spirits they have seen, marvels they have witnessed, and supernatural feats they can perform. This "banquet of mendacity" was visited by one of the interlocutors, Tychiades, who complains that "my overloaded stomach needs an emetic as much as if I had been drinking new wine. I would pay something for the drug [*pharmakon*] that should work oblivion [*lethedanon*] in me: I fear the effects of haunting reminiscence; monsters, demons, Hecates, seem to pass before my eyes."[4]

Tychiades fears nightmares, and he wishes to save himself from the corruption of the lies he's had to swallow by means of some pharmakon lethedanon, "drug that causes forgetfulness." His partner in the dialogue, Philocles, fears that even he, too, has been infected by the mere report: "You, it seems, have been bitten with many bites by the liar Eucrates, and have passed it on to me; not otherwise can I explain the demoniacal poison that runs in my veins."[5] But Tychiades proposes a cure for both of them: "Truth [*aletheian*] and good sense [*epi pasi logon orthon*]: these are the drugs [*alexipharmakon*] for our ailment; let us employ them, and that empty thing, a lie, need have no terror for us."[6] It is proposed, then, that truth, the alethes, be used as a drug to cause forgetfulness, lethedanon, as a cure for the effects of lies.

The *True History* is intended to be a pharmakon to cure the reader from the effects of lies, an emetic for the overloaded stomachs of those who have read too much Homer, Ctesias,

---

[3]Fowler and Fowler, *Works of Lucian* 3:231. The Greek text is that of Sommerbrodt, vol. 3.
[4]Fowler and Fowler, *Works of Lucian* 3:252.
[5]Ibid.
[6]Ibid.

Herodotus, Aristophanes, and so on. But Lucian's strategy here is not simply to give the antidote (alexipharmakon) that Tychiades recommends but rather to use the poison (also pharmakon) of untruth against itself by providing it in overdose. Such an excess of untruth, such a banquet of poison, is expected to make the reader so sick of the stuff that he'll never want to touch it again. His incredulity will be aroused, and this will guard him in the future. The drug offered by the *True History* is not the pharmakon lethedanon sought by Tychiades so much as a pharmakon alethedanon—or at any rate it is intended as such. Lucian does not want his reader to forget either his lies or the world. He wants us to remember, to consider the real world more important than the word, and to trust only words that conform to this reality. In short, he is writing in the alethetic mode.

The efficacy of the pharmakon offered in the *True History* depends to a great degree on its ability to be a stand-in for something else. Lucian solicits disbelief in his story, but not really because he wants the reader to disbelieve Lucian and Lucian's words. The reader's incredulity is meant to be redirected to those writings that Lucian's writing is meant to represent and parody. The *paroidia,* the "song beside (another song)," is a supplementary text that is always intended to remind the audience of the "original" that it supplements. No parody can, in principle, be composed in the lethetic mode. It is true that a few parodies, such as some of Lewis Carroll's, outlast the memory of the texts they burlesque and thus become (unwittingly) lethetic poems, but in such cases they also lose their parodic function. The parody is meant to stand beside its original and to "show it up." It must, therefore, essentially repeat the original so that the necessary recognition and comparison can take place: "I have only refrained from adding a key because I could rely on you to recognize as you read."

The pharmakon must be recognizably like the text it is to supplement and cure, but it must also be different. This difference is effected by exaggeration, by overdose. If the texts to be parodied lie but pass these lies off as truth, then the pharmakon will tell bigger lies and make broader and more explicit claims for veracity. That is surely the tactic employed by the *True*

History, but Lucian finds himself faced with at least one substantial problem: the untruths propounded by the authors he wishes to satirize are already so great that they defy exaggeration. How could an author propose anything more outrageous than the plot of the *Birds,* for example? Could anything be more unbelievable than Pisthetairos's victory over Zeus and elevation to the rank of *daimonon hupertatos?* Pisthetairos does not believe it himself. If that was not in itself sufficient overdose of the incredible, it is hard to imagine what would be.

Lucian cannot imagine it either, and it is for this reason, I suspect, that the reference to the *Birds* is as slight as it is. The only way to satirize Aristophanes is to call him a wise and veracious man who has met unmerited incredulity. Such a statement, surely, every reader can be expected to recognize as untrue and therefore ironic. (There is a difficulty even here, since there is not a shred of evidence that Aristophanes ever expected anyone to believe him. But that is my story, not Lucian's.) It is a form of the second sort of exaggeration, the making of broader claims for veracity. The narrator extends the assertion of his own truthfulness to cover Aristophanes as well, and that is intended to be damning enough, since the narrator's claims are obviously unwarranted.

It remains an open question, however, whether such a strategy is adequate to transform the poisonous pharmakon into a beneficial one, the evil kind of writing the story *imitates* into the curative writing it proposes to *be.* The *True History* is genuine alethic irony in that it employs the reader's disbelief in an effort to make the text mean the very opposite of what it says. Much as it resembles the literature it represents, it tries to remain in essence different and indeed opposed. But it may not entirely succeed. Ernst Bloch has noted that, "as is quite often the case with irony, the tale-telling [*Fabelei*] is satirized so much that the satire copies and surpasses its object. Lucian provided a studied, almost itself utopian fantasy of the nonexistent [*Phantasterei über Unvorhandenes*], and he did it lightly, in a perfectly carefree manner, as if he were himself an inhabitant of the happy isles."[7] Bloch believes that "the Lucian mode provides a

---

[7]*Das Prinzip Hoffnung* (Berlin: Aufbau, 1954), 1:467.

very good, that is, very amusing antidote against poets who lie, even against the Münchhausens who make up utopias," but his belief is beset by doubt.[8] Though Bloch does not makes these doubts explicit (his concerns lie elsewhere), we may wonder to what degree the pharmakon whose essence it is to copy and stand for the thing it is to act against may have done the first part of its job so well as to make the second impossible. Among Lucian's most illustrious readers are some who found the *True History* so charming that they chose to borrow from and imitate it. Some, like the Münchhausen stories and Rabelais's kingdoms in Pantagruel's mouth, are meant to be satirical—though the original objects of Lucian's satire are no longer at issue; others, like More's *Utopia*, are not satirical at all. Elements derived (perhaps indirectly) from Lucian's fantasy can be found in a work as recent as Brian Aldiss's *Hothouse,* where we meet, for instance, the giant space-faring spiders mentioned in the early part of the *True History* (A 15). There is no trace of satire in Aldiss's novel, no concern at all for the familiar world we know. *Hothouse* uses elements identical to elements in Lucian's alethetic fantasy to make a lethetic fantasy. The ambiguous nature of the pharmakon can be shown no more clearly than in this example of the giant moon-dwelling spiders, an element that is intended to work in precisely the opposite ways in the two stories that employ it.

The *True History* can therefore be said to have generated at least as much untruth as it has prevented, to have been more popular among the philopseudeis of this world than among the philosophers. If one ignores the introduction and reads the narrator's expressions of concern about the limits of his readers' credulity as genuine, it is not difficult to read the *True History* obliviously, in the lethetic mode. So well does it copy the material it satirizes that the satire often seems to evaporate, leaving a drug that is the very pharmakon lethedanon that Tychiades wished for—except, of course, that it causes us to forget the world rather than any untruth. The waters that feed the Pierian Spring are the very same as those that flow in the river of Lethe.

[8]Ibid., 468.

Everything we know about Lucian argues for an alethetic reading of his satirical fantasy, and yet even this almost certain knowledge of the author's intention has not prevented an occasional oblivious reading. The *True History* thus illustrates for us the conflict of authority between author and reader that no theory of reading is able to evade or definitively resolve. It is a conflict that is frequently reformulated in terms of an opposition between the *text* (as the representative of the author) and the reader. The opposition between two sorts of reading, one that submits to the authority of the text and the other that does not, is one of the most vexing, as well as one of the most durable, in our tradition. "The question is," in the words of one prominent philosopher of language, "which is to be master [people or words]—that's all."[9]

When it comes to the relation between text and gloss, the common assumption has been that the text was to be the master and that the writer of glosses should subordinate himself to the master text as much as possible. (By "master text" I mean the text as repository of authority.) A gloss is a secondary thing, generated from a primary original, and it is assumed that the primary has authority over the secondary. In this regard it is interesting to remember that Plato, in the *Phaedrus*, regards all writing as a king of marginalia upon spoken language: the myth of Theuth emphasizes this "hypomnemic" aspect of writing. What is written down is viewed as simply a set of memoranda that will have the undesirable effect of hindering the development of true, living memory. The gloss threatens to supplant the text it supplements, to overthrow and kill it. For this reason Socrates agrees with the judgment of Thamus-Amon that writing is more a destructive than a healing pharmakon and that it is likely to "implant forgetfulness in [men's] souls."[10]

There is another tradition, though not a dominant one in our culture, that questions such assumptions about the relation between text and gloss, between what is written and the reading of it. This alternative tradition proposes that the reader should be

[9]Humpty Dumpty in *Through the Looking-Glass*, chap. 6.
[10]This topic will be treated at length in Part Four.

the sole authority governing the reading process. Such a sovereign reader is under no obligation to treat the text as it seeks to be treated, and the reader's glosses may ignore the purposes of the author even when these are clear. Italo Calvino engages in such an oblivious reading of scientific texts in his cosmicomic stories. Before examining Calvino's practice, however, it will be helpful to take a brief look at the theory of this kind of glossing as it appears in one of the most interesting—though very short—discussions of glossing, the opening section of Poe's *Marginalia*.

One of Poe's principal contentions is that a gloss intended to be a reminder should in fact instill forgetfulness. Glossing, whatever else it may be, is certainly not useful as reminding:

> This making of notes, however, is by no means the making of mere *memoranda*—a custom which has its disadvantages, beyond doubt. *"Ce que je mets sur papier,"* says Bernardin de St. Pierre, *"je remets de ma mémoire et par conséquence je l'oublie;"*—and, in fact, if you wish to forget anything upon the spot, make a note that this thing is to be remembered.[11]

The marginal note thus cannot serve as a mere hypomnemic supplement to the text that occasions it, since the act of making a note is alleged to cause instant oblivion of the thing noted. The supplement supplants and destroys the "original." The relation between text and gloss, from Poe's point of view, cannot be understood in terms of its service to the "primary" text:

> But the purely marginal jottings, done with no eye to the Memorandum Book, have a distinct complexion, and not only a distinct purpose, but none at all; this it is which imparts to them a value. They have a rank somewhat above the chance and desultory comments of literary chit-chat—for these latter are not infrequently "talk for talk's sake," hurried out of the mouth; while the *marginalia* are deliberately pencilled, because the mind of the reader wishes to unburthen itself of a *thought;*—however flippant—however silly—however trivial—still a thought indeed, not merely a thing that might have been a thought in time, and under more favorable circumstance. [Pp. 1–2]

[11]*Marginalia—Eureka* (New York: Thomas Y. Crowell, n.d.), 1. Page references, henceforth in the text, refer to this edition.

Though Poe is not prepared to defend "talk for talk's sake" (though he might have done so under other circumstances), he is prepared to defend what might be called writing for writing's sake. Poe seems to have supposed the act of writing to possess a certain value above that of spoken language, which inverts the Platonic valorization. The marginal note derives its value not from the text it glosses but from itself and indeed to some extent because of the very absence of con-text. Poe's comments, we must remember, are in preface to a collection of marginal glosses deliberately taken from the texts in which they were written. They are a defense, however hasty, of the gloss as a genre independent of the text that originally gave them birth. Only minimal editing was done to free the glosses from the texts which bore them:

> I concluded, at length, to put extensive faith in the acumen and imagination of the reader:—this as a general rule. But, in some instances, where even faith would not remove mountains, there seemed no safer plan than so to re-model the note as to convey at least the ghost of a conception as to what it was all about. Where, for such conception, the text itself was absolutely necessary, I could quote it; where the title of the book commented upon was indispensable, I could name it. [P. 4]

The "original" text becomes nothing more than a point of departure for the gloss, upon which all attention and interest is focused. Poe's set of values finds worth to reside within things themselves and not in a "something else" for which they may be exchanged or for which they stand. The idea of "representation," of regarding things as traces of other things, is uncongenial to those who, like Poe, prize immediacy above all else. A gloss, then, whose initial purpose was mediation between text and reader could only be a hindrance and a barrier, *unless* one could make the gloss itself the object of attention, transform it from the mediator of the reading experience into the reading experience itself. For this transformation to be successful, though, it is necessary to remove the "original" text as much as possible from sight lest it reintroduce an element of supplementarity and dependence into what we now want to be a self-suffi-

/ 153

cient gloss. So a new genre is born, the oblivious gloss-without-a-text, and this new genre eventually wins an interesting sort of approval from the intellectual community: Paul Valéry published in 1927 his edition of selections[12] from the *Marginalia*, and therein he provided his own marginal glosses, which take issue with and go beyond what Poe sketches in his text. Poe's glosses, in other words, are taken up by Valéry as the point of departure for his own, which indeed do *depart* substantially from a text that surely can no longer be considered "primary."

It is possible that Poe's conception of the gloss was even more radical than his own glossator, Valéry, was prepared to admit. Lawrence Lipking has observed that the concluding sentence of Poe's introductory comments, a particularly interesting and important sentence, was left out of Valéry's version. Poe's final comment is: "It may be as well to observe, however, that just as the goodness of your true pun is in the direct ratio of its intolerability, so is nonsense the essential sense of the Marginal Note" (p. 4). Lipking supposes that Poe intends by this remark to say that the marginal note "offers the reader a kind of puzzle; divorced from the context that first stimulated it, it renders no more than a fragmentary clue to buried possibilities of meaning. The more outrageous the clue, the better the puzzle. Poe challenges the ingenuity of his reader." The removal of the context, then, is a kind of challenge to the reader to reconstruct or discover the absent text to which the "clue" refers. The *Marginalia* would thus be analogous to others of Poe's stories involving buried treasures and hidden clues in which it is the task of both the hero and the reader to "decipher the apparent nonsense . . . [by] decoding the keys or intentions secreted in the text."[13]

Lipking's reading is a persuasive one, particularly becasue it seems to put the *Marginalia* neatly into the context of Poe's poetry and fiction. But I think it would be possible to understand the last sentence of Poe's introduction more radically and more correctly by abandoning the assumption of an alethetic viewpoint. There is no reason to assume that, when Poe says "nonsense," he

[12]"Quelques fragments des *Marginalia*," *Commerce* 14 (1927), 11–41.
[13]"The Marginal Gloss," *Critical Inquiry* 3:4 (1977), 610.

has to mean "*apparent* nonsense." There is good reason, as we have seen from our earlier discussion of Poe's fiction, to suppose that he really means "nonsense," that he means to stress the lack of connection between the marginal note and the text that engendered it. The allusion, earlier in the prefatory remarks, to the power of notes to make one forget is highly relevant to this closing comment. The connection between nonsense and forgetfulness—to which I have been paying particular attention in this chapter and which is presented thematically in the tales of Calvino treated in detail below—is at the heart of the issue in *Marginalia*. The unconnectedness of the marginal notes, both to the "primary" text and to each other, is their very charm. While it is true that Poe was a lover of puzzles and mysteries, there is no support in this text for the notion that Poe meant to contrive this unconnectedness merely as a puzzle for his reader to solve. To "solve the puzzle" would be to make the "apparent nonsense" into sense, and that would destroy the qualities that Poe says make the marginal gloss worthwhile. If they are no longer forgetful of their origins, they are no longer interesting.

We might think of Poe as playing the role of "*arche* debunker" (in Paul de Man's outrageous and therefore memorable formulation),[14] of demystifier and even devaluer of origins, by thus turning things upside down and putting the "secondary" gloss in the primary role. Poe himself wonders if he is not engaged in an act of "translation" that may both betray and invert the ordinary function of the gloss: "What, then, would become of it—this context [that is, the glosses]—if transferred?—if translated? Would it not rather be *traduit* (traduced) which is the French synonym, or *overzezet* (turned topsy-turvy) which is the Dutch one?" (pp. 3–4). The answer is, to be blunt, yes: when transferred from its original place (in the margin of a particular book), the gloss as supplement to an *arche*-script is *traduit* and *overzezet* and becomes out of place, *atopos*. That is exactly the point of the whole procedure.

Poe's glosses are intended as this sort of oblivious nonsense, as an inversion of the normal position of the text and its note. That topsy-turvy situation is particularly evident in those portions of

---

[14]*Allegories of Reading* (New Haven: Yale University Press, 1979), 9.

the *Marginalia* in which the "original" text is present only as a note on the note. Consider this example, typical of the notes included in the collection:

> In reading some books we occupy ourselves chiefly with the thoughts of the author; in perusing others, exclusively with our own. And this* is one of the "others"—a suggestive book. But there are two classes of suggestive books—the positively and negatively suggestive. The former may suggest by what they say; the latter by what they might and should have said. It makes little difference, after all. In either case the true book-purpose is answered.
>
> Sallust, too. He had much the same free-and-easy idea, and Metternich himself could not have quarrelled with his *"Impune quae libet facere, id est esse regem."* [Pp. 36–37]
> *Mercier's *L'an deux mille quatre cent quarante.*

The volume of Mercier that had stimulated Poe's gloss and in which that gloss had resided is now a relatively unimportant supplement appended as a reference, a convenience for the reader, to the marginal note. The gloss has become text; the text stands as gloss.

The note itself, we observe, proposes the existence of a relatively large class of texts whose only function is to stimulate marginal notes, which are our own thoughts, the thoughts of readers as opposed to those of writers. Since Poe had earlier defined the marginal note as "a thought indeed, not merely a thing that might have become a thought in time," we are authorized to equate the two. It really does not matter whether such books stimulate because they are clever or because they are foolish, because the text that is read does not itself matter. The author no longer possesses any authority when his book is considered in this way: instead, the reader takes all authority to himself, making himself the ruler of the reading process. "To be a king is to do what you want with impunity," Sallust said, describing what for Poe is the situation of a reader of a book like Mercier's. Such a text does not end a process in which a writer's thoughts are brought together and recorded; nor does it mediate in a process of communication between author and reader; rather, it initiates a process that begins in the reader's mind when a stimulus is provided. No matter the quality of the stimulus: good, bad, or indifferent texts may initiate thought and thereby fulfill "the true book-purpose."

This kind of glossing represents the result of reading in the lethetic mode. The gloss ignores the purpose of the author and appropriates his text for purposes the reader alone must determine. The word of the text is valuable not as the trace of the world, not as something corresponding to states of affairs, but as a means to produce more words. Whether the text to be glossed is wise or foolish, true or untrue, makes no difference, because the process of lethetic glossing treats them all as untrue. Whether the text is credible or incredible, the reader *acts as if he disbelieves it and as if the text solicited that disbelief.* Though the text in fact solicits belief, the reader's imposition of disbelief is obviously not in this case an assumption that the text is in error, because the reader does not (for the purpose of his lethetic reading) posit the belief of the author. Such posited belief is essential (as noted in Chapter 2) if the reader is to assume that a text is in error. In the case of lethetic glossing, the oblivious reader ignores the author's known intention to obtain belief, to convey some particular meaning. In other words, the reader *pretends* that neither he nor the author believes the text to propose some connection between its words and the world. But, as we will see shortly, even fictional disbelief functions effectively: a genuine assumption and a hypothetical assumption are indistinguishable, since reading, lethetic or otherwise, is a process of assumptions.

CHAPTER 8 /

The Text as Propulsive Charge:
Italo Calvino

SOME EXAMPLES OF contemporary science fiction
are the result of oblivious reading applied to scientific theory. In
other words, they result from an uninvited employment of the
lethetic mode; they are a kind of lethetic gloss (I use the word
"gloss" to refer to all texts that explain or elaborate another text)
upon texts that earnestly solicit belief. Such stories do not purport to speculate seriously on the possible ramifications or consequences of scientific discoveries but rather take the text of the
theory as a point of departure, using it as an object of logomimesis and paying no attention whatever to what the scientific
theory is really trying to mean. Such stories represent quite a
different attitude from that of more orthodox science fiction,
and it is not unusual for writers of these stories to distinguish
their work from the main body of science fiction. Both orthodox
and unorthodox sorts can be properly seen as glosses on scientific texts, but one is alethetic glossing, the other lethetic.

Orthodox science fiction typically attempts to illustrate the
practical effects of scientific hypotheses that have not yet had
such practical consequences. An early favorite subject was space
flight and the possible effects on human spacefarers of extreme
acceleration, weightlessness, the airless environment of space,
and so on. Many of Arthur C. Clarke's stories continue this
tradition. *Rendezvous with Rama* attempts to show what it would
be like for a group of astronauts who discover an interstellar

space probe from an alien civilization to confront and deal with such a situation, what the probe itself might be, how it might be made, how it might function, and so on. Clarke assumes nothing that current scientific theory cannot sanction: he supposes, for example, that the alien probe does not travel faster than light and that the aliens themselves are not on board. *The Fountains of Paradise*, an even more recent novel (1979), chronicles the construction of a "space elevator," a tower extending from the earth to a satellite in geostationary orbit. The concept had been discussed among scientists during the sixties, and Clarke's novel simply fictionalizes the practical problems of carrying out this (technically difficult but theoretically feasible) project. Perhaps not surprisingly, another scientist/science fiction writer, Charles Sheffield, was working on the same premise almost simultaneously, and he published his novel *The Web between the Worlds* within a few months of Clarke's book. The stories are similar enough that the publisher of Sheffield's book requested, and received, a statement from Clarke that the two novels had developed independently and that "the parallels were dictated by the fundamental mechanics of the subject."[1]

Both novels are in effect fictional glosses upon the scientific hypotheses of Artsutanov, Isaacs, and others, scientists and engineers interested in a more efficient way to convey objects and people from the earth to nearby space. They are alethetic glosses because they take seriously the possibility of such an "orbital tower" and want to discuss seriously (though fictionally) what it might *really* be like to build such a thing. Such fictions serve as a speculative supplement to the scientific texts that stimulate them and attempt to conform to the intention of those texts, their scientific import, in a faithful manner. That two science fiction novels with parallel plots should be produced independently can be understood as the result of the process of alethetic glossing: both novels seek to conform to the same scientific texts and so inevitably conform to some extent to each other.

The stories of Italo Calvino's *Cosmicomics*, along with the Qfwfq tales of *t zero*, also gloss scientific theories. In the manner of Poe's *Marginalia*, however, the (original) text is turned into a

---

[1] *The Web between the Worlds* (New York: Ace Books, 1979), iv–v.

gloss, while the fictional gloss becomes the text. The story "The Distance of the Moon," for example, the first of the cosmicomic stories, is provided with the following headnote: "At one time, according to Sir George Darwin, the Moon was very close to the Earth. Then the tides gradually pushed her far away: the tides that the Moon herself causes in the Earth's waters, where the Earth slowly loses energy."[2] Such headnotes precede all the *Cosmicomics* and the tales in part 1 of *t zero*, and many, like this one, cite the scientists (Kuiper, Hubble, Darwin, and so forth) whose work provides the stimulus for the story. That Calvino is not really interested in the theories themselves or in their scientific truth is indicated by a number of things, including the fact that he unabashedly uses contradictory theories as texts for his glosses. The headnote to the story "The Soft Moon" takes as its authority a theory of the origin of the moon incompatible with Darwin's. According to this hypothesis of Gerstenkorn and Alfven, as cited by Calvino, the moon was once an independent planet that was captured by the earth. Gravitational forces eventually broke the moon apart, and fragments of its mass, originally much greater than now, fell to earth and formed the continents.[3] The narrator of both "The Distance of the Moon" and "The Soft Moon" is the same character, the immortal Qfwfq, and Qfwfq himself is completely oblivious to the fact that he participates in incompatible versions of reality. Calvino obviously does not care what the truth might be about the origin of the moon; he is interested in these theories the way Poe was interested in Mercier, as a point of departure for his own thoughts.

Another feature of the headnote to "The Distance of the Moon" that engenders a suspicion that Darwin's hypothesis did not interest Calvino *as science* is this: the headnote itself begins to

---

[2] I cite the *Cosmicomics* from the standard Italian edition (Torino: Einaudi, 1965) and from the translation of William Weaver (New York: Harcourt Brace Jovanovich, 1976). This passage is from the Einaudi edition, 9; *Cosmicomics*, trans. Weaver, 3. "Una volta, secondo Sir George H. Darwin, la Luna era molto vicina alla Terra. Furono le maree che a poco a poco la spinsero lontana: le maree che lei Luna provoca nelle acque terrestri e in cui la Terra perde lentamente energia."

[3] *t zero*, trans. William Weaver (New York: Harcourt Brace Jovanovich, 1976), 3–4.

personalize, to anthropomorphize, the relationship between the earth and the moon. The phrase "the tides that the Moon herself causes [*le maree che lei Luna provoca*]" indicates an issue of human responsibility, as if the moon, through her excessive influence upon the earth, had caused a falling out between them. To treat the motions and positions of the heavenly bodies as parallel to human relations is an ancient practice, of course; what is surprising here is that Calvino uses a modern scientific theory as if its language were primarily figurative. What Calvino does, as I will try to show in more detail below, is to treat scientific theory as pure language, as a storehouse of potential objects for logomimesis. In other words, he acts as if he does not believe these texts whose prime function is to be believed.

Sir George Darwin's analysis of the effects of the lunar tides on the earth-moon system provides an especially interesting example for us, partly because Darwin himself took pains to provide an exposition of his theory in layman's terms and partly because it provides the stimulus for one of the most interesting stories in the collection of *Cosmicomics*. A close look at Darwin's theory will enable us to see how Calvino uses only those aspects of the theory that he finds useful, ignoring its actual scientific import.

The main lines of Darwin's discussion, as first published in *The Atlantic Monthly*,[4] were concerned with the effects of tidal friction upon planetary bodies. Darwin provides this summary of his argument:

> If a planet consisted partly or wholly of molten lava or other fluid, and rotated rapidly about an axis perpendicular to the plane of its orbit, and if that planet was attended by a single satellite, revolving with its month a little longer than the planet's day, then a system would necessarily be developed which would have strong resemblance to that of the earth and moon. [P. 314]

The argument develops from the fact that the movement of material caused by gravitational attraction (that is, tides) does

[4]April 1898. I will cite the text as reprinted later in 1898 in his book *The Tides and Kindred Phenomena in the Solar System* (Boston: Houghton Mifflin), chaps. 16 and 17.

not take place without friction and therefore some loss of energy, resulting finally in the slowing of the earth's rotation. But because the earth is not alone, because the earth and moon are essentially one energy system, this slowing has an effect on the moon as well: "If we are correct in supposing that the friction of the tides is retarding the earth's rotation, there must be a reaction upon the moon which must tend to hurry her onwards" (p. 265). By examining the way in which the tides act on both the earth and the moon, Darwin is able to show that the "absolutely certain and inevitable results of the mechanical interaction of the two bodies" is that "both the day and the month are being lengthened" and that "the spiral in which the moon moves is an increasing one, so that her distance from the earth also increases" (pp. 271–72).

Armed with these mechanical considerations, and with the important assumption that the early earth and moon were "molten and plastic" and thus subject to "tidal oscillations in the molten rock" (p. 264), Darwin proposes an evolutionary history for the earth-moon system. If we run the cosmological clock backward, we can posit a situation in which the earth and moon are synchronized in their revolution/rotation: there is only one day in the month, "the moon always looks at the same side of the earth, and so far as concerns their motion they might be fastened together by a rigid bar." They go around each other at a very rapid rate, a period of "between three and five of our present hours. A satellite revolving in so short a period must almost touch the earth's surface" (pp. 276–78).

This is the condition with which Calvino plays in the story "The Distance of the Moon." Yet he does not attempt to consider seriously the consequences of such a state of affairs—as, for example, Arthur C. Clarke likes to do—but constructs his own version of the earth-moon system, based initially on the language of Darwin's theory (for example, "her distance from the earth also increases") but departing substantially from its scientific meaning in crucial respects. Essentially, Calvino tries to reconcile the situation proposed by Darwin with our own experience of the moon and tides, so that the moon of which Qfwfq speaks is recognizably the moon as we ordinarily experience it, with phases, eclipses, and ocean tides:

We had her on top of us all the time, that enormous Moon, when she was full. . . . it looked as if she were going to crush us. . . . But the whole business of the Moon's phases worked in a different way then. . . . Orbit? Oh, elliptical, of course: for a while it would huddle against us and then it would take flight for a while. The tides, when the Moon swung closer, rose so high nobody could hold them back. . . . Climb up on the Moon? Of course we did.[5]

Darwin's theory, cited so prominently in the headnote, has already been essentially (though not linguistically) disregarded before the first paragraph of the story is complete. In the system described by Darwin, the moon would have no phases as we understand them; and certainly that moon could never be "full," since the bulk of the earth would stand between it and the sun at such a time. Every full moon would also be a total eclipse of the moon. Calvino undoubtedly understands this system perfectly well, and he does have Qfwfq comment, "We had eclipses every minute." But it does not suit his story for *every* full moon to be an eclipse, so he ignores this consequence of the theory his story obliviously glosses.

The elliptical orbit Qfwfq mentions is also an invention of Calvino's, though one that sounds very scientific. Every orbit of a planetary body may be properly called elliptical, no matter how closely it approaches the circular, and so Qfwfq's "elliptical, of course" is strictly speaking true. But the situation described in the story, which would make apogee much, much further from the earth than perigee, has no basis at all in Darwin's theory. It is a very clever touch, a feature that looks very much as if it belongs to the theory of the evolution of the earth-moon system but in fact departs from that theory and serves a purely literary function. It strengthens the story by reinforcing the theme of closeness and distance, here presumed to be part of the monthly cycle, which is Calvino's central concern.

[5]*Cosmicomics*, Einaudi edition, 9–10; *Cosmicomics*, trans. Weaver, 3. "L'avevamo sempre addosso, la Luna, smisurata: quand'era il plenilunio . . . pareva che ci schiacciasse. . . . Ma tutto il meccanismo delle fasi andava diversamente che oggigiorno . . . L'orbita? Ellittica, si capisce, ellittica: un po' ci s'appiattiva addosso e un po' prendeva il volo. Le maree, quando la Luna si faceva più sotto, salivano che non le teneva più nessuno. . . . Se non abbiamo mai provato a salirci? E come no?"

Perhaps the most fundamental alteration Calvino makes in Darwin's hypothesis is to suppose an earth more or less like today's. The tidal friction that is essential to cause the retardation of the earth's rotation and the consequent receding of the moon from her original close proximity is the result of tidal oscillations in the molten lava of the young earth. The fundamental assumption of Darwin's theory is that the earth and all the planets were, at this early stage in the solar system's history, molten and plastic. It is the tidal friction in this molten material that causes the moon to slowly spiral out from near the earth.

Why does Calvino ignore this and other fundamental features of the theory that, his headnote indicates, is the basis for his story? "In reading some books we occupy ourselves chiefly with the thoughts of the author; in perusing others, exclusively with our own." As Poe read Mercier, so does Calvino read Darwin, Kuiper, Hubble, and the rest, occupying himself chiefly with his own thoughts rather than with those of the authors he reads. Such an author possesses no authority whatever. This sort of reading *pretends* that the relationship between the author's word and the real world does not exist or does not matter; that is, the reader acts as if he does not believe the text before him. Calvino, by ignoring many of the fundamental premises and consequences of Darwin's theory, treats it as if it were an apistic fiction and simultaneously uses it as the object of his logomimesis.

If we presume an absolute authority for the scientific text, a situation presented by the conflicting theories of Darwin and Gerstenkorn/Alfven puts the reader in a difficult position. He must accept the authority of one or the other, or of neither, but he cannot accept both. Only one theory can be the right one, and the reader must choose the one to believe. When theories conflict, one may disbelieve any number (including all), but one may believe only a single one. Calvino, by using both Darwin and Gerstenkorn as authorities, shows that, as far as these glosses are concerned, he believes neither.

I do not mean to suggest that Calvino, outside the context of these lethetic fictions, disbelieves all the theories used in the *Cosmicomics* and *t zero* or indeed all scientific theories as a group. It would be easy to assume, as readers of Calvino's fiction have occasionally done, that the purpose of these stories is to satirize science, to urge our skepticism for these theories that the glosses treat so cavalierly. After all, the narrations of Qfwfq are obviously incredible, and these narrations are explicitly based upon the scientific theories mentioned in the headnotes. Is it not reasonable to assume that Calvino, like Lucian in the *True History*, wants to use his text to lead our disbelief from the gloss to the authority it supplements, that the gloss is meant to "demystify certain attitudes" of the scientific text, such as the "cult of theory and the consequent detachment from reality, the absolute faith in objectivity," and so on?[6]

This is the position taken by one of the most knowledgeable of Calvino's readers, Francesca Bernardini Napoletano. She finds elements of science satire in many of the cosmicomic tales and suggests that the chief function of the headnotes is to strengthen the parody:

> The same parodistic function is fulfilled, more subtly, by the brief extracts that introduce the stories, taken from scientific texts, in which are reported theories and hypotheses on the origin of the Universe, often contradicting each other (as, for example, those on the origin of the Moon); the narrator confirms precisely by his own testimony each theory, of which the facts he is in the process of narrating, absurd facts based on nonsense, are the logical result. Thus in "The Distance of the Moon" the adoption of an hypothesis of Darwin and of scientific, deductive method makes credible the story of the excursions on the Moon and of the collection of the lunar milk.[7]

These comments seem to me misleading on a number of counts. First of all, Bernardini is simply wrong in calling the headnotes "extracts . . . taken from scientific texts [*brani . . . tratti da testi scientifici*]." The headnote gives a general idea that is drawn from a scientific text but no extracts from the text itself; it is an invocation of authority, but it never quotes the scientists in question. The headnote itself is already Calvino's interpretation, his reading, of a scientific text. In the second place, it is not quite true that the narrator "confirms precisely by his own testimony each

---

[6]Francesca Bernardini Napoletano, *I segni nuovi di Italo Calvino* (Roma: Bulzoni, 1977), 35. The translation is mine.
[7]Ibid.

theory." The narration of "The Distance of the Moon," as we
have seen, radically alters the terms of Darwin's hypothesis.
What Qfwfq does "precisely" (*puntualmente*) is to give Calvino's
version of the theory, a version that is on the whole quite oblivious of the assumptions and consequences of the text in question. Third, the facts that are narrated in the stories are not by
any means the "logical" result of the scientific theories cited, not
unless we change our definition of "logic." Bernardini is more
correct in pointing out that these facts are "absurd" and "based
on nonsense." They participate in the "sense" that Poe attributed to all marginal glosses: nonsense.

But the last sentence in the passage of Bernardini quoted
above seems to me the most misleading of all. Yes, Calvino
adopts *part* of Darwin's hypothesis, but only part of it; he ignores
or alters more than he adopts. One cannot properly say that he
begins by accepting Darwin's theory. Nor can one properly say
that Calvino has used a "scientific, deductive method" in choosing or arranging the facts of his narrative. One might be able to
make such a claim for Arthur Clarke or Charles Sheffield, who
indeed try to apply the scientific theory upon which their stories
are based in a manner consistent with the assumptions made by
the theory. That procedure might be called using the "scientific,
deductive method." Calvino, however, does not do so, and I
think it is quite clear that he wished it to be evident that he does
not. Scientific reasoning does not lead from Darwin's hypothesis
to Calvino's "facts"; it leads to the "facts" supposed by Darwin,
which are very different from those supplied by Calvino. How
can we suppose that Calvino intends to satirize the scientific
method when he pays no attention to that method? Calvino
begins to disregard Darwin's theory the moment he starts to
write about it.

The last thing Calvino has in mind is to "make credible" the
characters and actions set forth in the *Cosmicomics*. He would not
want to do so even if Bernardini were correct in thinking that
parody of science is a major concern of these tales. The point
then would be not to use the scientific theory to make credible
the fantastic story but to use the fantastic story to render incredible the scientific theory. That is the parodistic method of Lucian
and all satirists: one uses the text as a stand-in for the "target"
text, thus engendering disbelief (or whatever form of disap-

proval is desired) for the outrageous stand-in, with the expectation that the disbelief will then be transferred to the target. But for this sort of satire to succeed, the stand-in must recognizably resemble the target, and the closer the resemblance, the more likely the success of the parody—at least until that point is reached at which the parody so closely imitates its target that it can no longer be distinguished from it. Calvino has made no attempt in any of the Qfwfq stories to match the events narrated with states of affairs deducible from the theories mentioned in the headnotes. While it is true that the idea of climbing a ladder from the earth to the moon is nonsensical, it is not a notion that one could actually derive from Darwin's theory, so it says nothing against that theory.

The evidence seems to me very clear that Calvino does not care a whit about the adequacy or inadequacy of Darwin's or anyone else's theory of the origin of the moon. He as much as says so in a passage that Bernardini, since she quotes it, must have considered important. Calvino comments on the difference between the cosmicomic stories and science fiction:

> The first difference, already noted by several critics, is that science fiction deals with the future, while every one of my stories looks back to a distant past, and thus seems to copy a "myth of origins." But it's not only this: it's a matter of a different relation between scientific data and fantastic invention. I wish to make use of the scientific datum as a propulsive charge to depart from the habits of the imagination, and to live daily life too in terms/conditions [*termini*] farther from our experience; science fiction [*fantascienza*], on the other hand, seems to me to try to bring closer that which is distant, that which is difficult to imagine, to try to give these things a realistic dimension or at any rate to bring them within a horizon of imagination which already participates in an accepted habit.[8]

[8]Quoted by Bernardini in *I segni nuovi*, 70–71. The translation is mine. "La prima differenza, osservata già da vari critici, è che la 'science-fiction' tratta del futuro, mentre ognuno dei miei racconti si rifà a un passato remoto, ha l'aria di fare il verso d'un 'mito delle origini.' Ma non è soltanto questo: è diverso rapporto tra dati scientifici e invenzione fantastica. Io vorrei servirmi del dato scientifico come d'una carica propulsiva per uscire dalle abitudini dell'immaginazione, e vivere anche il quotidiano nei termini più lontani dalla nostra esperienza; la fantascienza invece mi pare che tenda ad avvicinare ciò che è lontano, ciò che è difficile da immaginare, che tenda a dargli una dimensione realistica o comunque a farlo entrare in un orizzonte d'immaginazione che fa parte già d'un' abitudine accettata."

I think we ought to take seriously the imagery of the "propulsive charge." It is a characteristic of propulsive charges that one places near them only that which one wishes to send far away and that the most successful charge is the one that propels our missiles the farthest. Likewise the most successful contact between Italo Calvino and a scientific theory, the most successful reading, will be one that results in a story that departs the furthest from the habitual practices of the imagination *and* from that theory itself. One might also note that a propulsive charge destroys itself in the act of doing its work. The story "The Distance of the Moon" is indeed a long way from the meaning of Sir George Darwin's theory of the evolution of the earth-moon system, and by the time the story gets under way, the language of the theory is all that is left; the theory itself has already been blown to pieces.

Traditional science fiction, in Calvino's view, tries to make credible the distant, difficult scientific datum; the cosmicomic stories, on the other hand, exploit the language of the theory, the energy in its "propulsive charge" to carry the narrative away to something distant from our experience, counter to expectation. The power that resides in the language of a scientific text is not, in this view, the power to bring enlightenment, the power of truth; it is rather the power to initiate a process of logomimesis that results in a text that takes us away from the world we know. Calvino's fictional glosses are lethetic, then, not only because they are "oblivious" to the intention of the texts they read but also because they use the language of those texts in a way typical of lethetic reading.

Calvino practices and advocates the exploitation of language intended to bring the reader closer to the truth as a source of energy to propel him "out of this world" into atopia. What he is about here is not parody or satire of the scientific text but rather its appropriation as an object of logomimesis. Calvino uses scientific language the way Pisthetairos uses puns and metaphors: as sources of materials for the construction of a fantasy. Calvino makes fact (or, at the least, the intention to uncover fact) the source of fantasy, the serious into toys to play with, logic into the alogos. This transformation is not effected without cost, for in making it the propulsive charge represented by the scientific datum must be exploded and thereby destroyed. One cannot create distance without losing, at a minimum, proximity.

The loss of proximity through the creation of distance, the loss of immediacy by the creation of mediation, the loss of useful seriousness through the creation of games—these problems will be recognized by readers of the *Cosmicomics* as the very stuff Calvino's dreams are made on, the themes they regularly treat in a fantastic and playful manner. The story with which we have been particularly concerned, "The Distance of the Moon," documents a series of relationships altered radically by the sudden intrusion of great distance. The plot, comical and fantastic though it may be, has all the makings of a Racinian tragedy: The narrator Qfwfq is in love with the Captain's wife, Mrs. Vhd Vhd; she in turn nourishes a passion for his cousin, the Deaf One; and the Deaf One loves—purely and absolutely—only the moon. As things turn out, Mrs. Vhd Vhd is caught on the moon when it has moved away from the earth too far for her ever to return. Qfwfq, who has been stranded there with her, just barely manages to leave. Qfwfq thus loses Mrs. Vhd Vhd, who loses the Deaf One, who loses the moon.

But these losses are in a sense the price paid for certain gains. Because the Deaf One loves the moon, anything the moon does is by definition good. When the moon begins to move away and the two adventurers are trapped there, the Deaf One appears with a means of rescue, a long pole that spans the newly great distance between the surface of the ocean and the moon. The narrator explains, however, that rescue may not have been the Deaf One's principal purpose after all: he was not trying to bring his friends back,

> he was playing his last game with the Moon. . . . And we realized that his virtuosity had no purpose, aimed at no practical result, indeed you would have said he was driving the Moon away. . . . And this, too, was just like him; he was unable to conceive desires that went against the Moon's nature, the Moon's course and destiny, and if the Moon now tended to go away from him, then he would take delight in this separation just as, till now, he had delighted in the Moon's nearness.[9]

[9]*Cosmicomics*, Einaudi edition, 23; *Cosmicomics*, trans. Weaver, 15. "Faceva il suo ultimo gioco con la Luna. . . . E ci accorgemmo che la sua bravura non mirava a nulla, non intendeva raggiungere nessun risultato practico, anzi si

This action of the Deaf One, his loving and playful acceptance of the moon's distance, suddenly makes distance itself a quality to be prized. Mrs. Vhd Vhd, seeing what her beloved is doing, can only demonstrate her love by accepting this distance: "If what my cousin now loved was the distant Moon, then she too would remain distant, on the Moon."[10] She gains in this way what she most desires, though she gains it metonymically, through making herself one with the moon by remaining with it, forever apart from the Deaf One but forever the object of his affection. If she cannot possess the body of her lover, she can at least participate in the symbolic act of copulation he has performed with the moon. She actually achieves a complete merging of herself with the distant moon, much to the grief of the lovesick Qfwfq: "She was there where I had left her . . . and she said nothing. She was the color of the Moon. . . . I could distinguish the shape of her bosom, her arms, her thighs, just as I remember them now, just as now . . . I imagine I can see her . . . , she who makes the Moon the Moon and, wherever she is full, sets the dogs to howling all night long, and me with them."[11]

Here we find Calvino in the role of *arche*-debunker, creating a pseudoetiological myth that turns out to explain—charmingly but absolutely incredibly—the origin of dogs' baying at the moon. If there is satire in the *Cosmicomics*, this is where it is most readily found. But the satire is not directed toward any particular explicatory principle. The etiologies of science (the theories of Darwin, Gerstenkorn, and so forth) and those of myth are

---

sarebbe detto che la stesse spingendo via, la Luna. . . . E anche questo era da lui: da lui che non sapeva concepire desideri in contrasto con la natura della Luna e il suo corso e il suo destino, e se la Luna ora tendeva ad allontanarsi da lui, ebbene egli godeva di questo allontanamento come aveva fino allora goduto della sua vicinanza."

[10]*Cosmicomics*, Einaudi edition, 23; *Cosmicomics*, trans. Weaver, 15–16. "Se quel che ora mio cugino amava era la Luna lontana, lei sarebbe rimasta lontana, sulla Luna."

[11]*Cosmicomics*, Einaudi edition, 24; *Cosmicomics*, trans. Weaver, 16. "Era là dove l'avevo lasciata . . . e non diceva nulla. Era del colore della Luna. . . . Si distingueva bene la forma del petto, delle braccia, dei fianchi, così come ancora lo ricordo, così come anche ora . . . m'immagino di vederla . . . , lei che rende Luna la Luna e che ogni plenilunio spinge i cani tutta la notte a ululare e io con loro."

balanced in these narratives, so we cannot readily say that Calvino is parodying science *or* mythology. He makes gentle fun of both and thereby calls into question the entire process of etiology. What is primary here and what secondary? Is Mrs. Vhd Vhd "she who makes the Moon the Moon," or has the moon made her? Is Calvino's story a gloss upon the text of Darwin's theory, or is Darwin's hypothesis merely a note supplementing the fictional narrative?

This very notion of the impossibility of establishing priority becomes material for Calvino to play with in another of the *Cosmicomics*, "A Sign in Space." This is a mock etiology on the origin of language in whch Qfwfq attempts to measure the rotation of the galaxy by making a sign "at a point in space, just so I could find it again two hundred million years later."[12] The moment this sign is made, the question of the priority of the signifier and signified arises: "The sign served to mark a place but at the same time it meant that in that place there was a sign . . . , the name of that point, and also my name that I had signed on that spot; in short it was the only name available for everything that required a name."[13] The issue is further complicated by the fact that confusion arises over the originality of signs themselves. Upon his return to the place that he had marked with his sign, Qfwfq finds only "a shapeless scratch, a bruised, chipped abrasion of space. I had lost everything."[14] He falls into despair but is roused again to excitement when he finds something in another place that looks very much like his sign, "a sign unquestionably copied from mine, but one I realized immediately couldn't be mine"[15] because it does not possess the "ineffable purity" of the original. Qfwfq reasons that someone, "a certain

[12]*Cosmicomics*, Einaudi edition, 41; *Cosmicomics*, trans. Weaver, 31. "In un punto dello spazio, apposta per poterlo ritrovare duecento milioni d'anni dopo."
[13]*Cosmicomics*, Einaudi edition, 43; *Cosmicomics*, trans. Weaver, 32–33. "Il segno serviva a segnare un punto, ma nello stesso tempo segnava che lì c'era un segno . . . , il nome di quel punto, e anche il mio nome che io avevo segnato su quel punto, insomma era l'unico nome disponibile per tutto ciò che richiedeva un nome."
[14]*Cosmicomics*, Einaudi edition, 45; *Cosmicomics*, trans. Weaver, 35. "Un fregaccio informe, un'abrasione dello spazio slabbrata e pesta. Avevo perduto tutto."
[15]*Cosmicomics*, Einaudi edition, 46; *Cosmicomics*, trans. Weaver, 35. "Un segno senza dubbio copiato dal mio, ma che si capiva subito che non poteva essere il mio."

Kgwgk," had erased his sign, from pure malice and envy, and then had tried to make his own. "It was clear that his sign had nothing to mark except Kgwgk's intention to imitate my sign, which was beyond all comparison."[16] Already here, at this very first attempt at reading, the reader (Qfwfq) cannot establish priority, neither the priority of the signified over the signifier, not the priority of one signifier over another. And once the fashion of making signs really catches hold, things can become only much worse. Everyone starts making signs, and even when Qfwfq is able to identify with certainty the point where he had made his original sign, it is so full of signs that he cannot recognize his own. It becomes impossible to determine what is a sign and what is not: "World and space seemed the mirror of each other, both minutely adorned with hieroglyphics and ideograms, each of which might be a sign and might not be."[17] Finally, it becomes impossible to make any decisions about priority:

> In the universe now there was no longer a container and a thing contained, but only a general thickness of signs. . . . There was no longer any way to establish a point of reference: the Galaxy went on turning but I could no longer count the revolutions, any point could be the point of departure, any sign heaped up with the others could be mine, but discovering it would have served no purpose, because it was clear that, independent of signs, space didn't exist and perhaps never had existed.[18]

[16]Ibid. "Era chiaro che quel segno non aveva niente da segnare se non l'intenzione di Kgwgk d'imitare il mio segno, per cui non c'era nemmeno da metterli a confronto."

[17]*Cosmicomics*, Einaudi edition, 50; *Cosmicomics*, trans. Weaver, 38. "Mondo e spazio parevano uno lo specchio dell'altro, l'uno e l'altro minutamente istoriati di geroglifici e ideogrammi, ognuno dei quali poteva essere un segno e non esserlo."

[18]*Cosmicomics*, Einaudi edition, 51; *Cosmicomics*, trans. Weaver, 39. "Nell'universo ormai c'erano più un contenente e un contenuto, ma solo un spessore di segni. . . . Non c'era più modo di fissare un punto di riferimento: la Galassia continuava a dar volta ma io non riuscivo più a contare i giri, qualsiasi punto poteva essere quello di partenza, qualsiasi segno accavallato agli altri poteva essere il mio, ma lo scoprirlo non sarebbe servito a niente, tanto era chiaro che indipendentemente dai segni lo spazio non esisteva e forse non era mai esistito."

This, the end of the story, proposes an undecidability that mirrors the beginning, except now it is the universality of signs rather than their total absence that makes it impossible to establish a point of reference. Every word of the story's title, "Un segno nello spazio," has been shown to be ambiguous. Is there, was there ever, *one* sign? Where does *space* end and *sign* begin? And which, after all, is *in* which, since container and contained can no longer be distinguished?

At the same time that he is obliviously reading scientific texts, then, Calvino is practicing this same oblivious reading upon semiotic theory. The abstract semiotic concept of "sign," along with all its theoretical context, is made concrete, literalized into an actual mark scratched into "space." Like Darwin's theories of the origin of the moon, the semiotic theories of *Tel Quel* become part of the linguistic resources of the fiction. Literary critical texts, no less than scientific texts, are used as storehouses of signifiers to be played with.

The process of reading as described in "A Sign in Space" is inevitably forgetful of origins, with the result that the priority of signatum over signans, of the world over the word, cannot be maintained. When the reader of the first text in the history of the universe, who happens also to be the author of that first text, tries to prepare himself for his first act of reading—that is, for recognition of the sign he made in space—he finds that something crucially important has already escaped him: he cannot really remember just what his sign looked like. No matter how hard he tries, his sign will not return to his memory. But: "Did I despair? No, this forgetfulness was annoying, but not irreparable."[19] Reading does take place, even though the loss of certainty about that original sign, imitations of which all other signs must be supposed to be, throws every act of reading into question. Qfwfq, the *arche* reader/writer, finds that he must inevitably disbelieve *every* text, because all the signs fail to be that original sign, that "ineffable purity." But since everything is now a sign—"The fire-streaks against a wall of schistose rock, the four-

[19]*Cosmicomics*, Einaudi edition, 44; *Cosmicomics*, trans. Weaver, 35. "Ma disperai? No, la dimenticanza era seccante, ma non irrimediabile."

hundred-and-twenty-seventh groove—slightly crooked—of the cornice of a tomb's pediment, a sequence of streaks on a video during a thunderstorm."[20] and so forth—it does not matter any more. The space that was to be marked by Qfwfq's original sign "didn't exist and perhaps never had existed" apart from signs. To focus all our attention on signifiers and remain forgetful of signifieds is proper in a universe in which the world does not exist independent of the word.

In such a universe, all writing must be glossing. The very first act of reading, Qfwfq's discovery of Kgwgk's "wretched counterfeit," discloses a gloss upon that original lost text. And all glossing must be lethetic glossing, which adverts to the text only at the level of the signans and does not care about what such a sign means to mark. All this glossing is explicitly logomimesis: "It was clear that [Kgwgk's] sign had nothing to mark except [his] intention to imitate my sign, which was beyond all comparison." It is a universe composed entirely of marginalia.

---

[20]*Cosmicomics*, Einaudi edition, 50; *Cosmicomics*, trans. Weaver, 38–39. "Le striature del fuoco contro una parete di roccia scistosa, la quattrocentoventisettesima scanalatura—un po' di sbieco—della cornice del frontone d'un mausoleo, una sequenza di striature su un video durante una tempesta magnetica."

Part Four /

THE ORIGINS OF
ALETHETIC READING

CHAPTER 9 /

Reading as Possession:
Influence and Inspiration

IF THE LETHETIC GENRE is at least as old as Aristophanes' *Birds*, and if the lethetic mode is a form of reading
potentially available to every reader who wants to make use of it,
the question must arise as to why lethetic literature does not
occupy a more prominent place in our tradition. I claim to have
identified an interaction between text and reader that is both
interesting and important, but it is clearly not an interaction that
has received much attention in past discussions of poetics and
rhetoric. One might be tempted to object, then, that our traditional literary theory did not focus on lethetic fiction because it
was not worth attending to. In a sense, this objection would be
absolutely correct: we do not attend to that which we do not
value, and lethetic reading has certainly not seemed valuable to
the main line of literary orthodoxy.

But I will argue below that a powerful cultural bias makes it
almost impossible to acknowledge the importance or interest of
lethetic reading. The philosophical presuppositions that under-
lie our approach to literary texts are such that an "untrue" text
as defined earlier is virtually ruled out of existence. The radical
distinction between "surface" and "intention," along with a
deeply held belief in the possibility of reconciling a fictional
surface with a truthful intention, leads to an assumption that the
text, no matter what it might appear to say, must somehow disclose the truth. Boccaccio, for one, exemplifies this assumption

when he asserts the presence of an underlying meaning even in the fireside tales of a "maundering old woman."[1] My hope here is that if we once understand the origins of our traditional preference for alethetic reading we will be more willing in the future to accept the reality, and the importance, of lethetic reading.

If Calvino has focused on the origins of a universe filled with *marginalia,* Harold Bloom in *The Anxiety of Influence* has trained his gaze upon its latest state of evolution. What is the would-be maker of signs to do in a world that is now so thick with signs that there is no room for him (as sign maker)? "Poetic history, in this book's argument, is held to be indistinguishable from poetic influence, since strong poets make that history by misreading one another, so as to clear imaginative space for themselves."[2] Every modern poet is of necessity a Kgwgk who goes about erasing the signs of others and putting in their place new signs that yet counterfeit in a recognizable way the old ones. Qfwfq sees the motive in Kgwgk's action to be envy, spite, vandalism, all acts of pure aggression. Bloom's "strong poet" is also aggressive with regard to his precursors, but his aggression arises from the anxiety of being a latecomer in a universe already full to bursting with texts, so full in fact that he must "clear imaginative space" for himself by deliberately *mis*reading the signs of his precursors. "Every poem is a misinterpretation of a parent poem" (p. 94).

Bloom inverts the image of reading presented in "In the Penal Colony"[3] so that, instead of the paternal scripture impressing itself by an act of violence upon the reader, the reader, in becoming himself a poet, performs an act of violence upon the paternal text. Bloom provides a taxonomy of such acts of violence, but the particular varieties are secondary in importance to the central concept of poetry as a particular kind of glossing, glossing that is not lethetic glossing, though it shares some of the

[1] Vincenzo Romano, ed., *Genealogie deorum gentilium libri* (Bari: Laterza & Figli, 1951), 2:711.

[2] (New York: Oxford University Press, 1973), 5. Citations below in the text refer to this edition.

[3] For a full discussion of Kafka's imagery of the reading process, see my *"In der Strafkolonie:* Kafka and the Scene of Reading," *German Quarterly* 55 (November 1982), 511–25.

features of that activity. Lethetic glossing *ends* by reducing the "original" text to a gloss upon the new text, to a footnote supplementing what is now no longer itself a supplement; "strong poets" *set out* to achieve this inversion, to turn the texts they read into supplements, "precursors," of themselves. Goethe's *Faust* might properly be seen as a lethetic gloss on the *Faustbuch* and other versions of the Faust legend that sprang from it, since Goethe really was interested only in his own thoughts when he read these texts, used them merely as points of departure without caring about their intentions. Thomas Mann's *Doktor Faustus,* on the other hand, is no such lethetic gloss; it is the product of a strong poet's attempt with all of his considerable resources to make Goethe's *Faust* into a precursor of his own larger and more "complete" version of the story. Mann cares urgently about Goethe's intention; it is Goethe that he must somehow efface if he is to make space for his own poetic self. This is not Mann's *only* reason for taking up Goethe's story, but it is an important one.

Calvino, the lethetic glossator of science, is not worried about securing for his story priority and authority over those theories. He may act as if he disbelieves them, but his own myths are—deliberately—even more incredible than the most outlandish scientific hypothesis. He throws the concept of priority into question and plays games with the etiology of the universe. For Bloom's anxious poet, issues of priority and authority are everything. Bloom presents his book as "part of a unified meditation on the melancholy of the creative mind's desperate insistence upon priority" (p. 13), desperate because those who try to establish authority over the past by the discovery of some means to be *prior* to the past cannot help but fail:

> A Wordsworthian critic, even one as loyal to Wordsworth as Geoffrey Hartman, can insist upon clearly distinguishing between *priority*, as a concept from the natural order, and *authority*, from the spiritual order, but Wordsworth's ode declines to make this distinction. "By seeking to overcome priority," Hartman wisely says, "art fights nature on nature's own ground, and is bound to lose." The argument of this book is that strong poets are condemned to just this unwisdom; Wordsworth's Great Ode fights nature on nature's ground, and suffers a great defeat, even as it retains its

greater dream. . . . Vico, who read all creation as a severe poem, understood that priority in the natural order and authority in the spiritual order had to be one and had to remain one, *for poets*, because only this harshness constituted Poetic Wisdom. [Pp. 9–13]

For anxious poets, then, the past is a threat, and earlier poems are giants that must be slain or at least diminished somehow so that the ephebe, the would-be poet, can establish poetic space and personality. For the lethetic glossator, though, the authorities of the past are a treasure house to be plundered and represent not a threat but a great natural resource. This *Wortschatz*, this treasury of texts, may be ransacked for whatever is useful to the glossator, for whatever signs it might be desirable to imitate, without worrying about why an earlier writer wrote, what the intention of that writer's text might have been. The glossator may simply use it or any part of it for his or her own purposes.

This view of a precursor text as a storehouse of signifiers requires readers who can maintain some distance between themselves and that text, a distance that can be maintained by disbelief or even by the pretense of disbelief. Bloom does not admit the possibility of this kind of reading or will not admit it as "good" reading, so that the act of reading becomes synonymous with the absolute proximity, indeed the flowing together, of author and reader. The text becomes dangerous because the author is so overwhelmingly present:

> Freud, in defining anxiety, speaks of "angst [*sic*] vor etwas." Anxiety *before* something is clearly a mode of expectation, like desire. We can say that anxiety and desire are the antimonies of the ephebe or beginning poet. The anxiety of influence is an anxiety of expectation of *being flooded.* Lacan insists that desire is only a metonymy, and it may be that desire's contrary, the anxiety of expectation, is only a metonymy also. The ephebe who fears his precursors as he might fear a flood is taking a vital part for the whole, the whole being everything that constitutes his creative anxiety, the spectral blocking agent in every poet. Yet this metonymy is hardly to be avoided; every good reader properly *desires* to drown, but if the poet drowns, he will become *only a reader.* [P. 57]

Since to be a good reader, for Bloom, is to drown, and to drown is to be merely a reader and thus no independent poet, ephebes must find ways to be bad readers, to misread the texts that threaten to drown them. The "revisionary ratios" identified in *The Anxiety of Influence* are the ephebe's defense against "good," that is, drowning, reading.

The anxiety of influence is the result of the threat of the power of speech—the speech of the other—that is allegedly experienced by every reader who is neither "oblivious" nor "revisionary." The danger can seem especially strong when the power of the word is set free from all constraints of conformity to the world, as it is in the *Birds* and indeed in every lethetic fiction. And if an element of belief is allowed to enter, if the reader suspects for a moment that such a liberated word might actually control the world, the anxiety must necessarily become overwhelming. As is vividly demonstrated in Ursula Le Guin's novel *The Lathe of Heaven,* a world in which language (in this case a young man's dreams) could instantly alter reality would be perhaps the most terrifying world imaginable, particularly for the possessor of such unlimited power of speech. Dream language, like all forms of language, is not under the absolute control of its user; it has its own structures and its own development; and a world ruled by such language is a world in fact ruled by language alone, wherein even the speaker/dreamer is at the mercy of his or her own protean utterance.

Aristophanes, however, has shown in the *Birds* that the power of speech is ultimately self-limiting, since that power is released by cutting the bond with reality (that is, with the world of things). The power of the unreal world is necessarily a dunamis adunate, an impossible power, and readers who are aware of its unreality must know that it is therefore a powerless power and that it cannot harm them. A lethetic fiction like the *Birds* is thus a kind of magic reactor in which the conditions that allow for the release of fantastic power are the very conditions that prevent that power from getting loose and harming us. The reader of such a lethetic text is always protected from the anxiety of drowning in the mighty sea of language by the disbelief that the text itself solicits.

But a reader may read any text lethetically, even texts (such as scientific theories) that earnestly seek our belief. Italo Calvino and Edgar Allan Poe practiced this mode of reading—not all the time but certainly in the texts we have discussed—and were able by this means to use the heritage of the past's numerous texts as a resource for their own personal exploitation. It may well be that those who refuse to read this way, even when invited to, who suppose, as Bloom does, that "good" reading must submit to the authority of the precursor text and must therefore drown in it, are inevitably faced with an anxiety of expectation of self-loss, self-effacement at the hands of the paternal scripture. And the anxiety could only be increased if the ephebe were to read in an aggressively alethetic fashion, combing the text for traces of an absent transcendental signified. If the text is understood as the paternal logos, there is every reason to fear drowning, as the would-be poet is possessed by the overwhelming presence of the authoritative precursor.

But this "good" reading, this possession of the reader's soul by a foreign power, in short this *influence*, has not always been the object of the poet's anxiety. One of the oldest and most powerful currents in our tradition assumes on the contrary that the would-be poet wants to drown, indeed cannot become a poet without being possessed by a power superior to that poet. Socrates argues along these lines in Plato's *Ion:*

Socrates: . . . this gift you have of speaking well on Homer is not an art; it is a power divine, impelling you like the power in the stone Euripides called the magnet, which most call "stone of Heracles." This stone does not simply attract the iron rings, just by themselves; it also imparts to the rings a force enabling them to do the same thing as the stone itself, that is, to attract another ring, so that sometimes a chain is formed, quite a long one, of iron rings, suspended one from the other. For all of them, however, their power [dunamis] depends upon that lodestone. Just so the Muse. She first makes men inspired, and then through these inspired ones others share in the enthusiasm, and a chain is formed, for the epic poets, all the good ones, have their excellence, not from art [techne], but are inspired, possessed [katechomenoi], and thus they utter all these admirable poems. [*Ion* 533 d-e][4]

[4]All English translations from Plato are from Edith Hamilton and Huntington Cairns, eds., *The Collected Dialogues of Plato* (New York: Bollingen Foundation, 1963), which anthologizes translations by various hands. Of principal concern here are the *Ion* and *Phaedrus*, translated by Lane Cooper and R. Hackforth, respectively. The Greek texts to which I refer come from J. Burnet, ed., *Platonis*

Aristophanes' hero Pisthetairos achieved divinity by means of the power of speech. Socrates argues here that the poets achieve their power of speech by the intervention of divinity, an "influence" if anything more powerful than that feared by Bloom's anxious ephebe. Socrates is trying to convince the rhapsode Ion that he (Ion) possesses neither art nor knowledge of the things about which he speaks but merely acts as the conduit through which the Muse communicates to us. Like a lodestone, the Muse transmits her power to the poet (that is, to Homer) and thence again to those who recite the poem (that is, to rhapsodes like Ion) and thence again to those who hear the recitation. The poets themselves, Socrates reminds him, report this very thing: "And what they say is true, for a poet is a light and winged thing, and holy, and never able to compose until he has been inspired, and is beside himself, and reason [nous] is no longer in him" (534 b). The influx (influence) of power that would prevent the making of a poet according to Bloom is in Socrates' view the only thing that will make one. The wings that Pisthetairos could only achieve by means of his words are in Socrates' opinion the essence of the poet's nature, a symptom of the quality that makes the poet able to receive the gift of words from the Muse. Poets are less like birds than like bees who buzz about the gardens of the Muses. Only when they have fed on the honey-dew provided by divinity are they able to utter their sweet speech.

But Socrates sees the divine Muse as the source not of all poetic speech but only of that which is powerful. He adduces the example of Tynnichus of Chalchis: "He never composed a single poem worth recalling, save the song of praise which everyone repeats, well nigh the finest of lyrical poems, and absolutely what he called it, an 'Invention of the Muses'" (534 d). The certain sign of the divine source of the poem is that poem's success, its ability to transmit power to reciters and listeners. Speech, even poetic speech, is not divine, but only the power that resides in some particular examples of poetic and oracular

---

Opera (Oxford: Clarendon Press, 1901 et seq.), vols. 2 and 3. Once again, I will forgo lengthy transliterations of the original Greek, since the texts are easily accessible, and will provide, in the text, only those words and phrases of the original that seem to me pertinent. I have, on occasion, modified the translations to make a point clearer.

speech. Poets, then, "are nothing but interpreters [*hermenes*] of the gods, each one possessed [*katechomenoi*] by the divinity to whom he is in bondage" (534 e), and the rhapsodes who "interpret the utterance of the poets" are no more than "interpreters of interpreters" (535 a). The dunamis that has its origin in the divine is transported along a hermeneutic chain from gods to poets to reciters to listeners, each one stage further removed from the source. The hermeneutic process assumed by Socrates is not, however, a mental discipline or application of intelligence. If poets try to think, if their "reason" (nous) is functioning, they will be powerless. "So long as he has this possession [that is, his nous], a man is powerless to compose poetry or to chant oracles [*adunatos pas poiein anthropos estin kai chresmoidein*]" (534 b).

This same argument is repeated by Socrates in the *Phaedrus*, near the beginning of his second speech on the merits of the lover and the nonlover, as part of a demonstration that "the greatest blessings come by way of madness, indeed of a madness that is heaven sent" (244 a).

> There is a third form of possession or madness, of which the Muses are the source. This seizes a tender, virgin soul and stimulates it to rapt passionate expression, especially in lyric poetry, glorifying the countless mighty deeds of ancient times for the instruction of posterity. But if any man come to the gates of poetry without the madness of the Muses, then shall he and his words of sanity with him be brought to nought by the poetry of madness, and behold, their place is nowhere to be found. [245 a]

Here again we have the contrast of mania and techne, madness and skill, that was at the center of Socrates' attention in the *Ion*. Techne requires that the artist be in possession of self and of nous, so as to construct something, whereas mania is a kind of katakoche, "possession," that supposes an external control that merely uses the poet.

Closely related to the mania of poetry, according to the Socrates of the *Phaedrus*, is a fourth form of madness, also divine in origin, and that is love (eros). The discussion of this fourth type of madness is long and complex, but much of it hinges on a pun found in "a couple of verses on love quoted by certain Homeric scholars from the unpublished works":

> Ton d' etoi thnetoi men Erota kalousi potenon,
> athanatoi de Pterota, dia pterophutor' anagken.
>
> Now surely mortals call the winged one Eros,
> But immortals Pteros, because of his need
> to produce feathers. [252 b]

The play on *eros* and *pteros*, stressing the wings with which the god of love is supposed to be equipped, proposes a connection between lovers and winged creatures of which Socrates makes much. (He is not above making use of a logomimetic narrative himself, if it suits him.) The soul (psuche), he claims, is also a winged creature, according to a myth he tells by way of explaining its essence (idea), but it can happen that the soul can lose its wings and can become immersed in earthly corporeality. The soul's wings need the nourishment of truth: those that behold the "ideas" keep their wings, but those who do not grasp them completely sink down to earth and are embodied in men, to go through various cycles of reincarnation. Only those souls that have had some glimpse of the "ideal" truth can become human. Philosophers, having the clearest memory of the truth their souls once saw, are able to approach in some measure the divinity in whose company their souls once traveled. "Standing aside from the busy doings of mankind, and drawing nigh to the divine, he [the philosopher] is rebuked by the multitude as being out of his wits, for they know that he is possessed by a deity" (249 c-d). This fourth form of madness is the best of all, the highest and closest to the divine,

> and when he that loves beauty is touched by such madness he is called a lover. Such a one, as soon as he beholds the beauty of this world, is reminded of true beauty, and his wings begin to grow; then he is fain to lift his wings and fly upward; yet he has not the power, but inasmuch as he gazes upward like a bird, and cares nothing for the world beneath, men charge it upon him that he is demented. [249 d–e]

If, as the pseudo-Homeric verses would have it, Eros is really Pteros—from the point of view of the immortals—then it should also hold true in reverse, that the philosophical soul whose wings begin to grow in the presence of truth is properly called a lover. The pteros is an eron. Of course, having only the memory of a partial truth, the philosophical soul lacks wings strong enough to attain the heaven of pure ideas but gazes up there "after the manner of a bird [*ornithos diken*]" in longing for that which is recalled but cannot be reached. The image of the bird is in keeping with the allusions to wings, but it also serves to illustrate why the philosopher is considered mad. To behave like a bird is, as Pisthetairos observes to the birds themselves, silly and undignified as far as men are concerned. It involves "being unmindful of the world below [*ton kato de amelon*]."

Socrates uses the same imagery here as that employed in the *Birds* but in the service of an opposite concept. For Pisthetairos, words are the source of wings and thus of the power to take leave of the world down below. But the source of the power of his words is their unconnectedness to the world, their participation in the alogos. The world "up there" in Cloudcuckooland is an impossible world formed out of the immense and yet "unreal" power of language. The play lets us be "unmindful of the world below" in the manner of a lethetic fiction by drawing our attention away from the power of that world to the power of speech. But for Socrates, the world that the philosopher ignores is in fact not the "true" world at all, since only the world of ideas, the world "up there," is true, and the world of experience is a play of shadows. What gives power to the wings of the philosopher's soul is the truth of ideal forms, which truth is only imperfectly reflected down here. The thinking man becomes birdlike by contemplating and longing for the divinity that resides above, a divinity that is remembered by the reincarnated soul.

The mania of eros is the yearning for *that which is remembered* (*aletheia*). It is to be "as close in memory as one's power will allow to those things nearness to which makes a god divine [*pros gar ekeinois aei estin mnemei kata dunamin, pros hoisper theos on theios estin*]" (249 c). This imagery of proximity closely parallels that of the magnet and rings in the *Ion,* but here the divinity is not the source of the power but one of the entities that draws power

/ 186

from closeness to the source. The process of receiving that power is called in the *Ion* "interpreting" (*hermeneunein*), but more often Plato refers to it as logos (dialectic, discourse, and so forth). "Dialectic, for Socrates, is the true art of making love," writes Herman Sinaiko,[5] and this connection between logos and eros is again reinforced linguistically by the fact that one of the chief features of dialectic is *erotesis*, "questioning."[6] Contact, albeit sometimes remote or secondhand contact, with divinity is the link that makes lunatic, lover, poet, and philosopher of imagination all compact. Wings, the sign and means of contact with divinity, cannot function save through the divine power. Poets, possessed by the Muse herself, are able to fly up on the wings of their poetry, not through any virtue or skill they possess, but rather through the power that possesses them.

The mania of the philosopher/lover differs radically from that of the poet in one way, in that the former is in possession of nous and will make use of a techne, the "art" of dialectic, to nourish the wings and draw nearer to the power that emanates from the divine realm of truth. In fact, it is only the power of truth (as opposed to conformity with *doxa*, "belief, opinion") that makes the logos a genuine skill: "It would seem to follow, my friend," Socrates says to Phaedrus, "that the art of speech displayed by one who has gone chasing after beliefs, instead of knowing the truth, will be a comical sort of art, in fact no art at all" (262 c).

We may observe, then, that Plato proposes two sources for the power of speech: one is the result of direct contact with (possession by) divinity and involves no skill on the part of the speaker; the other seeks to recollect the soul's direct contact with divinity through a process that requires the utmost skill and devotion to truth. "Arts" that claim such power without a concern for the truth (such as sophistical rhetoric) really attain such efficacy as they possess by means of the power of truth. Socrates attacks, for example, the claim that the "plausible" (*pithanos*) and "probable" (*eikos*) are more effective than truth. Those who feel they are can

[5]*Love, Knowledge, and Discourse in Plato: Dialogue and Dialectic in "Phaedrus," "Republic," "Parmenides"* (Chicago: University of Chicago Press, 1965), 117.
[6]See for instance *Meno* 185 d.

"say good-bye to the truth [*chairein toi alethei*]" (272 e) by recourse to the eikos are only deceiving themselves, since "the multitude get their notion of probability as the result of a likeness to truth, and we explained just now that these likenesses can always be discovered by one who knows the truth" (273 d). The true art of discourse (*techne logon*) approaches the divine by way of truth, as poetry approaches truth by way of the divine: "Poets, you know, singing as they do under the divine afflatus, are among the inspired and so, by the help of their Graces and Muses, often hit upon true historical fact."[7] Since it is truth, the realm of forms, "nearness to which makes a god divine," it follows that the ultimate source for all power of speech, whether that of logos or of poetry, is the truth.

An effective logos cannot say good-bye (*chairein*) to the truth, but Socrates seems to claim that it can and will say good-bye to *muthologein*, "myth-making, story-telling." At the beginning of the dialogue Phaedrus notes that he and Socrates are near the spot where Boreas was said to have seized Orithyia, and he asks Socrates if he thinks the story (*mutholomega*) is true. "I would not be out of place [*atopos*]," Socrates replies, "if I were to disbelieve it [*apistoien*], the way the men of science [*sophoi*] do" (229 c); that is, to disbelieve it by giving a "scientific" explanation of it. To explain the Pegasuses, centaurs, Gorgons, and other atopiai (229 e) of legend would be a tall order. Socrates has no time for such *allotria* (extraneous stuff), since he is still trying to know himself "in conformity with the Delphic inscription [*kata to Delphikon gramma*]" (229 e). "Therefore I say good-bye [*chairein*] to such things" (230 a). Not wishing himself to be atopos, Socrates gives his chairein to atopiai.

Socrates' chairein to myths "takes place in the name of truth," according to Jacques Derrida, and by that he wishes to emphasize both "truth" and "place." Socrates intends to seek the truth about himself and to let allotria go, "but this imperative to know oneself is not immediately felt or dictated in the transparent immediateness of the presence of the self. It is not perceived. Merely interpreted, read, deciphered."[8] It is obedience to an

---

[7] *Laws* 682 a.

[8] "La Pharmacie de Platon," first published in *Tel Quel*, 1968; quoted here from *La dissémination* (Paris: Seuil, 1972), 77. Page numbers in this edition are cited henceforth in the text. All translations of passages from this essay are mine.

inscription, the *gramma* of the Delphic Oracle. The *place* of the chairein has a related importance in that it happens in the context of the myth concerning Orithyia, "this *virgin* cast headlong into the abyss, surprised by death *while playing with Pharmacia*" (p. 78). Derrida shows in brilliant detail how closely related are the concepts of writing and "pharmacy" in Plato's dialogues, particularly the *Phaedrus,* and how ambivalent this concept of pharmakon really is. It is very telling that Socrates dismisses myth at the very moment when he acquiesces to the power of an inscription and interprets a legend understandable (in Plato's own terms) as a myth of the power of writing. It initiates Derrida's deconstruction of the Platonic oppositions of muthos/logos and of graphesis/logos.

The power of the word (logos) derives from the connection (logos) between speech and truth. But "truth" for Plato is not a matter of "reality," since the real world "down here" is only a shadow of the true world. The famous image of the cave at the beginning of Book VII of the *Republic* is one of the clearest explanations of this notion. The inhabitants of this cave, chained immobile in one spot, can see only the shadows of things outside projected against one of the walls of the cave. "Then in every way," Socrates explains, "such prisoners would deem reality to be nothing else than the shadows of the artificial objects" (515 c). And if it should happen that one of the prisoners were released and had the opportunity to see the objects that had cast the shadows, "do you not think that he would be at a loss and that he would regard what he formerly saw as more real than the things now pointed out to him?" Furthermore, if such a prisoner, having seen the originals in the full light of the sun, were to return to the cave, he would no longer be very skillful at making judgments about the shadows flickering in the cave's darkness, and the other inhabitants would consider him ridiculous and ruined.

The mania of philosophers and lovers is directly comparable to the condition of the returned cave prisoner. They do not behave in ways others consider normal; they do not seem to perceive the world accurately; they speak about things that have no connection to the world of sensible "reality"; in short, they speak and act in a manner that goes *para ten doxan,* both "counter to expectation" and "counter to reason" as well as "counter to opinion." And one of the things they do is to speak in fictions—

myths, parables, images—like the parable of the cave and countless others spread throughout the dialogues. The language of
the truth is "perforce poetical" (272 a), not simply because the
philosopher wants to entertain his friends, but because there is
no other way to express truth. Myths prove not to be allotria at
all.

Derrida, in quite another context—a discussion of Lacan's
"Seminar on 'The Purloined Letter' "—states the issue clearly:

> Once the distinction is made, as the whole philosophical tradition
> does, between truth and reality, it is self-evident that the truth is
> "confirmed in a structure of fiction." Lacan insists much on the
> opposition truth/reality, which he advances as a paradox. This
> opposition, as orthodox as can be, facilitates the passage of truth
> through fiction: common sense will always have made the distinc-
> tion between reality and fiction.[9]

The orthodoxy to which Derrida refers, the "whole philosophical tradition," is initiated by Plato. Lacan himself cites as his
philosophical authority not Plato but Heidegger, who is equally
orthodox in this regard. But it does not matter whose name is
invoked: the notion that Derrida understands Lacan to be ad-
vancing here as news is surely the same old story. Whether or
not Derrida correctly understands Lacan, his point about the
orthodoxy of the distinction between truth and reality is certainly valid. The assumption that appearance and essence do not
coincide lies behind all alethetic reading, all irony and allegory.

The point that Derrida makes about Lacan, which speaks to
"the whole philosophical tradition," including Plato, cannot be
overstressed: *once the assumption is made that truth and reality differ,
there can be no other structure for truth than the structure of fiction.*
This statement does not mean, of course, that every fiction reveals the truth, but it strongly suggests that every fiction needs to
be interrogated closely to determine whether in fact it might
reveal the truth or might at least lead to such a revelation. Socrates may reject the literal belief in the myths of the gods (as he
seems to do in *Euthyphro* 6 a ff.); he may reject the "overly subtle
[*sophizomenos*]" rationalizing interpretations of the sophists (*Phae-*

9"The Purveyor of Truth," *Yale French Studies* 52 (1975), 89.

drus 229 c); but he uses myths regularly to illustrate and clarify his notions of the truth.

We may begin to see the outline of an answer to the question implicit in much of this book and formulated explicitly at the beginning of this chapter: Why is it so hard for us to make use of the lethetic mode of reading, even in the case of texts (like the *Birds*) that invite such reading? The core of the answer must be that the disjunction between word and world, even the "forgetting" of reality, that characterizes the lethetic mode has been taken up by Plato and the entire Western tradition up to and including Heidegger in the service of the-truth-that-is-not-reality. The-truth-that-*is*-reality has, of course, been served as long and as well by mimetic literature and by its theorists from Aristotle onward. Poetry that conforms to the world and is credible represents one kind of truth, while poetry that does not so conform represents another. Where are we to fit in a poetry that represents untruth? When confronted with a text that apparently does so, the reader is provided by the orthodox tradition with a procedure for turning disbelief into belief, forgetting into remembering, lethetic into alethetic reading. We must investigate this process further, a process that I will call, in both its particular application and its historical development, the sacralization of fiction.

CHAPTER 10 /

Plato and the
Sacralization of Fiction

THE DISTRUST OF mimetic poetry evidenced by So-
crates in the tenth book of the *Republic* has as its chief target not
poetry as much as imitation—that is, poetry as a species of imitation: "We were entirely right in our organization of the state,
and especially, I think, in the matter of poetry . . . in refusing to
admit at all so much of it as is imitative" (595 a). Such poetry,
insofar as it imitates a reality that is itself no more than an
imitation of the truth, is rejected by the Platonic system but is
reclaimed for othodoxy by Aristotle's contention that poetry is
"more philosophical and serious than history [*philosophoteron kai
spoudaioteron poiesis historias*]" (1451 b). According to Aristotle,
history, and not poetry, imitates reality in its particularity (*ta
kath' hekaston*), whereas poetry abstracts general qualities (*ta ka-
tholou*) from reality and imitates these. As a result poetry is closer
to the truth of "forms" than history and points the way toward a
theory of fiction as a "higher" type of imitation.

A theory of fictions expressing "unreal truth" is easily con-
vertible into a mimetic theory if we espouse the notion of a
"higher form" of mimesis, a "superior realism." Derrida supposes that Lacan is doing just this when the latter says in a note:
"The novel will prove that it can paint something other than
reality . . . , will show that it may be a work of art, completely
composed, of a realism not of little facts and contingent, but

superior."[1] This is, as a historical process, the conversion of Platonism into Aristotelianism, a conversion that Aristotle (probably consciously) initiated in the *Poetics*. For it is quite true that Plato, concerned with the truth-that-is-not-reality, did not find in poetry as imitation the power that he found in poetry as divine madness. It is poetry as imitation, not as divine madness, that is at issue in *Republic* X.

Plato's distrust of poetry-as-imitation is applied to other forms of language that can be interpreted as imitations, the case being made most powerfully against writing as opposed to living speech. This opposition is most forcefully presented in the *Phaedrus* (which in a sense is about nothing as much as that opposition) and is made explicit near the end of the dialogue by Phaedrus, prompted of course by Socrates: "You mean no dead discourse, but the living speech, the original of which the written discourse may fairly be called a kind of image [*ton tou eidotos logon legeis zonta kai empsuchon, hou ho gegrammenos eidolon an ti legoito dikaios*]" (276 a). Writing is the image (*eidolon*) of logos, and as such it cannot provide aletheia but merely doxa (275 a), not wisdom itself but the appearance of wisdom (*sophias doxa*). It is a system of "external marks [*allotrion tupon*]" (275 a) that proposes to provide "a recipe for memory and wisdom [*mnemes te gar kai sophias pharmakom*]" (274 e) but instead "will implant forgetfulness in [men's] souls [*lethen men en psuchais parexei*]" (275 a).

Derrida's essay on Plato's attitude toward writing, "La Pharmacie de Platon," analyzes and deconstructs the opposition between *logos empsuchos*, "living speech," and writing. Derrida finds the crux of the *Phaedrus* in the notion of the pharmakon with which the concept of writing is associated. This association occurs not only in the myth of the origin of writing, in which Theuth calls his invention a pharmakon (274 c ff.), but at several other crucial points as well. I have already mentioned the myth of Orithyia and Pharmacia, which Derrida understands as telling of the destruction of purity and innocence apparently caused by *playing with* "one who administers *pharmaka*." "By her game [*jeu*], Pharmacia has lured toward death a virginal purity

[1]"The Purveyor of Truth," *Yale French Studies* 52 (1975), 88.

and an unbroached interior [*un dedans inentamé*]" (p. 78). The word *entamer* is a key word in the "Pharmacie." Derrida uses it as an equivalent of the Greek *kolapto*, "peck at (as of birds), open up by pecking, broach," and by extension "carve, chisel, inscribe, note down," as Derrida apparently assumes (p. 71). Thus the "unbroached interior" is one that is unwritten upon as well as unopened, unbroken, uncontaminated by exteriority. The game [*jeu*, Greek *paidia*], or "playing," another key concept, is that which leads to the opening up of the virgin interior; it is a pharmakon that can be deadly, that writes upon what was pure and contaminates and kills it. The letter kills.

It also seduces. Only a few lines later, Socrates calls the volumes of speeches that Phaedrus has with him "a recipe [*pharmakon*] for getting me out" (230 d). Derrida writes:

> This *pharmakon*, this "medicine," this philtre, remedy and poison at the same time, already creeps into the discussion [*discours = logos*] with all its ambivalence. This charm, this power [*vertu*] of fascination, this sympathetic magic can be—in turn or at once—beneficent and maleficent. The *pharmakon* would be a *substance*, along with all the word can bring up by way of connotation, an actual stuff possessing occult powers and a hidden depth defying analysis of its ambivalence, already preparing the place of alchemy, if we were not on the verge of recognizing it a bit further on as the antisubstance itself: that which resists all philosophizing, exceeding it indefinitely as nonidentity, nonessence, nonsubstance, and furnishing it in that very way with the inexhaustible adversity of its resources [*fonds*] and its bottomlessness [*absence de fond*]. [Pp. 78–79]

The conversation that makes up the *Phaedrus* is made possible, Socrates has said, by the written word [*logoi en bibliois* = "words in leaves"]: "only hidden letters [*lettres cachées*] could thus get Socrates moving . . . if in the limiting case an undifferentiated/undeferred [*non differé*] logos were possible, it would not seduce" (p. 80). When Derrida says *lettre* he also always means *l'être,* and vice versa, because he sees a metaphor of inscription as central to our traditional notion of "being." "Hidden letters" are also "hidden Being." Since in the Platonic system the truth of forms is "hidden Being," and since we know that it is such truth that motivates Socrates, we can understand how *lettres cachées/ l'être caché* would be enticing.

But this same Socrates who is enticed by written letters is also the voice that opposes writing later in the dialogue. The distrust of writing is, in fact, one of the hallmarks of Plato's writing, a paradox that has long been recognized and puzzled over. The condemnation of writing that is set forth in the *Seventh Letter* (341 b ff.) and in the myth of Theuth in the *Phaedrus* would seem to preclude the very activity of setting forth (in writing) such condemnations. Derrida, however, believes that "this contradiction is not contingent" (p. 182); that the game of writing[2] that indicts both games and writing follows therein a strict necessity; that an image or metaphor of writing must inevitably compose both the core and origin of such a philosophy (for example, *tupos* as "ideal form") and the thing most destructive of that philosophy (for example, *tupos* as "written sign"); and that the pervasiveness of the imagery of the pharmakon that both kills and cures is no casual accident. L'être caché, the true Being that is the arche and telos of the whole metaphysical system, is of necessity both opposed to and indistinguishable from lettres cachées, which can seduce and kill.

The eidos, the true form of things, can only be expressed by figures—that is, the truth reveals itself in the structure of a fiction. What Derrida has shown is that the most characteristic (because most appropriate) figure in Plato's discourse is a metaphor of writing, whose metaphor in turn is the pharmakon. Why? Because no other figure seems to capture so well for Plato the ambivalence and insubstantiality of the *triton ti*, the tertium quid or "third something," that Plato knows to be essential to the structure of his system and to the possibility of any logos.

Although writing is conceived as a supplement and imitation of speech in the *Phaedrus* and other dialogues, we discover that the highest and most successful logos is described by Socrates as a certain sort of writing. What Phaedrus calls *logos empsuchos*, animate speech, Socrates calls "the sort that goes together with knowledge, and is written in the soul of the learner [*hos met'*

---

[2]Plato frequently refers to his dialogues as games, as, for example, in *Parmenides* 137 b, *Politics* 268 d, and *Timaeus* 59 c–d.

epistemes graphetai en tei tou manthanontos psuchei]" (276 a). In other words, putting spirit (psuche) into logos is the same as inscribing logos in the spirit. That which is condemned for being exterior—writing is outside the subject—is resanctified upon becoming once again interior. But this writing upon souls is an image of violence, a forcing of the exterior into the subject that makes the reader, the one written upon, a suffering victim, a ravished Orithyia. Not everyone might wish to submit to having his soul written upon. Kafka has in fact demonstrated in "In the Penal Colony" how horrifying such psychic inscription can become.[3]

The opposition between logos and graphesis is transformed at the end of the *Phaedrus* into an opposition between two kinds of writing. Derrida observes:

> According to a scheme that will dominate all of Western philosophy, a good sort of writing (natural, living, knowing, intelligible, interior, speaking) is opposed to a bad sort (artificial, moribund, ignorant, sensitive/sensible/perceptible, exterior, mute). And the good kind can only be designated by the metaphor of the bad. Metaphoricity is the logic of contamination and the contamination of logic. [P. 172]

The good sort of writing is associated with memory (*mneme*), the bad sort with reminding (*hupomnesis*). Plato believes in the trace left by the soul's vision of the truth before incarnation, a memory of which can be "re-minded" but which nevertheless remains essentially *interior*. It is a kind of writing on the soul, a soul that is like Freud's mystic writing pad in that the traces may disappear from the surface while they remain permanently etched in the wax beneath. Theuth's invention of writing is condemned by Thamus as hupomnesis, a reminder that will bring about the atrophy of true memory. Derrida observes, however, that, because memory is like an organism and is limited like one, it cannot be in itself a perfect presence; it "needs signs to remind it of the nonpresent with which it is necessarily connected. The

---

[3]I discuss this demonstration at length in *"In der Strafkolonie:* Kafka and the Scene of Reading," *German Quarterly* 55 (November 1982), 511–25.

movement of dialectic testifies to it.[4] Memory thus lets itself be contaminated by its first outside, by its first substitute: *hupomnesis*" (p. 124).

The good form of writing, the dialectic that writes upon the soul of the learner, is itself already the movement of exteriority inward (reminding). It is hupomnesis and thus a form of writing. The true logos cannot rid itself of its need for exterior aids: in fact, it consists of nothing but such exterior language itself. Therefore it can only be described by a metaphor of "exterior marks [*allotrion tupon*]" that is itself a kind of "language of the exterior," that is, allegory. Metaphoricity is the contamination of the interior by the exterior by means of "speaking what is other" (*allos* = "other, exterior" and *agoreuein* = "to speak in public"). The truth becomes expressible only in fictions (language that does not conform to reality) *and* only in figures, metaphors, allegories (language that *says* other than what *is*). The language of the truth thus conforms neither to "reality" nor indeed to itself. It is always a language of alterity, of "otherness," of absence. In other words, it is always *écriture* in Derrida's sense.

Derrida's "Pharmacie" demonstrates that this alterity, this absence, is at once the thing the Platonic system most urgently seeks to exclude and that without which it cannot function. "That about which Plato *dreams* is a memory without a sign. That is to say, without supplement. *Mneme* without *hupomnesis*, without *pharmakon*" (p. 124). He dreams also of a memory without myth, and without metaphors as well, which are the linguistic pharmaka most efficacious and most dangerous. But what he *has* is memory that requires reminders, language that requires fiction and figure, because the truth, the fully present eidos, manifests itself only in repetitions, imitations, figures whose presence is the mark of the absence of the eidos. "The disappearance of the truth as presence, the stealing/concealing [*dérobement*] of the present origin of presence is the condition of every (manifestation of) truth. Untruth is truth" (p. 194). Untruth, particularly the untruth of poetry, is precisely the precondition for the

---

[4]Compare *Meno* 81 e ff., in which dialectic serves itself as the method of "reminding" the boy of geometric propositions.

revelation of truth, and every reading must necessarily become, in the root sense, alethetic. Here the deeper connection between my term and Heidegger's aletheia begins to show: Heidegger's conception of truth involves this same precondition of untruth[5] that tends to transform all untruth into the source of truth, at least potentially. Heidegger is still fundamentally a philosopher of *presence*, who finds the element of absence in every present truth "curious" and paradoxical but by no means an aporia leading to a radical questioning of the presence/absence opposition. He explicitly states what Plato implicitly requires, but he does not depart from the basic orthodoxy.

The philosophical enterprise in general, Derrida and perhaps Nietzsche set aside, assumes presence as the highest value and dreams of a language of presence uncontaminated by exteriority and alterity, a language that is of course precluded by the very nature of language. Presence is truth (as well as beauty and goodness) for Plato and his posterity, so that language that seems more present is assumed to be more truthful and thus also more powerful. It is for this reason (as Derrida analyzes the situation) that the philosophy of language we find in Plato, Rousseau, and Saussure is logocentric and indeed phonocentric. It values the spoken over the written word. For Plato, the presence embodied in living speech is expressed by a family image: the speaker is the father, his speech the son. The father is present to defend the child, who is himself not strong enough, not flexible enough, to defend himself. The written word is an orphan whose father is absent, who cannot alter as circumstances change and who cannot act in self-defense. Socrates makes such an analogy, which is itself a logomimesis on the Greek locution *pater logou* ("father of the word" = "speaker"), as part of an explanation and defense of the rejection of writing by Thamus in the myth. Written words, Socrates says,

> seem to talk to you as though they were intelligent, but if you ask them anything about what they say, from a desire to be instructed, they go on telling you just the same thing forever. And once a thing is put in writing, the composition, whatever it may be, drifts

[5]Heidegger says that truth "always withholds itself at the same time in a concealedness."

all over the place, getting into the hands not only of those who understand it, but equally of those who have no business with it; it doesn't know how to address the right people, and not address the wrong. And when it is ill-treated and unfairly abused it always needs its parent to come to its help, being unable to defend or help itself. [275 d–e]

Derrida observes that this imagery "is doubtless explained by the fact that writing is a written discourse (*logos gegrammenos*). As a living thing, the logos is the issue of a father. For Plato, then, there is no written thing. There is a *logos* more or less living, more or less close to itself. Writing is not an independent order of signification, it is a weakened speech" (p. 165). Strong speech, powerful speech, is characterized by a high level of presence, conceived here as the presence of the speaker and father of the words. *The central problem of writing for Plato is the absence of the author.* It is not a problem that can be solved completely, but two strategies for coping with it are proposed in the dialogues. One is to make the reader responsible for the paternal care of the written logos, since the reader is present when the author is absent; the other is to make the absence of the author part of the (fictional) structure of the logos itself. The dialogues are a kind of inter vivos trust, in which the author at the time of writing pretends he is already dead, already absent, and makes a pact with the reader to care for the orphaned logos. I will examine both of these strategies in detail.

One form of writing can survive the absence of its true parent, that which is "written on the soul of the learner." This sort of writing, Socrates argues, "can defend itself, and knows to whom it should speak and to whom it should say nothing [*dunatos men amunai heautoi, epistemon de legein te kai sigan pros hous dei*]" (276 a). While this is advanced not as a description of actual writing but as a metaphor of "living speech," it proposes a transfer of responsibility from speaker to listener, from teacher to learner. What is meant, of course, is not that the words themselves will magically acquire the power to defend themselves in the absence of the father but that the "learner" upon whose soul the words are written will become their stepfather. He who receives the words given him with due regard will make them part of his own psyche, where they will stand engraved like hieroglyphics. *He* will know when to speak and when to keep silent, will know to whom he should pass on the orphaned word and to whom he should say nothing. Furthermore, he will be able to defend and amend the word as the situation demands. He will act, in short, in loco parentis on behalf of the absent father/speaker/writer.

Plato's imagery for this situation, though, does not extend the family metaphor, as I have, but essentially abbreviates a metaphor of writing. The reader becomes not a reader, but the surface on which writing takes place. Here again we see the attempt to circumvent the problem of absence, this time the absence of the reader at the time of writing. What is *present* at the time of writing is the writing surface itself, and a reader who could somehow be like a writing surface could in effect become present at the scene of writing, could overcome the distance between the self and the writer that the text itself represents. The task of reading, of all hermeneutics, becomes the effacement of the distance between author and reader by making the reader one with the text. This is the goal of philosophical discourse, in Plato's view, and the only way one can hope to overcome (or at least to ameliorate) the problem of absence that writing represents.

The strategy, we must note well, is to make the reader one with the text, *not* to make the author one with it. Socrates wants readers ("learners") who are texts, but he does not wish himself to become one. In fact, making the author one with the text is an effective way to neutralize the author's writing. That is precisely what Socrates does to Lysias in the course of the *Phaedrus*. We should recall that the dialogue itself is a scene of reading in which Phaedrus, who has a text of one of Lysias's speeches with him, reads it to Socrates and then discusses it with him. The whole of the *Phaedrus* can be understood as the "reading" (that is, reading out loud plus discussion) of Lysias's text. It is only at Socrates' insistence, however, that the reading out loud takes place. Phaedrus is prepared to act as Lysias's writing surface and the foster parent of his logos, but Socrates prevents him:

Phaedrus. Then here is what I will do. It really is perfectly true, Socrates, that I have not got the words by heart, but I will sketch

the general purport of the several points in which the lover and
the nonlover were contrasted, taking them in order one by one,
and beginning at the beginning.

Socrates. Very well, my dear fellow, but you must first show me what
it is that you have in your left hand under your cloak, for I surmise
that it is the actual discourse [*ton logon auton*]. If that is so, let me
assure you of this, that much as I love you I am not altogether
inclined to let you practice your oratory on me when Lysias himself
is here present. Come now, show it to me. [228 d–e]

It is revealing that Socrates calls a piece of writing "the actual
discourse." Derrida describes this as one of the clearest examples
of the indistinguishability of logos and gegrammenos in a dialogue that insists upon such a distinction. But we may also
understand this as an effective strategy on Socrates' part for
rendering Lysias's speech defenseless. By pretending that having the text is equivalent to having Lysias himself, he separates
Phaedrus from the speech and from any obligation he may feel
toward it. If Phaedrus had done as he intended, given his own
version of the argument, he would have felt personally involved
with it and obligated to defend it. But as matters stand, the text
being Lysias himself, Phaedrus can stand apart from it and can
let Lysias—who is in fact far away and unable to participate—
defend himself. When Socrates afterward attacks the speech, it
is in precisely the position outlined by Socrates in his gloss on the
myth of the invention of writing: it maintains "a most majestic
silence" and is "unable to help or defend itself" (275 d–e). And
that, of course, is exactly the position Socrates wants it to take.

But Socrates is also careful not to let himself be placed in such
a position: in fact, he denies authorship of both the speeches he
makes on the subject of love. The first of these he regrets having
made and calls it "that discourse of yours which you caused my
lips to utter by putting a spell on them [*kaktapharmakeuthentos*]"
(242 d–e), and he introduces the second by assuring the fictional
beloved that "whereas the preceding discourse was by Phaedrus,
son of Pythocles, of Myrrhinus, that which I shall now pro-
nounce is by Stesichorus, son of Euphemus, of Himera" (243
e–244 a). He assumes the identity of Stesichorus ostensibly because the latter had written a poem recanting his "defamation"
of Helen, just as Socrates now recants his defamation of love.

But the fictional persona is primarily a way of keeping Socrates separate from his logos so that he may criticize it (as he does the first speech) or praise it (as he does the second) as if he were absent. Speech making, just as much as speech writing, is a form of fixed and therefore "weakened" utterance of which Socrates disapproves, though he engages in it from time to time. But when he does engage in it here in the *Phaedrus*, he protects himself against a logos alienated from its father by denying paternity. This is the second of Plato's two strategies for dealing with the absence of the author.

The obvious but insufficiently regarded fact is that Plato does the same thing in his own writing. Plato never says anything in the dialogues, never appears *in propria persona*, never lends the authority of the author to anything inscribed for posterity. One exception might be the *Seventh Letter*. (The authorship of all the *Letters* is doubtful, but the seventh is generally regarded as genuine.) But the *Seventh Letter* says precisely that philosophical writing of any kind can have no authority:

> I certainly have composed no work in regard to [the subjects to which I devote myself], nor shall I ever do so in the future, for there is no way of putting it in words like other studies. Acquaintance with it must come rather after a long period of attendance on instruction in the subject itself and of close companionship, when, suddenly, like a blaze kindled by a leaping spark, it is generated in the soul and at once becomes self-sustaining. [341 c–d]

The *Letters* are the only Platonic words that Plato ascribes to himself. "The most philosophically significant passage in all the *Letters*, however," as Herman Sinaiko notes,

> is precisely the so-called digression in the *Seventh Letter* from which the quoted statement is taken. That is to say, in the one piece of writing generally accepted as authentic in which Plato speaks directly to his readers he explicitly denies that he has ever written his philosophy or ever shall. The historical Socrates could not have been more ironical.[6]

---

[6]*Love, Knowledge, and Discourse in Plato: Dialogue and Dialectic in "Phaedrus," "Republic," "Parmenides"* (Chicago: University of Chicago Press, 1965), 289, n. 3. Cited henceforth in the text.

Sinaiko's *Love, Knowledge, and Discourse in Plato* tries to deal head-on with this fact, this apparent contradiction, in terms rather different from Derrida's. Whereas Derrida has shown why the prime value placed on presence makes the absence of the "father of the speech" a problem, Sinaiko demonstrates how Plato reacts to that problem and turns it into a strategy for using writing in philosophical activity without "writing philosophy." Plato writes *and* does not write. Derrida shows why Plato was suspicious of *and* devoted to writing, why Plato had no alternative but to make himself fictionally as well as actually absent; Sinaiko shows how Plato uses the dialogue form as a way to transfer responsibility for the logos from the absent writer to the present reader, to make that reader the stepfather the orphaned word must have. Derrida's "Pharmacie" gives the etiology of the apparent paradox represented by the condemnation of philosophical writing in the *Seventh Letter*. Sinaiko's *Love, Knowledge, and Discourse* takes that paradox as its starting point and shows how the dialogue form is a response to it.

Sinaiko argues that the dialogues themselves represent the "good" kind of writing that Socrates mentions near the end of the *Phaedrus:* "For like a living person, the dialogues 'know when to be silent' and 'when to speak'" (p. 15). The dramatic structure is calculated to engage the reader in the issues with which the text is concerned, to then interrogate it for answers, "and the dialogues *may* answer him; for there are answers to these questions in the dialogues, although the reader must find them the hard way by exercising his own creative intelligence" (p. 16). The reader may not rely on the author to give him the truth or even a procedure by which to calculate the truth: *there is no author;* he is even more absent fictionally than actually. The reader is faced with a choice of either dismissing the dialogues completely or taking responsibility for their logos himself. Sinaiko stresses again and again this responsibility of the reader: "The reader must [see the dialogues as coherent] himself. . . . each dialogue is an invitation to the reader to enter into a dialectical discussion of sorts with the dialogue itself" (pp. 287–88). As such it is also an invitation for the reader to disbelieve a great deal of what is said, by Socrates as well as by others: "Admittedly, Socrates' arguments are more often fallacious than not, his tactics are frequently unfair, he repeatedly contradicts himself, and he sometimes seems more interested in confusing an issue than clarifying it. The reader must realize, however, that he is not the object of Socrates' wiles. . . . the reader must, as I stated earlier, view the dialogues as dramas" (p. 16). In short, Sinaiko recommends that we read the dialogues as alethetic fictions.

What we have learned from Derrida and Sinaiko is that Plato had no alternative, either intellectually or practically, but to use structures of fiction to point the way toward a truth that is by its very definition always absent. Plato turns what Derrida sees as an aporia into what Sinaiko understands as an effective rhetoric by a gesture of escape, a self-dérobement that effectively allows authors to take themselves out of what they know to be a very chancy game. Since they cannot, as writers, be present to do their paternal duty toward the logos they engender, they efface themselves utterly from the scene by creating a fictional structure in which they do not exist. But since no logos can hope to prosper without someone to care for it, the absent parent must arrange for the adoption of the orphan by a foster parent who is present. There is no choice but to enlist the reader, the only living presence at the scene of reading, as trustee. Readers (as long as they consent to remain readers) are seduced and ensorcelled (*katapharmakeuthentos*] by the same pharmakon of language that makes all this indirection necessary, and they take on the trusteeship not entirely consciously and perhaps not altogether willingly.

But they take it on, and it is a sacred trust. What is at stake is not simply the logos that stands before us in the text, but the divine truth that it ambivalently and imperfectly represents. And it is up to the reader to understand how to discover the connection (logos) between a text that looks unconnected (alogos) and that sacred truth. As Sinaiko understands Plato's position, the expression in language, particularly written language, of coherence, "connectedness" (that is, logos) must inevitably be accomplished in structures that are, one way or another, alogos. Plato does the reader the service of foregrounding these aloga so that the reader realizes the need to confront and wrestle with them: neither Plato nor any other author can assume that responsibility. In other words, Sinaiko understands Plato to be contriving an exercise in Heideggerian aletheia, a bringing-out-of-concealment, a bringing-out-of-untruth. The gesture that begins in Plato, in the words of the dialogues, as the banishment of the alogos ends up, in the dialogue form itself, as its embrace.

The sacralization of fiction is therefore also the sacralization of the alogos, for it is from this (written) alogos that the reader catches the spark, according to Sinaiko, that kindles the (living) logos in the soul. This living logos can be the means by which the reader comes in contact with the divine. We return, in a sense, to the image of the magnet that Socrates introduces in the *Ion,* through which the divine power is transferred along a chain of "rings" from that which is closest to the source of power—the gods themselves—to an audience that is many removes distant. In the same way the power that ultimately resides in the truth, the eidos, the "one," is transferred in weakened form to the reader of fictions through a chain of language that *is* a species of the alogos but *stands for* the ideal logos, though it may contain only the dimmest spark of that ultimate perfection. The present poet stands for the absent god and has been granted a tiny portion of his power; the present alogos stands for the absent logos; the present reader stands for the absent author; the present beloved stands for the absent idea of beauty. Lyric poetry, oracles, philosophical dialogues, dialectic, and love: all are examples of a transfer of power from the divine realm to the human, from the sun that is too strong for us to look upon to the shadows we may perceive with impunity.

Let me briefly recapitulate. I have argued for the possibility of an apistic (that is, disbelieving) mode of reading that ignores the relation between the word and the world and adverts instead to the power of the word. This is the lethetic mode, and I have demonstrated how it functions in works of ancient and modern literature. But another apistic mode reverses the priorities and values the world above the word, values especially the *connection* between the two that the lethetic mode disregards. Such alethetic fictions, an example of which I have discussed in Lucian's *True History,* present themselves as pharmaka having the power to be both themselves and something else at the same time. Both

Lucian and Plato understand fiction to be such a pharmakon, but for Plato *all language* is such a pharmakon. Since Plato assumes that reality itself is only a shadow of the truth, to be distinguished from it and indeed opposed to it, it follows that truth must take on a structure that is unreal, that is, a fiction. Unconnectedness with the world of reality—one of the chief features of lethetic fictions—is assumed by Plato and the tradition that he initiates to be a characteristic of the truth. Thus, the behavior that sets a man apart from the world of reality—madness—is for Plato a sign of a man's participation in some form of contact with the unreal realm of truth. The mania of the poet, lover, and philosopher is to be understood in this way, as a mark of the presence of divine power. The same is true of incredible speech: language that does not conform to reality and is therefore unbelievable is precisely the language most likely to have some touch of the divine spark. Furthermore, Plato's system of presence and absence, his theory of the always-absent eidos, makes it inevitable that truth and untruth be forever commingled, forever contaminated by each other: metaphoricity is the logic of contamination and the contamination of logic. Plato finds that he has no way to express himself but in the language of fiction, no way to indicate the logos save through the alogos, no way to make his word present save by making himself absent and leaving to the reader the responsibility for discovering "connectedness." Untruth has been mobilized as the prime weapon in the army of Truth.

Untruth has been given a sacred mission and has been touched by the divine spark. Already in Plato's dialogues we have the complete sacralization of fiction, untruth, the alogos, but not, we must be sure to note, of *all* such fiction. To the degree that poetry attempts to conform with reality it is not sacred and has no place in the well-ordered state. Nor is every myth, or every reading of myth, touched by the power of the divine lodestone. Socrates is prepared to "say good-bye" to the making and interpreting of myths to the degree that these activities are not part of an earnest inquiry into the truth. When they do play a role in that inquiry, Socrates welcomes and makes extensive use of them. Sinaiko makes just such a distinction: "A careful reading of Socrates' remark [about the myth of Orithyia] will show that he is not objecting to the making or the interpreting of myths as such; he is only rejecting these activities to the extent that they interfere with his primary obligation" (p. 13). But when they assist Socrates to meet his obligation, they, too, become part of the sacred chain of power.

It is clear, then, that the virtue of a text or a speech or a dialogue or a myth does not so much reside within it as let itself be impressed by an external agency. In other words, the pharmakon of logos (écriture, in Derrida's terms), is exactly like the triton ti discussed in the *Timaeus* in a passage that Derrida calls "going beyond all the oppositions of 'Platonism,' toward the aporia of originary inscription" (p. 185):

> For the present we have only to conceive of three natures: first, that which is in process of generation; secondly, that in which the generation takes place; and thirdly, that of which the thing generated is a resemblance naturally produced. And we may liken the receiving principle to the mother, and the source or spring to a father, and the intermediate nature to a child, and may remark further that if the model is to take every variety of form, then the matter in which the model is fashioned will not be duly prepared unless it is formless and free from the impression of those shapes which it is hereafter to receive from without. [50 c–d]

The mother, the *matrix*, is referred to as "the natural recipient of all impressions," an *ekmageion*. She carries the impress of the father that generates the imitation which is the child. She is herself without form and can receive form only from an external source, which is the father but is also (because it imitates and copies the father) the child. If we conceive of readers as surfaces for inscription, they too become such recipients of impression and are expected to efface themselves in favor of the paternal form. This is the metaphor made the object of logomimesis in "In the Penal Colony." If the readers take on the duties of foster fathers of a text, they take on also responsibility for placing the paternal impression upon it. In a sense, then, readers as stepfathers are in a position to write the text they read, to be both father and child to the text matrix placed in their care, *so long as they write in a manner that conforms to the paternal model.*

Though Socrates, the Socrates of the *Phaedrus* at any rate, would like a reader who would act as an ekmageion, a thing written upon, it is clear from Derrida's and Sinaiko's analyses that such a reader is only a dream of presence that cannot be realized. The only effective, practical strategy left open for dealing with the distance between author and reader is to make the text a matrix and the reader a foster parent. In order to exert influence on the reader by means of the text, the author must yield some authority to the reader. As part of this strategy authors efface themselves, deny their paternity by fictionally removing themselves from the scene of writing. In Plato's theater, the name of Plato never appears on the list of the cast of characters. It is expected that this vacuum of authority will be filled by the reader on the author's behalf.

Why should readers assent to the trusteeship that is thus thrust upon them? One reason is suggested by Sinaiko's observation that "Plato, through his use of the dialogue form, invites the reader to ask questions and to look and listen for answers, invites him to participate in a dialogue in which Plato's own writings play the role Socrates plays within the dramatic world of the dialogues" (p. 16). Just as Socrates forever professes his ignorance and asks more questions than he gives answers, so, too, do the dialogues themselves severely limit their own authority. They, too, ask questions that they do not answer—not explicitly at least—and perform an ironic gesture of self-deprecation. A text possessing the appearance of self-sufficiency would be useless in Plato's enterprise, since that self-sufficiency would keep the reader out. What "invites the reader in," what engages the reader, are the text's evident insufficiencies—those illogical arguments, self-contradictions, and confusions of which Sinaiko speaks. Led to think that this text, poor flawed thing that it is, needs help, the reader volunteers for the position of foster parent.

The author, having contrived this well-meaning deception, this snare for the reader, is gone. And if we discover the insufficiencies of the text, we may not ascribe them to its author; we may not do so, even if we suspect that some of them are not deliberate. It is Socrates who is illogical, Socrates who contradicts himself, Socrates who is confusing. The writer we know as Plato has said nothing. Everyone remembers the scene from the *Odys-*

sey, Book IX, in which Odysseus is trapped by the Cyclops in his cave. The monster promises to give Odysseus a gift in return for the name of his unwilling guest, and the wily hero answers, not with his true name of *Odusseus*, but with a pun on the first two syllables of that name, *Oudeis*, "Nobody." When the band of Greeks manages to blind Polyphemus with a hot stake, the Cyclops calls to his neighbors, who gather outside his cave inquiring who it is that is hurting him. "My friends," he says, "it is the treachery of Nobody." So the other Cyclops go home, and the Achaeans are saved. Only when he is safely out to sea in his ship does Odysseus reveal his true name.

Plato, too, is trapped in a cave and forced to do something for which he does not want to take responsibility: he must write. He must make do with the tools available to him, and in that particular cave are only shadows, images, imitations, simulacra, the very things he wishes to discredit and destroy. How can the advocate of truth take up untruth as his sole weapon? But how, under the circumstances, can he do anything else? He must do it *and* not do it, write *and* not write, ascribe his writings to an Oudeis, a fictional Socrates and other fictional Athenians, none of whom is equivalent to Plato. Only in this way is there any hope for escape from the cave in which he sits, wondering if he is not himself Polyphemus, "the one who speaks many things, the many-voiced, abounding in songs and legends." But as a writer he may remain Oudeis until the book is complete, until the reader is safely distant, when he may put his real name on the *outside*. The voice of the *polutropos* can be heard from far away, acknowledging, "It was I, Plato, who made you blind from looking at the sun."

The sacred character of the task in which Plato enlists the aid of untruth has the effect of making it, too, sacred, in spite of the fact that the task's goal is the suppression and exclusion of that very untruth. It is the same contradictory process as that by which the knight's sword is Christianized and is actually rendered equivalent to a crucifix, a holy symbol of an ethic that seeks the exclusion of swords. The truth is holy. It is the very thing "nearness to which makes a god divine." It is the source of all divinity, and poetry, insofar as it is not simply an imitation of "reality," has been touched by the power emanating from this

ORIGINS OF ALETHETIC READING

source. The view of poetry put forth in the *Ion* is not really contradictory to that of the *Republic;* it has, rather, two different objects in the two dialogues. Poetry that merely imitates reality is condemned, while poetry through which divinity transmits its power is praised. It is quite in keeping with Plato's position on language in general that he should find both of these at once in Homer, for example. Homeric poetry is the same pharmakon that all language is, different only in that it is more extreme in the limits of its good and evil. It is *more* harmful than ordinary language in its capacity as imitation, because it imitates so well; and it is *more* direct and overpowering in its transmission of divine power, because the divine, the Muse, takes direct possession of the poet (something that does not happen so readily to the philosopher, whose nous is functioning). Poetry is "authentic language," for Plato as for Heidegger, the pure and undiluted form of this most potent elixir. Its power makes it dangerous and holy.

The Platonic strategy, particularly as Herman Sinaiko understands it, puts the potent pharmakon of fictional language in the care of the reader, who is then charged with the responsibility of making it holy and healing rather than poisoning and profane. The *pharmakeus,* the sorcerer, puts the magic bottle in the hands of the apprentice, pulls the cork, and disappears. The individual holding the bottle must decide what to do with the genie that emerges. The choices the pharmakeus has offered are few: the genie will do either great good (lead toward the truth) or great evil (lead us away from the truth) but will not tamely go back in the bottle. Given the irremediable absence of the pharmakeus, it is no surprise that the apprentice attempts to turn the acquired power toward the search for truth—in spite, even because, of disbelief in genies.

Plato makes possible and indeed necessary the conversion of disbelief into belief. There is only one value: truth. There is only one way to get there: untruth. Disbelief and untruth are thus essential tools in the search for the truth and the attainment of belief. All reading *must* be alethetic reading, must disbelieve the visible shadow in the quest for the invisible source, reject the present save as trace of the absent. Hermeneutics *must* seek to discover the characteristics of the absent through the minute examination of the present and must thereby somehow bring the absent closer. Lethetic reading, which is prepared to let the absent stay absent, is utterly excluded by such a system of imperatives, in which even the alogos can be seen as "connected" to the realm of ideal forms.

The sacralization of fiction thus set in motion continues to the point at which the alogos seems to cease to exist. Derrida understands this to happen when the opposition between seriousness (*spoude*) and play (*paidia*) follows the same pattern as that between logos and graphesis. Just as Plato makes writing a "weakened" form of logos, so does he suggest play as a special way of being serious. Two kinds of play seem to be implied, a genuine playful play and a serious variety, the *ernsthafte Witze* of which Goethe spoke. "The opposition *spoude/paidia* can never be regarded as a simple symmetry," Derrida explains.

> *Either* play is *nothing* (that's its only *chance*), can give rise to no activity, to no discourse worthy of the name, that is to say charged with truth or at least with sense. It is then *alogos* or *atopos*. *Or* play begins to *be* something, and its presence even provides a handle for a certain metaphysical confiscation. It takes on sense and works in the service of the serious, of truth, of ontology. Only the *logoi peri onton* can be taken seriously. To the degree that it comes to Being and to language, play effaces itself as such. [Pp. 180–81]

In other words, the alogos/atopos, the essential element not only of the literary marvelous and of lethetic fictions but of play itself, is excluded from the notion of play "in the better sense of the word." This "better sense," as Derrida reads the Platonic system, "is play supervised and contained by the guardrail of ethics and politics. It is play understood under the innocent and inoffensive category of the *amusing*" (p. 180).

By banishing the alogos/atopos or (what amounts to the same thing) by coopting it in the service of the sacred quest for the truth, Plato convenes the solemn conclave of Western literary theory. We may have our games and our jokes, our Witze, but only if they are ernsthaft. Anything else is condemned with the abusive term, "escapism." This escapism is the freedom of play granted to *readers*. The tradition is perfectly willing to let *writers* escape (as Plato himself did), to be playful and even irresponsible in their fictions. But it will not let readers escape, or if they do it makes them feel guilty and sinful, because then the hope for the discovery of truth must end. The fiction remains fiction, the absent remains absent, the play has been nothing. Plato has taught that the writer must be free to play, to use the aloga and atopiai forbidden to readers, because there is no alternative *for a writer*. But readers do not have to write, and the obligation that must necessarily be lifted from the author is set firmly on the shoulders of the reader. That obligation can become a substantial burden to one group of readers in particular, the readers-who-must-write, the professional readers, the literary critics. When critics begin to claim for themselves the same privileges granted to other writers, as Plato granted them to himself, orthodoxy recoils with shock. The strength of the tradition that authorizes the sacralization of fiction continues unabated.

Plato represents one of the formative impulses behind this sacralization, but there are others. When the West became Christendom, it added to its Greco-Roman heritage a set of cultural values firmly grounded on the sacred obligation of reading, the bibliocentrism of postexilic Judaism. The divinity of the Torah that was established by Ezra and his group was broadened to include the more recent revelations of the prophets and then of the New Testament and became one of the enduring characteristics of the Christian conception of the Bible. Christianity never became as bibliocentric as the Judaism of Mishna and Talmud, but the idea of a sacred text, of a word revealed by God, was nearly as important as the idea of an incarnation in human flesh of perfect divinity. In a very real sense, God first "became" the Word, the holy text that not only set forth the law but prophesied about the reestablishment of good relations between the Lord and his people; then that Word became flesh, particularly to the degree that Jesus' life story follows and fulfills various statements of Scripture. The central and sacred position of the text was maintained even by a Christianity that held in contempt the Scribes (*Soferim* = "men of the book") who looked to the keeping of the Torah. The Bible becomes the perfect embodiment of the trace of the absent Father.

The transfer of responsibility from author to reader that Plato's conception of language requires becomes more complete—indeed absolute—with regard to the postexilic Torah. The proper service of divinity becomes indistinguishable from the interpretation of Scripture. "For Ezra had set his heart to seek the law of the Lord, and to do it, and to teach in Israel statutes and ordinances" (*Ezra* 7.10). Morris Adler notes:

> In this verse from Ezra, the Hebrew word here translated as "to seek" is "lidrosh" which may also be rendered "to interpret." It suggests the method by which the Torah was made to be a functioning force relevant and applicable in the midst of the changes to which men are subject. The Torah was enlarged by interpretation, and the Hebrew word for this process is derived from the root Ezra employed. The process is "Midrash"—interpretation.[7]

The activity represented by the Hebrew root *darash,* the "seeking, inquiring, interrogating" of the text, gives rise to the necessary supplement of the Oral to the Written Law. "The view that along with the revelation of the Written Torah was a revelation of an Oral Torah," writes Judah Goldin, "that is, that interpretations and deductions from the Scriptures must have accompanied the Scriptures themselves, has at least this to recommend it: no written text, particularly if it is meant as a guide for conduct, can in and of itself be complete; it must have some form of oral commentary associated with it."[8] The unavoidable incompleteness of the text, even of the Divine Text, requires that God intervene a second time and inspire the reading as well as the writing of his Word. Thus the ancient Jewish tradition of the divine authority of the Oral Torah repeats precisely the gesture figured by Plato's familial image: the readers take on the role of foster father (with the Father's assistance) and in an important way help to write the text as they read.

But the obligation to read and to write-in-reading by way of supplementing what is read is also an obligation to obey the Father. The book that is the way to the truth must be read with a

[7]*The World of the Talmud* (Washington: B'nai B'rith Hillel Foundation, 1959), 24.

[8]*The Living Talmud* (New York: New American Library, 1957), 22.

heart submissive to the authority that stands behind its words. Right reading means for Plato a reading that helps the text conform to the truth, for Judaism a reading that conforms to the will of God. In short, we must already know what we seek if we are to seek it properly and successfully. The reader unable to count on some outside assistance will be forever caught in the "hermeneutic circle" of needing to know what he seeks to learn in order to be able to learn it. That assistance is provided either by Judaism's faith in God's inspiration of the Oral Law or by Plato's assumption of an inherent "memory" of truth in every human soul. Bad reading results when the reader fails to obey the promptings of God or of the soul's natural affinity for truth, when the reader therefore "forgets." Readers must not examine the book simply as language, as "dead letters" that may in turn kill them, but as a container for a divine spirit that "giveth life." If they suppose that language's power resides in language itself rather than in the absent thing or Being whose traces it is assumed to be, they become disobedient readers.

The institution of a divinely authored Scripture eliminates the difficulties of writing as Plato saw them, since such Holy Writ is in fact closer to ultimate perfection than the spoken word. But both Platonic and Jewish traditions agree on the transfer of responsibility from absent author to present reader, while at the same time retaining authority as the sole prerogative of the writer. The reader has all the responsibility but no authority. This is the pathos, and the power, of alethetic reading, for it gives into the reader's care something infinitely valuable if also infinitely difficult and unyielding of certainty. We are issued an invitation to find God or the truth hidden inside the most unpromising discourse, an invitation that appears to render all texts potentially divine. What it really does, of course, is to transfer value away from texts to the truth or divinity that is alleged to stand behind them. Still, the invitation is hard to resist, even if the text before us makes every effort to encourage us in another direction. The love of words, the "pleasure of the text," seems a small thing beside the love of God and the discovery of the truth. Lethetic reading, which is content to let the word go its own way and to delight in it, even to hurry it along as the Deaf One does the moon, will probably always appear less grand than alethetic reading. The sacralization of fiction remains a powerful and long-lived trend, and lethetic reading goes against it. Under such circumstances it is little wonder that the lethetic genre has existed only as a subversive tendency within the orthodoxy of alethetic reading.

Part Five /

CONCLUSION

CHAPTER 11 /

The Place of Lethetic Reading

> "That's the most important piece of evidence we've heard yet," said the King, rubbing his hands; "so now let the jury—"
>
> "If any one of them can explain it," said Alice, (she had grown so large in the last few minutes that she wasn't a bit afraid of interrupting him), "I'll give him sixpence. I don't believe there's an atom of meaning in it."
>
> The jury wrote down on the slates, "*She* doesn't believe there's an atom of meaning in it," but none of them attempted to explain the paper.   "If there's no meaning in it," said the King "that saves a world of trouble, you know, as we needn't try to find any."
>
> —*Alice in Wonderland* (chapter 12)

ALICE DOES NOT believe that the text in question (the White Rabbit's study in ambiguous antecedents, "She told me you had been to her / And mentioned me to him" and so forth) conveys any meaning. The King, however, despite his remark about the trouble that would be spared by such an assumption, is not really willing to give up the search: " 'And yet I don't know,' he went on, spreading out the verses on his knee, and looking at them with one eye; 'I seem to see some meaning in them after all.' " And indeed he tries to find something in the nonsense verses that applies to the matter at hand, which is

Alice's trial. Alice, however, plays the ultimate trump card in this particular game by withdrawing her belief, not just from the White Rabbit's confusing verses, but from the entire basis of the fiction: "Who cares for *you?*' said Alice (she had grown to her full size by this time). 'You're nothing but a pack of cards!'" And with that, the world of Wonderland shatters and the dream ends. Whatever form our text may take, if we cease to believe that there is any meaning in it, the text becomes nothing but a set of physical objects, and reading ceases.

We may, however, withdraw our belief less radically, in such a way as to allow reading to take place but at the same time to save ourselves that "world of trouble." This is the strategy of lethetic reading, which does not go as far as to deny that a text has "meaning" but denies that its "meaning" could consist of a correspondence between its statements and actual states of affairs in the world. If we are willing to accept such a distinction between "meaning" and "truth"—and philosophers of language are agreed that we must accept it—then there is no reason why untrue texts should not be meaningful and readable. The question is: What would the "meaning" of an untrue text consist of?

One interesting and useful answer has been given by Stanley Fish in his essay of 1970, "Literature in the Reader: Affective Stylistics."[1] Fish develops a method for the analysis of texts based upon what he calls the "simple" concept implied by "the rigorous and disinterested asking of the question, what does this word, phrase, sentence, paragraph, chapter, novel, play, poem, *do?* (p. 73). I am not so much interested in Fish's particular method of analysis as in the implications of the question he asks. If the crucial question to be asked of a text concerns what it does, then that action becomes in a real and important sense its *meaning.* For Fish, as for Wolfgang Iser and others who follow his phenomenological view of literature, that action is above all an experience. "The meaning of an utterance . . . is its experience—all of it" (p. 98).

While I do not share the view that the posing of the question "What does this text do?" necessarily implies that the reader's

---

[1] I will cite this essay, in the text, from Jane P. Tompkins, ed., *Reader-Response Criticism* (Baltimore: Johns Hopkins University Press, 1980).

experience must constitute its entire meaning, I am in general agreement with the basic thrust of Fish's inquiry in "Affective Stylistics"—as Fish himself may no longer be.[2] In any case, if we take the question "What does this text mean?" to be answerable by an investigation of what the text does, we will be able to agree with both Alice and the King, to accept the White Rabbit's verses as nonsense and to "see some meaning in them after all." As Fish very correctly observes, "Another advantage of the method [based on the question of what a text does] is its ability to deal with sentences (and works) that don't mean anything, in the sense of not making sense" (p. 81). The Rabbit's poem is certainly "meaningless" by such a definition, for it not only contains an assortment of pronouns referring to persons and objects unidentified anywhere in the poem, but it also follows no observable principle of consequence (for example, "She gave me a good character, / But said I could not swim"). It is also "meaningless" from the standpoint of the issue at hand, Alice's trial. The King would like to use the classic hermeneutic strategy of *applicatio* by identifying the antecedents of various pronouns with various persons in the case ("*'We know it to be true—'* that's the jury, of course—*'If she should push the matter on'*—that must be the Queen—" and so on). But Alice's objection holds up best against just this sort of arbitrary message hunting: there's no "meaning" of this kind in the Rabbit's poem. "Perhaps," Fish suggests, ". . . the word 'meaning' should also be discarded, since it carries with it the notion of message or point" (p. 98).

But from the point of view offered by Fish's key question, even the White Rabbit's nonsense verses become readable. The confusion created by the pronouns without antecedents and the non sequiturs is surely exactly what Carroll wished to create. And this confusion is akin to a confusion which will not be unknown to most of Carroll's readers. The poem is presented in the mode of *gossip,* and the reader, while reading it, feels precisely the perplexity that he or she might experience while overhearing some gossip about unfamiliar people and circum-

[2]Compare his essay on the Milton *Variorum* cited below. In a paper delivered at the Modern Language Association meeting in 1981, Fish seemed to be withdrawing (or progressing) further from the position offered in "Affective Stylistics."

stances. The poem is an imitation of a certain form of linguistic behavior and—more important—is the occasion for a certain form of hermeneutic behavior typical of listeners in such situations. We want to ask "Who is he (or she) talking about?" and "What could all this be referring to?" That it refers to nothing detracts not one whit from its effectiveness. I certainly do not say that the White Rabbit's poem is "about" gossip or even "about" interpreting confusing texts. I mean only that it successfully *does* something, something that is quite different from "telling the truth" or "delivering a message."

Lethetic fictions operate in two ways—the two ways identified by J. L. Austin in his famous lectures.[3] Their illocutionary force (that is, what they do *in* the act of uttering them) is a special one, in fact the very one identified in Chapter 2. We have no name for the special action performed by lethetic fictions, as we do for example for "lying," so we are reduced to calling the action "uttering-a-lethetic-fiction." That will be good enough as long as we realize that the circumlocution is only necessary because the action referred to is not considered one encountered frequently in everyday discourse. In a very real sense, the major purpose of this book has been to identify and illustrate the illocutionary act of uttering-a-lethetic-fiction.

Lethetic fictions, like other utterances, also have perlocutionary effects; that is, they do something *by* (as a result of) being uttered/written/read. Typically, lethetic fictions have the perlocutionary effects of amusing and frightening, as I argued in detail in Chapter 6. Many other perlocutionary effects are possible, and every work will be different in this regard. All lethetic fictions are the same kind of illocution, but they can be many different sorts of perlocutions, often more than one at the same time. Nye's *Merlin*, for example, has the effect of amusing; but at the same time it involves us in a special kind of intellectual chasing-of-our-tails that he identifies with the story of the Sleeve Job. Lethetic fictions are potentially infinitely variable in this regard, each calling forth different effects in different ways. The object of literary-critical analysis, when applied to such fictions, ought to be mainly the discovery of what effects are sought and achieved.

[3] *How to Do Things with Words* (Cambridge: Harvard University Press, 1962).

Such an approach to criticism is of course highly "rhetorical." It assumes that a text seeks to have a certain effect on an audience and that a successful text will have just those effects it solicits. This assumption in turn implies that there is indeed a text and that it has an important controlling influence on the reader. On this issue I part company with Fish, who has more recently "made the text disappear" (his own words) and has replaced it with "interpretive communities" and "interpretive strategies."[4] My notion of "lethetic fiction" depends upon the assumption that there is a text and that a text may solicit disbelief as well as other perlocutionary effects. I take such a "rhetorical" approach because lethetic reading demands it. Here we have a kind of "pre-Socratic" literature, a literature that is everything Plato rejected in rejecting the sophists. The lethetic text is precisely what Gorgias called his "Encomium on Helen," a paignion, a plaything.[5] Lethetic fictions, since they do not pretend to the seriousness that Plato and the orthodoxy following him have demanded, are properly understood as such playthings. They are "rhetorical" in this playfulness, as in their interest in obtaining effects—all sorts of effects—with their language. They may very well also be "rhetorical" in the more special sense introduced by Paul de Man (compare Chapter 4).

De Man has argued that literature is the special type of utterance that is aware of itself as language and performs upon itself the operation that Derrida performs on Plato's *Phaedrus*, Saussure's *Course in General Linguistics*, and other texts. De Man's point of departure from Derrida arises from de Man's perception that we do not need Derrida, in a sense, to deconstruct Rousseau—as he does in *De la grammatologie*—since Rousseau has really already done that job himself. The reader of literature is charged with the task of identifying not features of the text of which the author was unaware but rather what is in the text because the author put it there. "The deconstruction is not something we have added to the text but it constituted the text in

[4]See, for example, "Interpreting the *Variorum*," *Critical Inquiry* 2 (Spring 1976), 465–85.

[5]See "Gorgias' Encomium of Helen" in J. H. Hawthrone, *Gorgias of Leontini* (Ph.D. diss., University of Chicago, 1949), 81. Hawthorne argues on the basis of this word *paignion* that the "Encomium" is the work not of Gorgias himself but of an inferior student. Here is further testimony to the dominance of the alethetic, "serious" viewpoint.

the first place. . . . Poetic writing is the most advanced and re-
fined mode of deconstruction; it may differ from critical or
discursive writing in the economy of its articulation, but not in
kind."[6] The greater humility of de Man's stance vis-à-vis the
text, in comparison with Derrida's, his assumption that the writer knew as well as the reader what he was doing, may be a
remnant of the orthodox tradition that authorizes the sacralization of fiction, but it no longer serves to further that sacralization. The self-awareness that characterizes the poetic text does
not make it any more true, any freer of self-contradiction, than
other kinds of utterance, but it does make it more *honest*.

This special honesty of the rhetorical—that is, literary—text is
most rigorous and most evident, I would argue, in lethetic fictions. By soliciting the reader's disbelief, a lethetic fiction effectively forestalls any attempt by the reader to discover in it the
truth about anything, save possibly about the language that its
logomimesis elaborates and imitates. The self-revelation of lethetic texts, however, is not necessarily equivalent to the kind of
self-deconstruction proposed by de Man as a regular feature of
"poetic writing." Of course it can be argued that the very act of
writing a fiction that asks not to be believed constitutes a large
and forceful gesture of self-deconstruction, but the honesty of
lethetic fictions does not always consist in drawing our attention
to this gesture. What we discover in the course of lethetic reading is what language can *do* when it is not required to represent
reality. De Man's self-deconstructive text does not begin with
disbelief—such a text in fact gives every appearance of seeking
and deserving belief—but ultimately leads us to it: "After the
rhetorical reading of the Proust passage [in the opening essay of
Allegories of Reading], we can no longer believe the assertion
made in this passage about the intrinsic superiority of metaphor
over metonymy. We seem to end up in a mood of negative
assurance that is highly productive of critical discourse" (p. 16).
Though this "negative assurance" has the look of a kind of truth
("if truth is the recognition of the systematic character of a certain kind of error"), de Man finds in these readings no "negative

[6]*Allegories of Reading* (New Haven: Yale University Press, 1979), 17. Citations
below in the text refer to this edition.

certainty" but merely a "state of suspended ignorance" when faced with the "impossibility of knowing what [language] might be up to" (p. 19). The lethetic text, which begins by offering the negative assurance of its incredibility, then proceeds to play with the possibilities opened up by such an assumption. The lethetic fiction, in other words, offers a kind of security to the reader in the very certainty of its untruth. It frees itself of one of the possible functions of language in order more freely to explore some of the others, to examine what language "might be up to" when it does not aspire to tell the truth about the world.

The reader is always free, of course, to seize this security for himself with regard to any text and to read obliviously, as Calvino does with scientific theories or Poe does with Mercier. The reader can simply ignore whatever pretension to truth the text at hand may have and can treat it as a storehouse of signifiers to be used as the objects of logomimesis. This approach is as easy as its opposite, which is to treat a text that has no apparent intention of telling the truth as if it were a revelation of the deepest secrets of the universe. The latter procedure is far more common in our tradition, having as it does the illustrious precedent of such readings as that of the *Song of Songs* by generations of theologians; but it has no greater justification in theory than the former. But because the act of treating an apparently true text as if it were untrue seems to be a kind of destruction, whereas the discovery of truth under a surface of untruth appears constructive, it is not surprising that our natural desire to preserve and increase our heritage should manifest itself in a preference for alethetic reading.

In the context of this preference, one might well wonder what is to be gained by elaborate attempts to sunder the text as language from a reality in which we can believe. The gain, I think, is the following: language severed from the obligation to reflect some form of reality is free to reflect itself honestly, to do all things that language can do, to affect readers however it can and will, and yet to keep them safe from what could easily become a terrifying assault on their sense of reality. As long as we assume that language represents reality, we must be careful with it, because language might change reality in ways that we are not able to control and might not like. The characters who stand inside the boundaries of a lethetic fiction, like Strepsiades in the *Clouds* and the dreamer in *The Lathe of Heaven,* are unprotected by disbelief and suffer terrifying consequences from the restructuring of their reality by unfettered language.

This element of security offered by the lethetic fiction should not be underestimated. Those who study fairy tales as a special form of literature intended for children have stressed the importance of the child's recognition of the untruth of what he reads. Michel Butor, for example, accurately refers to

> the pleasure of knowing that all this isn't true, the pleasure of not being taken in by a fiction, the pleasure of feeling in deep agreement with the adult about what is real and what is not. The fairy tale liberates one from the immediate by the possibility it offers of withdrawing from it with the utmost confidence. It is because of the fairy tale that reality presents itself as something certain and solid, something easily distinguished, something one masters and understands.[7]

And Bruno Bettelheim, in a section of his book *The Uses of Enchantment* appropriately titled "Fear of Fantasy,"[8] quotes with approval the observation of J. R. R. Tolkien about his own experience of fairy tales: "I never imagined that the dragon was of the same order as the horse. The dragon had the trademark *Of Faerie* written plainly upon him. In whatever world he had his being it was of Other-world." Bettelheim's goals, of course, are entirely alethetic: he wants to show how "useful" structured literary fantasy is for the psychic health of children, and he reads fairy tales for their "personal meaning," to "go beyond the surface."[9] Even so, the point is still valid even in my context of lethetic fictions. Whether the reader is a child reading fairy tales or an adult reading the tales of Poe, the assurance that what is being read is not true keeps the story at a distance and thus allows one to take pleasure in it.

Lethetic reading assumes that language represents, not things in the world, but linguistic objects like tropes, proverbs, or even

---

[7]"On Fairy Tales," in Vernon W. Gras, ed., *European Literary Theory and Practice* (New York: Dell, 1973), 351.
[8]*The Uses of Enchantment,* (New York: Vintage/Random House, 1977), 118.
[9]Ibid., 19.

scientific theories. Disbelief protects the reader (if not its characters) by drawing a circle around the sovereign realm of language
and keeping the dangerous power of liberated speech away
from the reader. Of course, not all of that power is dangerous:
the power to affect the reader and move him psychically from
his place in the world to a linguistic atopia is something we want
to experience when reading lethetically, but we are provided
with a simple and ready means of reversing that power and
returning to the world at any time. It is safe to travel in literary
frigates—if our disbelief is intact—because our presence in
atopia is contingent upon a permission that we may instantly
withdraw. Without that disbelief, such a frigate would turn into
a specter bark, and our ride on it would not be any more enjoyable than the ancient mariner's. But the disbelieving reader's
presence is really absence, as if something other than ourselves,
some surrogate or astral projection, were taking the trip. We
find, in fact, that this is a favorite theme of dialeptic fantasy and
science fiction: numerous stories are based on the ability of a
character, by either supernatural or technological means, to
travel to distant places and to participate in adventures in the
body of some other, while "in fact" remaining relatively safe at
home. We must realize, as these stories often take pains to point
out, that the safety thus afforded is only relative: any experience, even a vicarious one, that is capable of having good effects
upon the subject is capable also of having bad ones. Still, when
readers give themselves up to the powerful effects that lethetic
literature can generate, they do so with a high degree of protection from the power that is released when language is liberated
from the constraints of veracity.

The orthodoxy that begins with Plato understands language
to be a dangerous thing from which we need to be protected, a
pharmakon that at any moment may turn from a remedy to a
poison. The play of language must be contained, according to
Plato, by what Derrida calls "the guardrail of ethics and politics,"
not to mention the obligation to conform to the truth. Plato sets
up a "restricted economy" of language, the restrictions of which
attempt to keep language safely under control and to channel its
power in the direction deemed socially desirable. But there is,
Derrida suggests, a "general economy" wherein nothing is held

back and only the rules of language itself apply to the process of writing and reading. Lethetic fictions represent what we might call a victory of the general over the restricted economy, because nothing that language can do is forbidden. This triumph of the general economy is characteristic of verbal comedy, which can be understood as rebellion (revel = rebel) against all authority, all restraints. The *Birds* is both a model comedy and a model of lethetic writing because it brings about the ultimate rebellion (that is, the overthrow of Zeus) by means of setting loose and finally deifying language itself in the person of the fast-talking Pisthetairos.

This realm of atopia, in which the only laws are those of speech itself, has always seemed to Western orthodoxy a place of illusion, a dreamworld in which the dreamer forgets the cold, clear light of day. "Although of the two halves of life—the waking and the dreaming—the former is generally considered not only the more important but the only one which is truly lived, I would, at the risk of sounding paradoxical, propose the opposite view."[10] Nietzsche justifies this notion by proposing that "we ourselves are the very stuff of such illusions" and "our dreams will appear to us [therefore] as illusions of illusions, hence as a still higher form of satisfaction of the original desire for illusion" (p. 33). If we desire to explore this realm of illusion, we may do so most readily by means of lethetic fictions, which guarantee the security of the reader. But the lethetic reader will not undertake such an exploration of illusion in the hope of protecting himself against the "terrors and horrors of existence," which is how Nietzsche would explain the ancient Greek development of a "shining fantasy of the Olympians" (pp. 29, 30). Illusion cannot protect us from reality unless we are willing to let the illusion displace that reality and eliminate it from our sight.

It should be clear to readers of this book that reading and writing in the lethetic mode is never naive, not even in the special and sophisticated way that Homer is naive in Nietzsche's understanding of him. The sophisticated naivete of Homer,

---

[10]*The Birth of Tragedy* and *The Genealogy of Morals,* trans. Francis Golffing (Garden City: Doubleday/Anchor, 1956), 32. Citations below in text refer to this translation of *The Birth of Tragedy* (secs. 3 and 4).

"that complete identification with the beauty of appearance," is "a complete victory of Apollonian illusion" over the "somber contemplation of actuality" (p. 31). That terrible actuality is "conquered—or at least hid from view—again and again by means of this artificial Olympus" (p. 30). Lethetic reading can never conquer or hide actuality; it can only make a strategic retreat and for a time escape it. But that is enough; it is all that is needed. The lethetic reader thus forgets the world in a very different way from that in which Nietzsche's dreamer "forgets the day," because his concern is not with covering up and hiding reality but with uncovering and setting forth the possibilities of sovereign language. The lethetic reader forgets, not because the dreamworld is a welcome distraction from a horrifying reality, but because reality is an unwelcome distraction from the linguistic atopia. The *aktive Vergesslichkeit* that Nietzsche proposes as a positive force for human good in *The Genealogy of Morals* (Second Essay, Section 1) assists the lethetic reader to escape. He escapes, however, not from something undesirable (the terrors of actuality) but into something desirable, which, though it may be terrifying in its power, is contained by the boundary of our disbelief.

The lethetic reader seeks to escape the world not because that world is too horrifying for him to bear but because the atopia of language is more valuable to him. The lethetic reader is not necessarily running away from a world with which he cannot cope. The escape of lethetic reading is not properly seen as an escape from something frightening, since it is the attraction of being carried away by the power of speech rather than the anxiety about reality that leads the reader to participate in lethetic reading. To read what we do not believe gives us the opportunity to take a vacation from the world, a world in which we may in fact be very comfortable and content, with every expectation that the world will be there, unchanged and unharmed, when we get back.

The dreamworld of the lethetic atopia therefore has little in common with our classical or biblical tradition of dreams and their place in human life, since this tradition understands dreaming as a mode of psychic inscription and therefore as alethetic writing. The sleeping mind is used by divine agency as a tablet upon which to write cryptic messages for waking consciousness, which somehow stands in the way of direct communication with the divine. Sleep lets the psyche be opened up easily by the delicate writing implements of the gods and lets them bypass the unreliable mediation of the senses to inscribe directly upon the soul their commands, prophecies, and so on. It is a way to make that which is most absent in the mortal world—that is, the divine world—as present as possible. Lethetic fictions are never dreams in this sense, because they can never be understood as the inscription of an absent authority upon the soul of the reader.

If we make the kind of assumptions necessary for lethetic reading, we are certainly saved that "world of trouble" of which the King of Hearts spoke, because we need not try to find the "hidden other" behind the surface of what we read; but it seems to be precisely that concealed and absent other that makes reading worthwhile. Reading that looks only to the surface, and writing that solicits such reading, seem condemned forever to be merely superficial. In one sense, it is impossible to argue with those who believe that only some transcendental signified (such as God or the Truth) can justify the energy and time expended upon ever-more-detailed acts of reading. Compared with the "macrocosmic values" provided by the assumption of the hidden presence of God, all other values not claiming transcendence pale and shrink to insignificance. On the other hand, if one believes that the search for transcendental values has always been illusory in the first place, its "loss" is no loss at all and need not be lamented. The endless reading of texts, the endless building of buildings, the endless battle with disease and death—all are equally vain or equally justified, depending on your point of view.

The viewpoint of this book obviously inclines to the assumption that the search for transcendent value has always been attended by mystification, self-deception, and an inevitable component of self-contradiction. At the same time, however, I must make something of a disclaimer: I have been examining only one kind of text and have been directing all my arguments toward the understanding of that particular sort of text. I do not suppose that all the claims made here for lethetic reading and lethetic fictions necessarily hold good for other modes and other texts as well, and my reader will readily understand that to do so would be not only unjustified but, in some cases, destructive of the very distinctions I have tried to make. I do not doubt that many texts ask to be read as the trace of a hidden other and that not to read them in this way can be seen as a sort of violence against them. But I do not doubt either that such violence, such lethetic reading of texts that seek to tell the truth, can in certain cases be extremely fruitful, as it is in the case of Calvino's reading of Sir George Darwin.

Surely even some forms of fantasy are properly seen as alethetic attempts to describe "alternative worlds," but the texts in which I am interested, lethetic texts such as the *Birds* and the *Galgenlieder,* are more properly understood as atopiai—that is, nonworlds—than as "other worlds." The "heterocosm" of romantic theory, as Meyer Abrams describes it,[11] is a "second nature" that is to be understood as natural in its own terms. It might be a utopia, a place better than this world, or what is sometimes called a *dystopia,* such as Huxley's *Brave New World,* which is considerably worse than this. In either case, however, the heterocosm is supposed to present a legitimate alternative— indeed, a credible alternative—to present reality. The linguistic atopia of the lethetic fiction, however, is not a place we can reach by restructuring society (as in utopian fiction) or by waiting for the future. Atopia is attainable only on the wings of sovereign speech, by adhering solely to the rules of language and scrupulously ignoring the laws of reality. Poetry of the heterocosm answers the question, "What would it *really* be like if . . . ?" Huxley's novel wonders what it would really be like if certain trends in present society were to continue unchanged for many years into the future. Arthur Clarke wonders what it would really be like to build a "space elevator." But we quickly realize that Calvino has *not* shown us and has not wished to show us what it would really be like if the moon and the earth were very close together.

Literature need not show us what "it would really be like," and lethetic literature surely does not. "If there's no *reality* in it," say

---

[11]In *The Mirror and the Lamp* (New York: Oxford University Press, 1953).

the authors of such literature, "that saves the reader a world of trouble, you know, as he need not try to find any." He need not fear that a reality represented by the text will overwhelm his reality and drown him. The text, for all its power to move, remains only a text behind which nothing lurks, no divine or paternal authority that wants to open up the reader and plant in him a simulacrum of itself. It remains just language and the effects of language. But that, for readers, is a very great deal.

Index

Hotspur, 138
Humor, 119
Huxley, Aldous: *Brave New World*, 231

Iago, 31
Iagoism, 31
Identification, 136
Identity crisis, 129
Igrayne, 103, 105, 109
Illocutions, 32, 222
Imagination, dialeptic, 133
Influence, 178, 182, 183
Inscription, 194, 229, 230
Insincerity, 91
Intentio, 38
Intentional error, 31
Intentionality, 122
Interpretation, 72
Interpretive communities, 223
Irony, 22, 23, 32, 33, 50, 57, 74, 83, 86, 87, 88, 97, 121, 144, 145, 149, 190, 208
Iser, Wolfgang, 45, 48, 220

Jauss, H. R., 46, 48
Jests, 46, 47
Johnson, Samuel, 139
Jokes, 47
Joke work, the, 48
Judaism, 212, 214
Julius Caesar, 111

Kafka, Franz: "In the Penal Colony," 178, 196, 207
Kgwgk, 172, 174, 178
Kopf verlieren, 51, 52, 53
Kovalyov, 120, 122

Lacan, Jacques, 39, 190, 192
Lady Bracknell, 92, 93, 97
Language: authority over, 76, 78; autonomy of, 122; as carrier of messages, 122; conformity to, 93; everyday, 44; expansion of, 121; face value of, 92; faith in, 24; figurative, 49; literary, 29; mastery over, 72; origin of, 171; philosophy of, 80, 198, 220; poetic, 35; power of, 41, 64, 96, 102; power over, 79; priority of, 68; self-referential, 65; sovereign, 37, 62, 229

Langue, 143
Laugh-track, 135
Lausberg, Heinrich, 83
Le Guin, Ursula: *The Lathe of Heaven*, 181, 226
Lesein, 146
Lethe, 36
Lethetic fictions (defined), 33–37
Lethetic genre, 61 ff., 177; (defined), 37–38
Lethetic mode, 49, 50, 143 ff., 177, 205; (defined), 37–38
Lethetic reading (defined), 38
Lethetic texts, meaning of, 45, 219 ff.
Leverkühn, Adrian, 106
Lexical norms, 50
Lipking, Lawrence, 154
Literary criticism, 108, 122, 173, 177, 211, 212, 222
Literature, mimetic, 191
Living speech, 198
Logomimesis, 41–57, 61, 70, 74, 80, 81, 82, 88, 91, 94, 109, 117, 118, 128, 129, 130, 136, 158, 161, 164, 168, 174, 185, 198, 207, 224, 225; in alethetic literature, 50; (defined), 41, 42
Logos, 61, 73, 182, 187, 188, 193, 194, 195, 196, 197, 199, 200, 201, 202, 203, 204, 207
Lucian, 23, 144–151, 206; *The Liar*, 146, 147; *True History*, 23, 144–151, 165, 205
Lucifer, 101, 102, 103, 107, 108
Ludus, 16
Lying, 30, 31, 147, 222
Lysias, 200, 201

Madness, 184, 185, 206
Malory, Sir Thomas, 100, 104; *Morte d'Arthur*, 104
Mann, Thomas, 20, 21, 22, 23, 24, 51, 52, 54, 55, 87, 94, 106; *Buddenbrooks*, 20, 88; *Doktor Faustus*, 179; *Joseph and His Brothers*, 94; *The Transposed Heads*, 21, 22, 23, 25, 26, 51, 52, 54; "The Wardrobe," 24, 25, 26
Marvelous, the, 22, 25, 26, 27, 37, 66, 89, 99, 115, 118, 137, 146, 211; subgenres of, 26

Library of Congress Cataloging in Publication Data

KOELB, CLAYTON, 1942–
    The incredulous reader.

    Includes index.
    1. Fantastic literature—History and criticism.
2. Literature—Psychology.   3. Belief and disbelief in
literature.   4. Reader-response criticism.   I. Title.
PN56.F34K63   1984   809'.915   83-18840
ISBN 0-8014-1645-0